Docker
Containers

Docker Containers

Build and Deploy with Kubernetes, Flannel, Cockpit, and Atomic

Christopher Negus
with William Henry

Visit us on the Web: informit.com/ph

Library of Congress Control Number: 2015948006

ISBN-13: 978-0-134-13656-1
ISBN-10: 0-134-13656-X
Text printed in the United States on recycled paper at RR Donnelley in Crawfordsville, Indiana.
First printing: December 2015

As always, I dedicate this book to my wife, Sheree.
—Christopher Negus

Contents

Preface

Docker is a containerization technology at the center of a new wave for building, packaging, and deploying applications. It has the potential to impact every aspect of computing, from the application development process to how applications are deployed and scaled up and out across massive data centers.

Despite its great popularity, Docker is still a fairly new project, with many people still not really knowing exactly what Docker is. If you are one of those people, this book can help you take that first step, while also opening your eyes to the huge potential that containerization promises for you down the road. My goals for leading you into the world of containerization with this book can be summed up in these ways:

- **Hands-on learning**: I often say this in my books, but I believe that the best way to learn how technology works is to get it and use it. To that end, I let you choose from among several popular Linux systems, show you how to install Docker on the one you choose, and provide working examples of using Docker for everything from running a simple container to building and managing your own container images. That learning then extends into tools and techniques for orchestrating and managing containers.

- **How Docker can benefit you**: I explain the benefits of creating and running applications in containers, instead of installing software packages (in formats such as RPM or Deb) and running uncontained applications directly from your hard disk. Beyond running applications, I also describe how containerization can benefit software developers and system administrators.

- **Essential qualities of Docker**: I describe how Docker uses technologies such as Linux Containers (LXC) to keep containers separate from other applications running on a host computer or selectively tap into the host system. These qualities include how Docker uses name spaces, metadata, and separate file systems to both manage and secure containerized applications.

To get started, you don't need to know anything about Docker or containerization; you can treat this book as your introduction to Docker. However, this book is also intended to offer an entry into more advanced Docker-related topics, such as orchestration and container development.

As you progress through the book, you see specific ways to run containers, investigate them, stop and start them, save them, and generally manage them. As you begin creating your own containers, I discuss techniques to help you make container images that build and run efficiently. I even step you through build files (which are called Dockerfiles) that others have created to make their own containers.

A knowledge of Linux Containers in general, or Docker containers specifically, is not needed to start using this book. That said, however, there are other technologies you will use both within your Docker containers and outside those containers to work with them. Understanding some of those technologies will make your experience with Docker that much more fruitful.

KNOWLEDGE TO HELP YOU WITH DOCKER

To get the most out of working with Docker containers, it helps to know something about the operating environment in which Docker will be running. Docker is built on Linux technology and is specifically integrated with advanced features, including Linux Containers (LXC) for managing Linux name spaces and Cgroups for managing container access to system resources (such as CPU and memory).

Even your most basic interactions with Docker containers rely on underlying Linux technologies. You may have heard that you can run Docker on your Windows or Mac systems. But adding Docker to those systems always relies on your adding a Linux virtual machine. In other words, there are no Docker containers without Linux. Likewise, each container itself is typically built from a base image created from a specific Linux distribution.

So if you have no experience working with Linux systems, you might find it useful to learn about some of the following aspects of Linux and related technologies:

- **Command shell**: There are graphical interfaces available for working with Docker. However, most of the examples of Docker in this book are done from a Linux command line shell. Knowing how to get around in a Linux shell makes it much more efficient to work with Docker.

- **Software packages**: Docker is itself a mechanism for delivering software packaged and delivered together as a bundled application. To build the container images themselves, however, most Docker base images are set up to allow you to install software packages from the specific Linux distribution on which they were based.

  So, for example, for an Ubuntu base image, you should understand how to install Deb packages with tools such as apt-get. For Fedora, Red Hat Enterprise Linux, or CentOS Docker images, the yum, dnf, and rpm commands are useful. When you use these base images to build your own Docker containers, those images are usually enabled to automatically grab the packages you request from online software repositories. Understanding how to get and install packages in your chosen Linux distribution is important for your success with Docker.

- **File ownership and permissions**: Every file in a Linux system, as well as within a container, is owned by a particular user and group and has certain permissions set to allow access to those files. At times, you want to grant access to files and directories (folders) from the host within the container. Some of those might be special files, such as devices or sockets, that the application needs to run. Processes also run as a particular user. Understanding how those permissions work can be critical to getting a container working properly.

I mentioned only a few of the more obvious features you need to know about to work effectively with Docker containers. You will run into many other Linux-related features as you continue to explore how to make the best use of the Docker containers you use and create yourself.

If you are not familiar with Linux, I strongly recommend you take a class or get a book that gives you at least the basics of Linux to help you get going with Docker containers. My humble suggestion would be to pick up the *Linux Bible*, Ninth Edition, written by this author (http://www.wiley.com/WileyCDA/WileyTitle/productCd-1118999878.html). It will not only help you specifically with the technology you need to build Docker containers, but will also help you to generally work in a Linux environment as you develop Docker container images.

WHAT THIS BOOK COVERS

This book is meant to be used from beginning to end by someone just starting up with Docker containers. Later, it can serve as reference material to remind you of different options and features associated with Docker containers. The book is organized into five parts.

Part I: Getting Going with Containers

In Part I, you learn what you need to know to start working with Docker containers. Chapter 1, "Containerizing Applications with Docker," describes what containers are and how they differ from applications that are not contained. In Chapter 2, "Setting Up a Container Run-Time Environment," you learn how to install Docker on different general-purpose Linux systems, such as Fedora and Ubuntu, as well as how to install Docker on specialized container-oriented Linux systems, such as CoreOS and Project Atomic. In Chapter 3, "Setting Up a Private Docker Registry," we complete a basic container setup by showing you how to configure a private Docker registry to hold your own Docker images.

Part II: Working with Individual Containers

Most of the coverage in this part relates to using the `docker` command to work directly with individual containers. In Chapter 4, "Running Container Images," I show you how to run your first container images. To help you find and get container images, Chapter 5, "Finding, Pulling, Saving, and Loading Container Images," describes how to search for container images from the Docker registry and then pull the image you want, save it to a file, and load it into another Docker system.

In Chapter 6, "Tagging Images," you learn how to tag images, to better identify what the image contains and to use that information to push images to registries. In Chapter 7, "Investigating Containers," I show you how to look inside a Docker container or container image to see the details of how that container or image works. In Chapter 8, "Starting, Stopping, and Restarting Containers," you learn just that—how to stop, start, and restart containers.

In Chapter 9, "Configuring Container Storage," you learn how to configure storage, primarily by mounting directories from the host inside your containers. To learn how to configure networking for containers, Chapter 10, "Configuring Container Networking," describes how to configure both the default networking used (or not used) by the Docker service in general, as well as ways someone running containers can set network interfaces for individual containers.

Docker caches a lot of data, for possible reuse. In Chapter 11, "Cleaning Up Containers," I show you how to clean out cached data left behind when you created or ran Docker images. In Chapter 12, "Building Docker Images," you learn how to build your own Docker containers, including how to build containers that build and run efficiently.

Part III: Running Containers in Cloud Environments

In Chapter 13, "Using Super Privileged Containers," I describe how to run what are referred to as super privileged containers (SPCs). To illustrate how SPCs work, I show you how you can get several images that can perform different administrative tasks on an RHEL Atomic system. In Chapter 14, "Managing Containers in the Cloud with Cockpit," I describe how to manage containers across multiple hosts in your cloud or local environment using the Cockpit web-based container management tool.

Part IV: Managing Multiple Containers

In this part, I get into the area of orchestration. For Chapter 15, "Orchestrating Containers with Kubernetes," I describe how to use Kubernetes master and node services all on one system to be able to try out Kubernetes. In Chapter 16, "Creating a Kubernetes Cluster," I go beyond the all-in-one Kubernetes system to describe how to set up a Kubernetes cluster. With that cluster in place, you can deploy applications in container pods to be managed on different node computers from the master computer.

Part V: Developing Containers

In the short time that Docker has been around, techniques have already been developed to make building containers more efficient. In Chapter 17, "Developing Docker Containers," I describe some tips and a few tricks for developing Docker containers. Finally, in Chapter 18, "Exploring Sample Dockerfile Files," I show you various Dockerfile files I have come across to illustrate what different people have done to overcome obstacles to building their own containers.

So if you are ready now, step right up and start reading Chapter 1. I hope you enjoy the book!

Acknowledgments

The help I have had producing this book has been extraordinary. In my day job, I have the pleasure of working directly with people at Red Hat who take the fine work being done on projects like Docker, Kubernetes, and Atomic and extend and integrate those projects together into operating systems that are ready for the most stringent enterprise environments. So, in general, I want to thank developers, testers, and other writers on the Red Hat Enterprise Linux Atomic, OpenShift, and Linux container teams for helping me learn on a daily basis what it takes to make Linux Containers ready for the enterprise.

As for having a direct impact on the book, there are a few people from Red Hat I want to call out individually. First, William Henry wrote two chapters in this book on storage and networking. I was fortunate that he was available to write those critical chapters. Beyond his work here, William has made significant contributions to Docker-related projects. In fact, William wrote dozens of `docker` command man pages that are delivered with the Docker software itself. Having William around to participate in helping develop the content of the book was priceless as well.

Another important contributor to this book from Red Hat is Scott Collier. Scott's public contributions to the general knowledge about Docker have included blogs on setting up Docker and Kubernetes, as well as sharing many sample Dockerfiles through the Fedora Cloud initiative. For this book, Scott was generous with his time, helping me sort through technology and examples illustrated throughout the book.

Because I wrote this book outside of work hours (which is why it took me longer than I had hoped), I often relied on interactions with my publisher (Pearson) during evenings and weekends. So, thanks to editors Chris Zahn and Elaine Wiley for reviewing my content, occasionally responding on Sunday nights, and compressing their schedules to help me meet mine. Also from Pearson, my dear friend Debra Williams Cauley, who developed this project with me, has shown extraordinary patience as I sought to balance a tight schedule with my desire to take the time to write the exact book I wanted to write.

Finally, I'd like to thank my family. When someone writes a book he must almost, by necessity, neglect his family for some amount of time. I'm so proud of you all. Despite my drifting off to write, my son Seth managed to do a great imitation of Zac Efron in *High School Musical* by having the lead in his school play while also playing on his high school soccer team. My son Caleb found his niche, settling in on his little organic farm in Maine. And my wife, Sheree, continues to amaze younger generations with her fitness and Spartan runs. Your love and support are what keeps me going.

About the Author

Christopher Negus is a bestselling author of Linux books, a certified Linux instructor and examiner, Red Hat Certified Architect, and principal technical writer for Red Hat. At the moment, projects Chris is working on include Red Hat OpenStack Platform High Availability, Red Hat Enterprise Linux Atomic Enterprise, Kubernetes, and Linux Containers in Docker format.

As an author, Chris has written dozens of books about Linux and open source software. His *Linux Bible*, Ninth Edition, released in 2015, is consistently among the top-selling Linux books today. During the dotcom days, Chris's *Red Hat Linux Bible* sold more than 250,000 copies in eight editions and was twice voted best Linux book of the year. Other books authored or coauthored by Chris include the *Linux Toolbox* series, *Linux Toys* series, *Fedora and Red Hat Enterprise Linux Bible* series, and *Linux Troubleshooting Bible* with Wiley Publishing.

With Prentice Hall, Chris helped produce the Negus Software Solution Series. For that series, Chris wrote *Live Linux CDs* and coauthored *The Official Damn Small Linux Book*. That series also includes books on web development, Google Apps, and virtualization.

Chris joined Red Hat in 2008 as an RHCE instructor. For that role, he became a Red Hat Certified Instructor (RHCI) and Red Hat Certified Examiner (RHCX). In 2014, Chris became a Red Hat Certified Architect (RHCA), with certifications in Virtualization Administration, Deployment and Systems Management, Cluster and Storage Management, and Server Hardening. In 2011, Chris shifted from his Linux instructor role back to being a full-time writer for Red Hat, which he continues to do today.

Early in his career, Chris worked at UNIX System Laboratories and AT&T Bell Labs with the organizations that produced the UNIX operating system. During that time, Chris wrote the first official UNIX System V Desktop system manual and cowrote the *Guide to the UNIX Desktop*. For eight years, Chris worked closely with developers of the UNIX system, from UNIX System V Release 2.0 through Release 4.2.

Part I

Getting Going with Containers

## CHAPTER 1

Containerizing Applications with Docker

IN THIS CHAPTER:

- Understand Docker containers
- Learn about challenges in containerization
- Understand the components that make up Docker
- Start on a path to enterprise-quality containers

Docker is an elegant and beautiful way to package and run applications. Using your favorite Linux system, you can have Docker installed and running as a service in just a few minutes. The ease with which you can then build, run, stop, start, investigate, modify, and otherwise manipulate containers is, honestly, awesome.

Docker's ease of use contributed to it becoming one of the most popular open source projects today. But Docker as a centerpiece for containerization of the data center has caused the most commotion. The potential is not less than the reinvention of how individuals and companies, large and small, create, test, deploy, and manage their most critical applications.

With containerization also comes the possibility of more efficiently deploying applications into cloud environments. Like containers themselves, the operating systems that run containers can be slimmed down. These new, container-ready host operating systems no longer have to carry all the dependencies that an application requires because the container is already holding most of what it needs to run.

The goal of this book is not only to introduce you to what Docker is and how it works, but also to expose you to the many ways you can extend it for special uses. While a single container can be straightforward to create and deploy, getting multiple containers to work together and access resources from other containers, and from the hosts they run on, requires a higher level of complexity. This book addresses several different ways of creating and deploying these complex sets of containers.

This book is not meant to be just used in theory. Nearly every aspect of container and container-related tools described in this book is backed up with real examples of how those features work. You are meant to be able to try them out yourself and then modify and extend them in ways that extend how you want to use Docker.

To begin, however, you need to know why you should care about containers at all.

UNDERSTANDING PROS AND CONS OF CONTAINERIZING APPLICATIONS

Docker provides a way to create and run applications that have been configured within a container. To truly understand what that means, it helps to start with what a containerized application is not. A containerized application is NOT...

...An Application Running Directly on a Host Computer

The traditional way to run an application is to install and run that application directly from a host computer's file system. That application's view of its environment would include the host's process table, file system, IPC facility, network interfaces, ports, and devices.

To get the application working, you often need to install additional software packages to go with your application. Normally, this is not a problem. But in some cases, you might want to run different versions of the same package running on the same system, which could cause conflicts.

The application could conflict with applications in other ways as well. If the application is a service, it might bind to a particular network port by default. It might also read common configuration files when the service starts up. This could make it impossible, or at least tricky, to have multiple instances of that service running on the same host computer. It could also make it difficult to run other services that want to bind to that same port.

Another downside of running an application directly on the host computer is that it can be difficult to move that application around. If the host computer needed to be shut down or if the application needed more capacity than is available on the host system, it might not be easy to pick up all the dependencies from the host computer and move them to another host.

...An Application Running Directly within a Virtual Machine

Creating a virtual machine (VM) for the specific purpose of running an application can overcome some of the drawbacks of running applications directly on the host operating system. Although a virtual machine is on the host, it runs as a separate operating system, which includes its own kernel, file system, network interfaces, and so on. This makes it easy to keep almost everything inside the operating system separate from the host.

Because a VM is a separate entity, you don't have the same issues of inflexibility that come from running an application directly on hardware. You could run an application 10 times on the host by starting up 10 different VMs. The service on each VM could listen on the same port number, but not cause a conflict because each VM could have a different IP address.

Likewise, if you need to shut down a host computer, you could either migrate the VM to another host (if your virtualization environment supports it) or just shut it down and start it again on the new host.

The downside of running each instance of an application in a VM is the resources it consumes. Your application might require only a few megabytes of disk space to run, but the entire VM could consume many gigabytes of space. Also, the startup time and CPU consumption of the VM is almost sure to be higher than the application itself would consume.

Containers offer an alternative to running applications directly on the host or in a VM that can make the applications faster, more portable, and more scalable.

Understanding the Upside of Containers

For running applications, containers offer the promise of both flexibility and efficient resource usage.

Flexibility comes from the container being able to carry all the files it needs with it. Like the application running in a VM, it can have its own configuration files and dependent libraries, as well as having its own network interfaces that are distinct from those configured on the host. So, again, as with the VM, a containerized application should be able to move around more easily than its directly installed counterparts and not have to contend for the same port numbers because each container they run in has separate network interfaces.

As for startup time and consumption of disk space and processing power, a container is neither running a separate operating system nor should it hold the amount of software needed to run a whole operating system. That's because the container can contain just what the application needs to run, along with any other tools you might want to run with the container and a small amount of metadata describing the container.

Docker containers don't have a separate kernel, as a VM does. Commands run from a Docker container appear in the process table on the host and, in most ways, look much like any other process running on the system. The difference between an application run in those two environments, however, has most to do with the different view of the world those two applications have looking out:

- **File system:** The container has its own file system and cannot see the host system's file system by default. One exception to this rule is that files (such as /etc/hosts and /etc/resolv.conf) may be automatically bind mounted inside the container. Another exception is that you can explicitly mount directories from the host inside the container when you run a container image.

- **Process table:** Hundreds of processes may be running on a Linux host computer. However, by default, processes inside a container cannot see the host's process table, but instead have their own process table. So the application's process you run when you start up the container is assigned PID 1 within the container. From inside the container, a process cannot see any other processes running on the host that were not launched inside the container.

- **Network interfaces:** By default, the Docker daemon defines an IP address via DHCP from a set of private IP addresses. Instead of using DHCP, Docker supports other network modes, such as allowing containers to use another container's network interfaces, the host's network interfaces directly, or no network interfaces. If you choose, you can expose a port from inside the container to the same or different port number on the host.

- **IPC facility:** Processes running inside containers cannot interact directly with the inter-process communications (IPC) facility running on the host system. You can expose the IPC facility on the host to the container, but that is not done by default. Each container has its own IPC facility.

- **Devices:** Processes inside the container cannot directly see devices on the host system. Again, a special privilege option can be set when the container is run to grant that privilege.

As you can see, Docker containers have the capability to run in plain sight to the host, but in a way that restricts what the container can see outside its boundaries into the host (unless you explicitly open those views).

Understanding Challenges of Containerizing Applications

Among the challenges of containerizing applications is the fact that they are different from applications not in a container. In every Linux system facilities are in place for starting and stopping services and viewing error messages. Linux also provides ways of monitoring services and rotating log files.

For running virtual machines, whole virtualization platforms, such as OpenStack and Red Hat Enterprise Virtualization, are built to start, stop, and otherwise work with VMs. Although efforts are underway to build tools for managing sets of containers, most are still in their infancy. Frameworks for deploying and managing sets of containers are being put in place in projects such as Kubernetes and OpenShift.

Docker containers are packaged as container images. Work has been done to be able to store container images in registries and manage them with the `docker` command. However, the tools for managing Docker images are not nearly as mature as those used to manage Linux software packages (such as those for Linux RPM or Deb based systems).

Tools are just now being developed to be able to verify where an image came from, to determine whether it has been tampered with, and to see exactly which software packages and their versions have been installed in the container. For now, however, be aware that it is difficult in most cases to be completely assured that random images you grab from the Docker Hub Registry are safe to use.

Another challenge to using containers comes from the fact that containers, by their nature, cannot see other containers by default. So, what about the times that you want your container to work closely with another container? For example, you might have a web server that you want to access your database server.

Some of the solutions for getting containers to see each other are features in Docker that let you link containers together and Kubernetes features that let you identify services that are used and provided between containers in pods. More container management tools are also becoming available to deal with these issues. Just keep in mind that they are in early stages of development, and multiple, sometimes conflicting, tools are being developed in almost every area of container management.

UNDERSTANDING WHAT MAKES UP DOCKER

Docker is a container format developed by the Docker Project. The `docker` command can run, stop, start, investigate, and otherwise manipulate containers. The `docker` command also can run as a service daemon, handling requests to manage Docker containers. This Docker service, by default, grabs the images you request from the Docker Hub Registry. You don't need to know much more than that to get started, but some additional words are in order.

The Docker Project

The Docker Project (`https://www.docker.com`) provides a focal point for Docker development. It refers to Docker as "an open platform for developers and sysadmins of distributed applications." Its goal is to simplify application development and distribution.

Solomon Hykes is the founder and CTO of Docker. He compares what Docker sets out to do in the software industry to what physical shipping containers have done for the shipping industry. Whether you are shipping cars, barrels, boxes, or pianos, by using a standard container to ship those diverse types of items, the tools you use for transporting and working with them can become standardized as well.

So, at its core, the Docker Project provides a format for software containers and creates a simple infrastructure that is set up specifically to work with software in that format. As the project has progressed, it has begun extending out beyond its initial focus on stabilizing the Docker format and providing the tools to manage single containers.

Today, the Docker Project is expanding its scope to include provisioning and orchestration tools, to help people deploy and manage groups of containers. It is also working on ways to manage computing resources and help run Docker containers in ways that offer high availability. As those tools become available, they will have to go head-to-head against more established container orchestration tools being developed by companies such as Google and Red Hat (tools that include the Kubernetes project covered in this book).

For now, however, the Docker Project's greatest achievements are the Docker container format, the tools for managing individual containers, and the capability to pull and push Docker container images between Docker clients and registries. The central registry, which is managed by the Docker Project, is referred to as the Docker Hub Registry.

The Docker Hub Registry

The Docker Hub Registry (https://registry.hub.docker.com) offers a place where individuals and organizations can store and develop their Docker container images. When you install Docker on your Linux system, by default Docker looks to the Docker Hub Registry when you make requests for Docker container images not already on your system.

Figure 1.1 shows the Docker Hub Registry page.

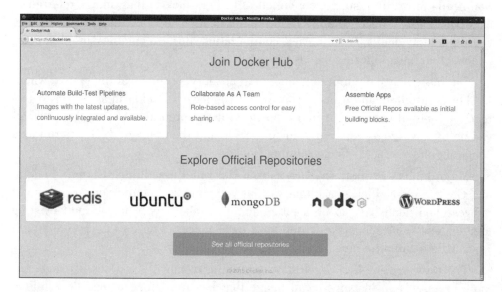

FIGURE 1.1 The Docker Hub Registry holds thousands of Docker images.

By signing up for a Docker user account, you can have your own Docker repository that you can push Docker container images to. After that, you can pull those images from any system running Docker that has an Internet connection.

There are Linux distributions and application projects that have official repositories available from the Docker Hub Registry. Along with the Docker container images themselves, the Docker Hub Registry also is a place where you can, in many cases, find instructions for using these images and the Dockerfile files used to build them. For container images that you don't want to share publicly, there are also ways to create your own Docker Registry that you can use to store images privately or purchase secure container storage directly from the Docker project.

You may notice that the words "image" and "container" come up when describing the form in which Docker stores and transports software. Understanding the differences between images and containers is important when it comes to using Docker.

Docker Images and Containers

The goal of containerization is to gather together all the components an application needs to run in a single, contained unit. For Docker, that unit is referred to as a *Docker image*. Inside the image is the application the container is intended to execute and, typically, any libraries, configuration files, executables, or other components that the application needs to execute.

An image is a static unit that sits in a repository, or the local file system where Docker is installed, and waits to run. When you save a Docker image to a file system, as opposed to storing it in a repository, it is stored as a tarball. That tarball can be transported as you would any other file and then imported later to run as a container on your local system running Docker.

Major Linux distributions, such as Red Hat Enterprise Linux, Ubuntu, Fedora, and CentOS offer official base images that you can use to build your own Docker images. You don't have to be a programmer to take a base image, add existing applications to it, and make it into your own images. You do this by creating a Dockerfile file and running a `docker build` command on it.

The term *Docker container* refers to a running instance of a Docker image. Or, more precisely, an instance of an image that has run, since it may be running, paused, or stopped at the moment. The distinction between images and containers is critical when you start to use Docker. The reason you need to understand that distinction is that there are different commands for working with images versus working with containers.

For example, when you want to see a list of images on your local system, you type `docker images`. To see a list of containers that are running, you type `docker ps` (or `docker ps -a` to see a list of containers no longer running, but still saved on your system).

To run a container from an image, you use the `docker run` command. To stop a running container, you use the `docker stop` command. After it has stopped, you use the `docker start` command to start the stopped container again. To just pause all the processes within a container, you use the `docker pause` command. Then type `docker unpause` to start the paused container again. Keep in mind that `docker run` runs a new container from the original image, while `docker start` restarts a container from its state when it was stopped (for example, software you added or files you changed will still be in place).

When it comes to working with containers, you may notice that all the examples just given have one thing in common. Every one of them is invoked using the `docker` command.

The `docker` Command

The `docker` command is the primary command you use to work directly with Docker containers and images. In fact, in some packaging of Docker software, it is one of only a couple of executable commands included.

Once you have installed Docker software, as described in Chapter 2, "Setting Up a Container Run-Time Environment," you need only to start the Docker service to be able to start using the `docker` command. One of the nice features built into the `docker` command is Tab completion (if you are running Docker from the default bash shell). So, once the Docker service is running, you can type `docker` as root user (or `sudo docker` in Ubuntu or in Fedora) followed by pressing the Tab key twice to see the available `docker` subcommands:

```
# docker <Tab><Tab>
attach    exec      inspect   port      rmi       tag
build     export    kill      ps        run       top
commit    help      load      pull      save      unpause
cp        history   login     push      search    version
create    images    logout    rename    start     wait
diff      import    logs      restart   stats
events    info      pause     rm        stop
```

Because most of the second section of this book is devoted to using `docker` with these subcommands, I don't spend a lot of time showing you how they all work. Instead, I give you an overview of what you can do with them:

- **Find information about Docker components**: Show version information about Docker features with `docker version`. View information about the system running Docker with `docker info`. View commands and options available with the `docker` command with `docker help`. Show the history of an image with `docker history`. View information about an image or container with `docker inspect`. List a container's port mappings with `docker port`.

- **Work with running containers**: List running containers with `docker ps`. Attach another command to a running container with `docker attach`. Run a command within a running container with `docker exec`. Inspect a container's metadata with `docker inspect`. Copy files from a container to the host system with `docker cp`. Check the changes made to a container's file system since it was started with `docker diff`.

- **Work with images**: List images on your system with `docker images`. Run images with `docker run`. Pull images from a registry to the local system with `docker pull`. Push images to a registry with `docker push`. Save an image as a tarball with `docker save`. Load a local image from a tarball with `docker load`. Export the file system from a container to a tarball on the local system with `docker export`.

- **Work with Docker Registries**: Search registries for images with `docker search`. Log in to the Docker Hub Registry (so you can push and pull images with your account) with `docker login`. Log out of the Docker Hub Registry with `docker logout`.

- **Modify an existing image**: Add a name to an image with `docker tag`. Change the name of an image with `docker rename`.

- **Change the state of a container**: Stop a running container with `docker stop`. Start a stopped container with `docker start`. Pause a container with `docker pause`. Restart a paused image with `docker unpause`. Send a kill signal or other signal to a container with `docker kill`. Stop and restart a container with `docker restart`.

- **Watch Docker activities**: Watch events from the Docker server with `docker events`. Watch a container's process activities with `docker top`. View log messages produced from a container with `docker logs`. View CPU and memory use statistics for a container with `docker stats`. Watch a container until it stops and then print its exit code with `docker wait`.

- **Create images and containers**: Build an image from scratch with `docker build`. Create an image from a container with `docker commit`. Create a container from an image without running it with `docker create`. Import a file system to an image with `docker import`.

- **Remove containers and images**: Remove a stopped container with `docker rm`. Remove an image with `docker rmi`.

Even though Docker was designed to help you get up and running containers with minimal fuss, this book is here to guide you through your first experiences with Docker and point out interesting features you may not find on your own. After that, it leads you into some of the less charted waters of Docker, related to deploying and managing multiple containers. In other words, it gives you a way to approach your Docker adventure.

APPROACHING CONTAINERS

With the fast pace of development surrounding Docker specifically and containers in general, the best any book can do for you these days is get you on a good path. In this book, that means starting with a solid set of examples to illustrate how Docker and a select set of supporting tools work today. After that, the approach is to lay out what is on the horizon for new features and new tools.

Whether you are someone who wants to use and manage containers or someone tasked to develop containers, this book starts you out with a few things that everyone needs, including

- **Setting up Docker**: Docker is available on many full-blown Linux systems and several special, container-oriented Linux systems. So instructions at the beginning of this book help you choose one or more of these systems and show you how to start up the Docker service.

- **Setting up a Docker Registry**: Docker is made to store container images in registries and make them available to pull (download) to systems running Docker. So you can learn how to create your own private Docker Registry and use it to hold your container images.

If you are someone who wants to use and administer containers, I present you with various procedures for working with:

- A regular individual container
- A set of containers (using Kubernetes and other tools to manage them)

Whether you are creating or just running containerized applications, it helps to understand the ways in which the underlying operating system features are made available to containers. Supporting features from the operating system you should know about to support containers include

- **Host privileges**: The scope of what a container can manipulate on the host is limited by design. Opening host privileges allows a container direct access to features on the host system, such as the host's process table, devices, particular CPUs, and IPC namespace. Containers designed to access and change the host system (referred to as super privileged containers) are demonstrated with a Fedora Atomic Host later in the book.

- **Storage**: Rather than store data inside the container itself, you can connect storage space from the host inside a Docker container using bind mounts.

- **Networking**: There are special rules and options for managing host network interfaces from within your containers.

As a software developer, containers both limit you and set you free. You have the ability to make sure all the files for your application are packaged with it in a form that is ready to run. But new challenges arise that require you to rethink your approach to development for such things as how to

- Efficiently handle container layers.
- Navigate software enhancements through stages of testing, development, and production.
- Divide up services across multiple containers.
- Deploy, start, and stop containers in your run-time environments.
- Deal with supporting services that your applications need from the host system.

Docker has many great features and works well today for building and running individual containers. But the world around Docker is not standing still. Even now, hundreds of people are working every day to extend what you can do with Docker.

An extraordinary number of tools are just on the horizon to support the development and deployment of enterprise-ready containers. Likewise, people are continuing to create clever containers, while offering those containers, and the Dockerfiles used to build them, to anyone who wants to use them and extend them. To help you take your next steps beyond this book, the last two chapters describe

- **More containerization tools**: So many tools are being developed to work with Docker containers that it can be difficult to make sense of it all. This chapter provides descriptions of up-and-coming tools you will soon be able to use to work with Docker containers.
- **Sample container images**: To illustrate the creative ways in which people are using Docker, I devote a whole chapter to showcasing cool containers that people have made public for you to try out.

That next to last chapter in particular is meant to help you evaluate which existing and upcoming tools will be most useful to you as you seek to extend your own path with containers. It sorts through what those tools can do for you today and how they are being developed to serve you tomorrow.

SUMMARY

By decoupling an application (and all that application needs to run) from the host system it runs on, Docker containers offer a simple, elegant way of deploying and running applications. Docker containers can offer greater flexibility of use than you can get with applications installed directly on a host computer. And, compared with virtual machines, Docker containers can offer less demands on system resources, such as CPU usage, memory consumption, and disk space usage.

This chapter described the different components that make up Docker. Those components, which are managed by the Docker Project (`https://www.docker.com`) include the Docker Hub Registry (which stores Docker Images), the Docker service, the `docker` command, and the images and containers you work with.

This book puts you on a path that starts with learning all the ins and outs of using Docker to work with individual containers. From there, it takes you through special use cases, such as special privileged containers, and introduces you to issues you need to know about storage and networking.

For programmers, you can learn some tips about best practices for developing containers. Finally, the book leaves you with examples of containers to spark your imagination for what you might build yourself and new developments surrounding Docker that you can expect in the near future.

## CHAPTER 2

Setting Up a Container Run-Time Environment

IN THIS CHAPTER:

- Set up Docker on standard Linux systems
- Set up Docker in a specialized container Linux system

Docker is built to run on Linux. Unlike a virtual machine, which consists of an entire operating system, by its nature a container relies on a separate operating system to provide the environment in which it runs. That said, you still have plenty of choices for how you can create a working Docker environment. Choices include

- **Standard Linux**: Docker has been packaged and made available with many major Linux distributions. To get the latest Docker features, you may need to install the latest version of that Linux distribution, however. Remember that Docker is closely tied to the operating system, so earlier versions of Linux may not include all the features that Docker needs to run. In this book, I show you how to set up Docker on popular Linux distributions such as Ubuntu, Fedora, and Red Hat Enterprise Linux. I provide links to instructions for installing Docker on other Linux systems.

- **Microsoft Windows, Mac OS X, or others as a VM**: Docker cannot run directly on a Windows or Mac system. However, if you have a version of Microsoft Windows or Mac OS X that can run virtual machines, and you have the hardware to support that as well, you can install Linux as a virtual machine and run Docker from there. Keep in mind that you may not get the best experience running Docker this way, if your computer is light on processing power and RAM. But if you have a recent Windows or Mac system and adequate hardware, Docker should run just fine.

- **Container-specific Linux**: To run a container, you don't need a full-blown desktop or server Linux system. In fact, because the container is meant to carry the software it needs to run with it, the underlying Linux system can be very lightweight. Linux distributions such as Project Atomic and CoreOS are particularly suited for providing container run-time environments. You might want to use a standard Linux distribution when you develop containers, so you have easy access to all the development tools you need. Later, you can use Project Atomic or CoreOS to deploy those containers, either directly on hardware or into cloud environments, such as Amazon EC2 or Google Cloud Platform.

This chapter describes how to prepare the computer systems just described to run Docker containers. Once you have one or more of those systems set up, you can work along with the examples for running, managing, deploying, and orchestrating containers throughout the rest of this book.

CONFIGURING A STANDARD LINUX SYSTEM FOR DOCKER

If you are new to Linux, I suggest you install a standard Linux distribution with a desktop interface (Server with Desktop, Desktop, or Workstation installation). This provides you with a full set of development, debugging, and monitoring tools as you create and run your containers. When you are ready to run your containers more permanently, consider deploying them using Project Atomic or CoreOS Linux systems.

Most of what you need to get started using Docker in Linux is the software package containing the `docker` command. In Ubuntu, the package that includes the `docker` command is called docker.io. The package was previously called docker-io in Fedora, so as not to conflict with a package named docker that provides unrelated desktop docking features. However, the latest versions of Fedora now call the package docker. In Red Hat Enterprise Linux, the Docker containers package is also simply named docker.

Configuring Ubuntu for Docker

Ubuntu (`http://www.ubuntu.com/`) is a popular Linux distribution among Linux enthusiasts. Besides offering a popular standard desktop system, Ubuntu is also available in lightweight desktops (such as Xubuntu and Lubuntu) and special spins for education and multimedia, among others. Although Ubuntu releases a new version about every six months, most of which are supported for nine months, some releases are designated as Long Term Support (LTS) releases and are supported for five years.

To use Docker in Ubuntu, start with the latest LTS version of Ubuntu available. I use Ubuntu 14.04 desktop edition (the most recent LTS) to start with. To get the Ubuntu 14.04 desktop live/installation medium and instructions, go to the following URLs:

- **Ubuntu download**: Go to `www.ubuntu.com/download/desktop` and download the ISO image that matches your computer. For most newer computers, the 64-bit PC version is the one to use. For older or low-end computers, choose the 32-bit ISO download.

- **Ubuntu installation**: Refer to the "Install Ubuntu 14.04 LTS" instructions (`www.ubuntu.com/download/desktop/install-ubuntu-desktop`) for information on installing that version of Ubuntu.

Install Docker in Ubuntu (docker.io package)

Once you have Ubuntu installed and ready to go, log in to it as the owner of the system and go through the following steps to get the docker.io service up and running:

1. **Update package list**: You should update your Ubuntu package list before proceeding to install Docker.

   ```
   $ sudo apt-get update
   . . .
   Reading package lists... Done
   ```

2. **Install docker.io package**: In Ubuntu, Docker is provided by the docker.io package. Installing that package also pulls in any dependent packages as needed:

   ```
   $ sudo apt-get install docker.io
   ```

3. **Start the docker.io service**: The Docker service should start automatically. To make sure this is true, type the following:

   ```
   $ sudo service docker.io status
   docker.io start/running, process 1236
   ```

The output shows that the docker.io service is up and running. The next thing you should do is investigate the contents of the docker.io package.

Look in the Ubuntu docker.io Package

To begin to get a feel for the components that make up Docker, take a look at the contents of the docker.io package. To list the contents of the docker.io package, use the following command:

```
$ sudo dpkg-query -L docker.io | less
/usr
/usr/share
/usr/share/man
/usr/share/man/man1
/usr/share/man/man1/docker.io.1.gz
/usr/share/docker.io
/usr/share/docker.io/contrib
/usr/share/docker.io/contrib/mkimage-alpine.sh
...
/usr/share/doc
/usr/share/doc/docker.io
/usr/share/doc/docker.io/README.Debian
/usr/share/zsh
/usr/share/zsh/vendor-completions
/usr/share/zsh/vendor-completions/_docker.io
/usr/bin
/usr/bin/docker
/usr/lib
/usr/lib/docker.io
/usr/lib/docker.io/dockerinit
/etc
/etc/bash_completion.d
/etc/bash_completion.d/docker.io
/etc/init
/etc/init/docker.io.conf
/etc/init.d
/etc/init.d/docker.io
/etc/default
/etc/default/docker.io
/lib
/lib/udev
/lib/udev/rules.d
/lib/udev/rules.d/80-docker.io.rules docker-io
/lib/systemd
/lib/systemd/system
/lib/systemd/system/docker.io.service
/usr/bin/docker.io
```

Documentation that comes in the docker.io package includes a single man page describing the docker command (type man docker.io to view it) and README files in the /usr/share/doc/docker.io directory. By the time you read this, the docker.io package available to you should have many more man pages included.

The `/usr/share/docker.io/contrib` directory holds scripts, some of which you can use to create minimal file systems and others you can use for other tasks, such as creating basic Docker images. Subdirectories of this directory hold Dockerfile files for building or importing and running Docker images yourself.

Tab completion is available with the `docker` command. Tab completion with the `docker` command for the `bash` (`/etc/bash_completion.d/docker.io`) and `zsh` (`/usr/share/zsh/vendor-completions/_docker.io`) shells are included in files that come with this package.

The `docker` command (`/usr/bin/docker`) is the primary command that comes with the docker.io package. The `docker` command is used to create, work with, and otherwise manipulate Docker images and containers. The same `docker` command is also run as a daemon to provide the Docker service.

Speaking of the Docker service, most of the remaining files in the docker.io package relate to how the Docker service starts up. Startup files are included that can start the Docker service whether your system uses Upstart (init) or systemd to initialize the operating system.

A directory that is not shown as part of the docker.io package but is created when you install it, is the `/var/lib/docker` directory. Keep an eye on that directory. When docker images and containers are created, they are stored in that directory structure, so you want to make sure you don't run out of disk space there.

At this point, Ubuntu is ready for you to start using Docker. You can go right to Chapter 3, "Setting Up a Private Docker Registry," if you want to get started using Docker.

Configuring Fedora for Docker

Fedora (`https://getfedora.org`) is the free, bleeding-edge Linux distribution sponsored by Red Hat, Inc. New releases of Fedora come out about every six months and are used as a proving ground for new software as it becomes available.

Many people who use Red Hat Enterprise Linux at work install Fedora on their laptops or home desktop system. That's because Fedora offers not only software development tools and a range of server and system administration software, but also a large selection of desktop tools and fun stuff (such as games) that you might want for your personal computing.

I recommend you install the most recent version of Fedora if you want to try out Docker with Fedora. I downloaded a Fedora workstation live ISO and installed it. Docker doesn't require a desktop system, so I could have just as easily installed a base system and worked entirely from the command line.

To get started with Docker in Fedora, you need to install Fedora and then install the docker package. Once that's installed, you can start the Docker service and begin pulling Docker images, building your own images, and managing containers that you start from those images.

To get the latest Fedora Workstation live/installation medium and instructions, go to the following URLs:

- **Fedora download**: Go to `https://getfedora.org/` and select Workstation. Then choose the Download Now button and select the Download button to choose the 64-bit Fedora Workstation installation medium. (Other media are available if you have a 32-bit computer or if you want a different type of install, such as server or cloud.)
- **Fedora installation**: See the Installation Guide for help installing Fedora (if a later version of Fedora is available, use that):
  ```
  http://docs.fedoraproject.org/en-US/Fedora/22/html/
  Installation_Guide/
  ```

Install Docker in Fedora (docker Package)

Once you have Fedora installed and ready to go, log in. Then either become the root user or use `sudo` to run the commands as follows. Before you install Docker, as root user make sure you update your Fedora software (`yum update`). Then install the docker (or, with older versions of Fedora, docker.io) package with `yum install` and start the Docker service as follows (as an alternative, you can use the `dnf` command in the latest Fedora distribution instead of `yum` to install software):

1. **Update packages**: Run the following command to install the latest versions of your Fedora software.

   ```
   # yum update
   ```

2. **Install docker package**: In earlier versions of Fedora, Docker is available from the docker.io package. By the time you read this text, the package will probably simply be called docker. Install the package as follows, which also pulls in any dependent packages as needed:

   ```
   # yum install docker
   ```

3. **Start the Docker service**: The Docker service is not set to start automatically in Fedora. To enable the Docker service and start it immediately, type the following:

   ```
   # systemctl enable docker.service
   Created symlink from /etc/systemd/system/multi-user.target.wants/
   docker.service to /usr/lib/systemd/system/docker.service.
   # systemctl start docker.service
   ```

4. **Check status of Docker service**: To make sure the Docker service is running, type the following:

```
# systemctl status docker.service
  docker.service - Docker Application Container Engine
  Loaded: loaded (/usr/lib/systemd/system/docker.service; enabled)
  Active: active (running) since Sun 2015-05-17 10:05:32 EDT; 2min
ago
      Docs: http://docs.docker.com
  Main PID: 3405 (docker)
    CGroup: /system.slice/docker.service
            └─3405 /usr/bin/docker -d --selinux-enabled
```

As you can see from the output, docker.service is enabled and active. The actual service consists of the `docker` command (`/usr/bin/docker`), run as a daemon process (`-d`), with SELinux enabled (`--selinux-enabled`). Next, take a look inside the docker package.

Look in the Fedora docker Package

Once docker is installed, run the `rpm -ql` command on the docker (or docker.io) package to take a look at the contents of that package. This gives you a sense of what you can do with Docker:

```
# rpm -ql docker | less
/etc/docker
/etc/sysconfig/docker
/etc/sysconfig/docker-network
/etc/sysconfig/docker-storage
/etc/udev/rules.d/80-docker.rules
/usr/bin/docker
/usr/bin/docker-storage-setup
/usr/lib/systemd/system/docker.service
/usr/libexec/docker
/usr/libexec/docker/dockerinit
/usr/share/bash-completion/completions/docker
...
/usr/share/doc/docker/README.md
/usr/share/man/man1/docker-attach.1.gz
/usr/share/man/man1/docker-build.1.gz
/usr/share/man/man1/docker-commit.1.gz
...
```

Many of the files are the same as you would find in the Ubuntu docker.io package. There are files for starting up the Docker service (systemd is used exclusively in the latest Fedora releases) and the docker command itself (`/usr/bin/docker`).

Likewise, there is a file to allow you to do tab completion of text you type when using the `docker` command in a bash shell. The tab completion file makes it possible for you to do tab completion for docker subcommands and options, names and IDs of containers and images, and repository names and tags.

Here are descriptions of some of the other files in Fedora's docker package that are particular to Fedora:

- **/etc/sysconfig/docker**: This file lets you add options to the `docker` command when it runs as a service daemon. By default, only the `--selinux-enabled` option is added to enable SELinux support for Docker. One other setting in that file (DOCKER_CERT_PATH) sets the directory path to key files needed to start the Docker service to `/etc/docker`.

- **/etc/sysconfig/docker-network**: Use this file to add networking options to pass to the Docker service.

- **/etc/sysconfig/docker-storage**: Use this file if you want to change how data are stored by the Docker service. By default, a sparse file mounted in loopback in the `/var/lib/docker` directory is used. If you choose, you can instead assign raw storage devices to hold metadata and data. Read the contents of this file for suggestions on how to do that. Using raw storage devices in this way can help improve performance and overcome the 100GB maximum storage limitation with loopback.

- **/etc/udev/rules.d/80-docker.rules**: The 80-docker.rules file tells the udev service to set up device mapper files used by the Docker service to access host features needed by the containers. **(The Ubuntu Docker software package includes a similar udev file.)**

- **/usr/share/doc**: In the **/usr/share/doc/docker** directory, you can see documentation files that come from the Docker Project. They include things such as information about software changes and licensing, as well as general README files about the project itself.

- **/usr/share/man documentation**: Man pages for the `docker` command itself are divided across multiple docker man pages stored in section 1 by subcommand. For example, to read about using `docker` with the `build` option (`docker build`), type the `man docker-build` command. The only man page in section 5 describes the format of the Dockerfile file you use to build Docker images. (Type `man Dockerfile` to view that file.)

With the docker package in place, you can go on and start using the `docker` command in Chapter 3.

Configuring Red Hat Enterprise Linux for Docker

Red Hat Enterprise Linux (RHEL) is the subscription-based Linux distribution from Red Hat. Its goal is to offer a stable, tested Linux distribution available with different levels of customer support from Red Hat. When security and stability are critical, Red Hat Enterprise Linux is often used on systems throughout the application development life cycle, as well as for production deployment.

Like Fedora, Red Hat Enterprise Linux is an RPM-based Linux distribution. However, a few steps are different from Fedora when you install Red Hat Enterprise Linux and add Docker.

Before you can download and install Red Hat Enterprise Linux, you need either to have an active subscription or to sign up for an evaluation subscription. Go to the following URLs to learn about how to download and install RHEL:

- **RHEL download**: Go to `https://access.redhat.com/downloads/` and either select the button next to Red Hat Enterprise Linux that says Download Latest (Server) or select Red Hat Enterprise Linux and choose the installation medium that suits you. If you are prompted to log in and you don't have a Red Hat subscription, select the Evaluations button to sign up for an evaluation subscription. Keep in mind that your need the RHEL server version of the software because other versions of RHEL don't include Docker.

- **RHEL installation**: Go to the Red Hat Enterprise Linux documentation page (`https://access.redhat.com/documentation/en-US/Red_Hat_Enterprise_Linux/`) and select the Installation Guide. The guide describes how to boot the installation medium you just downloaded and install the software in various ways.

Once you have installed RHEL, you need to register your system, install docker, and start the Docker service, as described in the following sections.

Install Docker in Red Hat Enterprise Linux (docker Package)

Assuming you have Red Hat Enterprise Linux subscriptions and an account to the Red Hat customer portal, here are the steps you can follow to subscribe that system and add docker software to it.

1. **Register and subscribe RHEL**: Use subscription manager to enable your Red Hat subscription and enable the repositories you need to get the docker package, as well as related packages you need later. Run the following command, identifying your Red Hat user name and password (when prompted):

```
# subscription-manager register --username=rhnuser --auto-attach
Password:
```

```
# subscription-manager repos --enable=rhel-7-server-extras-rpms
# subscription-manager repos --enable=rhel-7-server-optional-rpms
```

2. **Update packages**: Once the RHEL 7 system is properly entitled, update all installed packages to the latest versions and reboot as follows:

```
# yum update
# reboot
```

3. **Install docker**: After the system has come back up, install the docker package by typing the following:

```
# yum install docker
```

4. **Start and enable Docker service**: With Docker installed, to start using Docker all you have to do is start and enable the Docker service. To do that in RHEL 7, type:

```
# systemctl start docker.service
# systemctl enable docker.service
# systemctl status docker.service
docker.service - Docker Application Container Engine
    Loaded: loaded (/usr/lib/systemd/system/docker.service; enabled)
    Active: active (running) since Sun 2015-05-17 16:52:33 EDT; 8s ago
      Docs: http://docs.docker.com
 Main PID: 32147 (docker)
    CGroup: /system.slice/docker.service
            └─32147 /usr/bin/docker -d --selinux-enabled \
                    --add-registry registry.access.redhat.com
```

From the output, you can see that the Docker service is enabled and active. The docker command that provides the service (/usr/bin/docker) is started with options to run it as a daemon (-d), enable SELinux, and add a container registry to those searched by docker (in this case, registry.access.redhat.com).

With the docker package now installed and the Docker service running, you should familiarize yourself with the contents of the docker package in RHEL.

Look in the RHEL docker Package

To check out the contents of the docker package type the following command:

```
# rpm -ql docker
/etc/docker
/etc/docker/certs.d
/etc/docker/certs.d/redhat.com
/etc/docker/certs.d/redhat.com/redhat-ca.crt
/etc/docker/certs.d/redhat.io
/etc/docker/certs.d/redhat.io/redhat-ca.crt
...
/usr/share/man/man1/docker-attach.1.gz
```

```
/usr/share/man/man1/docker-build.1.gz
/usr/share/man/man1/docker-commit.1.gz
...
/usr/share/man/man5/Dockerfile.5.gz
/usr/share/rhel
/usr/share/rhel/secrets
/usr/share/rhel/secrets/etc-pki-entitlement
/usr/share/rhel/secrets/rhel7.repo
/usr/share/rhel/secrets/rhsm
...
/usr/share/vim/vimfiles/doc
/usr/share/vim/vimfiles/doc/dockerfile.txt
/usr/share/vim/vimfiles/ftdetect
/usr/share/vim/vimfiles/ftdetect/dockerfile.vim
```

The components in the docker package are nearly identical to those in Fedora's docker package. So you can refer to the section on installing Fedora for docker for descriptions of many of the components. Here are descriptions of components that are specific to the RHEL docker package:

- **Certificates**: The RHEL docker package is configured to point to registries other than the Docker Hub. In particular, Red Hat has its own registry for official RHEL container images. Directories under `/etc/docker/certs.d` contain certificates that the Docker service can use to validate that it is communicating with the Red Hat registry.

- **Secrets**: Any files placed in the `/usr/share/rhel/secrets` directory are copied into containers run on the system. In particular, the docker package for RHEL places files in the secrets directory that allow the container to use Red Hat subscription management. These and other files related to subscription management make it possible for the containers to use subscription entitlements from the host to install and manage RPM packages within the container without consuming additional subscriptions.

- **vimfiles**: Files in the `/usr/share/vim/vimfiles/` directory provide syntax highlighting when you use the `vim` command to edit a Dockerfile file. This can help you create and edit Dockerfile files.

Configuring Other Operating Systems for Docker

As mentioned earlier, Docker is available with operating systems other than those demonstrated here. For instructions on installing Docker on other operating systems and cloud environments, see the following Docker installation procedures:

- **Install Docker on Mac OS X**: Using Mac OS X 10.6 or later, the procedure described at this location uses an ISO image containing the Boot-2Docker tool (`https://github.com/boot2docker/boot2docker/releases`) to create a lightweight Linux virtual machine that runs in VirtualBox on the Mac:

  `https://docs.docker.com/installation/mac/`

- **Install Docker on Microsoft Windows**: For Windows 7.1 or 8 systems (and possibly others), you can use the procedure described at this URL if your computer supports hardware virtualization. Again, Docker only runs natively in Linux, so this procedure uses the Boot2Docker tool to create a Linux virtual machine in which you can try out Docker:

  `https://docs.docker.com/installation/windows/`

- **Install Docker on CentOS**: Running Docker on CentOS gives you the nearest experience to Docker on Red Hat Enterprise Linux without having to pay for a subscription. Keep in mind that CentOS comes with no guarantees and may lag behind RHEL in features and security patches. Go here to install Docker on CentOS:

  `https://docs.docker.com/installation/centos/`

- **Install Docker on Debian**: Go here for instructions on installing Docker on Debian GNU/Linux systems:

  `https://docs.docker.com/installation/debian/`

- **Install Docker on SUSE**: Both openSUSE and SUSE Linux Enterprise procedures for installing Docker are described in this location:

  `https://docs.docker.com/installation/SUSE/`

If the operating system you want to use is not listed here, see the Docker installation page (`https://docs.docker.com/installation/`) for instructions related to installing Docker on other operating systems. If you want to put Docker together yourself for your own operating system, see the Docker Binaries page (`https://docs.docker.com/installation/binaries/`).

One type of Linux system that has not been described yet for using Docker is the specialized Linux systems designed specifically for running containers. The next section describes how to set up Project Atomic and CoreOS operating systems to do the task they were created for: provide a run-time environment specifically for containers.

CONFIGURING A CONTAINER-STYLE LINUX SYSTEM FOR DOCKER

It makes no sense to containerize applications, making them small and efficient, if you end up deploying those containers in slow, bloated operating systems. In the evolving container model, as the executables, libraries, and other components an application needs to run are in its container, host operating systems are being slimmed down to little more than what is needed to run those containers.

Project Atomic and CoreOS are two projects aimed at producing operating systems tuned specifically for running containers. While the operating systems can run directly on hardware, they can also run as virtual machines on public clouds (such as Amazon EC2 or Google Compute Engine), private virtualization platforms (provided by OpenStack, VMware, or Red Hat Enterprise Virtualization), or individual computers (such as a Linux KVM host).

Likewise, there are different methods of installing and configuring Project Atomic and CoreOS operating systems. Project Atomic offers an installer ISO that is similar to installing a Fedora or RHEL system, where you click through steps for configuring networks, partitioning disks, and adding users. CoreOS provides an ISO that can simply copy its entire image to a selected partition and boot up within minutes.

When deploying to cloud environments, tools such as cloud-config (CoreOS) and cloud-init (Atomic and others) can be used to configure cloud images as you need them.

Configuring an Atomic Host for Docker

The Atomic Project (www.projectatomic.io) is an RPM-based Linux distribution builder, designed specifically for deploying and managing containers. There are versions of Fedora, Red Hat Enterprise Linux, and CentOS that are available to run as an Atomic host.

Atomic Host systems are offered in several different forms to make it easy for you to use in different environments. You can download an Atomic qcow2 image and use cloud-init to essentially inject configuration information (user accounts, hostnames, configuration files, and so on) to configure it. Vagrant files for quickly spinning up CentOS Atomic VMs are available for CentOS Atomic. The RHEL Atomic and Fedora Atomic projects offer installation ISOs you can use to step through a traditional installer to configure an Atomic system.

Here are the links to where you can find images to download for different Atomic host versions:

- **Fedora Atomic** (`https://getfedora.org/cloud/download`): From the Download Fedora Cloud page, there is a tab for Atomic Images. Select the Atomic ISO Image to download the image and install the Fedora Atomic system using a normal Fedora installer (anaconda). For other formats of Fedora Atomic, Atomic Images in qcow2 (for OpenStack) and raw formats are available for download. You also can launch Atomic images from Vagrant for VirtualBox and KVM (libvirt) environments. Finally, Atomic images also are available for Amazon EC2 cloud deployment.

- **CentOS Atomic** (`http://buildlogs.centos.org/centos/7/isos/x86_64/`): Images in qcow2 format are available from this site. Likewise, vagrant boxes are available that you can use to immediately spin up a CentOS Atomic VM if your system has vagrant installed (`https://www.vagrantup.com/`). The procedure used here is similar to what you use to deploy a RHEL or Fedora Atomic qcow2 image.

- **RHEL Atomic** (`https://access.redhat.com/downloads`): You need a Red Hat subscription (regular or evaluation) to download an RHEL Atomic image. From the Red Hat downloads page, select Red Hat Enterprise Linux. Then, under Product Variant, select Red Hat Enterprise Linux Atomic host. RHEL Atomic images are available in different formats (qcow2, ova, vhd, and installation ISO) that are suitable for different platforms (cloud, Red Hat Enterprise Virtualization, Microsoft Hyper-V, and VMware vSphere).

For more ways to get and install Project Atomic distributions, see the Project Atomic Quick Start Guide (`www.projectatomic.io/docs/quickstart`). For this example, I set up a Fedora Atomic Host, using the Fedora 22 installer. The same basic procedure can be used to configure RHEL from an Atomic installation ISO.

Configuring Fedora Atomic Host for Docker

Like CoreOS, Atomic Host systems are preconfigured to run Docker. To get started setting up a Fedora Atomic Host in this procedure, download the Fedora Atomic ISO installation image. You can burn that ISO to a CD or DVD and install it directly to computer hardware or use it on almost any system that supports virtualization (such as a Linux KVM system, using the virt-manager tool).

1. **Download Fedora Atomic ISO Image**: Download the latest Fedora Atomic installer image. Look for the official Fedora 22 or later version. I used the following:

```
https://download.fedoraproject.org/pub/fedora/linux/releases/22/Cloud_
Atomic/x86_64/iso/Fedora-Cloud_Atomic-x86_64-22.iso
```

2. **Start the Fedora Atomic ISO Image**: Start up the installer either physically (from the image burned to a CD in your drive) or as a virtual machine (using virt-manager, OpenStack, or some other tool for managing VMs). I recommend you have at least a 10GB disk partition to devote to Fedora Atomic, just to try it out.

3. **Make installation selections**: Step through the installation screens, providing information on how you want to configure your system. Most of the features are set from the Installation Summary screen, as shown in Figure 2.1. On the Installation Summary screen, do the following:

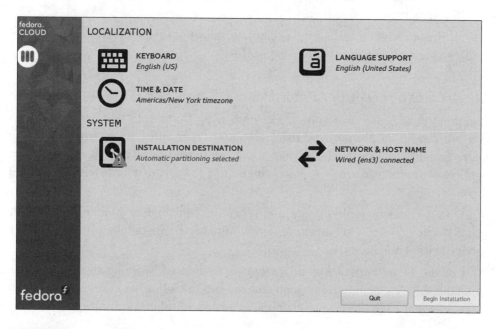

FIGURE 2.1 Identify disk partitions and networking settings from the Installation Summary screen.

- **Keyboard**: Choose your keyboard by language and location.
- **Time & Date**: Set date, time, and time zone. By selecting Network Time (the default) you have your system synced with an NTP time server.
- **Installation Destination**: Select this item and either take automatic disk partitioning or choose partitioning yourself.
- **Language Support**: Choose your language.

- **Network & Host Name**: Networking is turned on automatically (attempting to use DHCP to get address information). Select this item if you want to disable networking or set your host name. Select Done when you are finished.

4. **Select Begin Installation**: No changes have been made to your disk partition yet. If all your settings are done, select Begin Installation.

5. **Set root password and user**: As the installer is working, select ROOT PASSWORD and set the root password. Then select USER CREATION and add a user account (set a password for the user). You can also decide whether you want the user to have sudo privilege (select Make This User Administrator). Select Done and return to the Configuration screen and wait for installation to finish up.

6. **Reboot**: When installation is complete, select to reboot the system so you can start using your Fedora Atomic Host.

Check Out Your Fedora Atomic Host

You don't need to add any software to start using Docker. In fact, you can't even add software to an Atomic host using traditional rpm and yum software packaging tools. To add software to the system you have to add regular containers (to run applications) or super privileged containers (to add tools to access the host system directly).

What you can do immediately after rebooting your Fedora Atomic Host is start using Docker. The docker package should already be installed, with the Docker service started and enabled.

Updates to the Fedora Atomic system are performed by doing atomic upgrades using the atomic command. I recommend you run the following atomic command to make sure you have the latest version of Docker and related software available on your system:

```
# atomic host upgrade
```

Once the software is upgraded, reboot for the latest atomic upgrade to take effect. You can now start setting up a Docker registry, as described in Chapter 3, or start using docker commands, as shown in Chapter 4, "Running Container Images."

Configuring CoreOS for Docker

CoreOS offers several ways of getting a running CoreOS system going. In this example, I use a CoreOS live media. This image can be burned to CD and booted up directly on hardware or launched in a tool that can install a virtual machine (such as the Virtual Machine Manager tool available in many Linux systems).

The following section describes how to use the CoreOS ISO live media to boot to a live CoreOS system, install CoreOS to hard disk, and then boot the system from hard disk so you can start using Docker.

Go through the following steps to get, boot, and install CoreOS from a CoreOS live media ISO image:

1. **Get CoreOS**: To get CoreOS installation media, go to the following URL and select Download Stable ISO:

   https://coreos.com/docs/running-coreos/platforms/iso/

2. **Prepare installation medium**: Make the CoreOS live medium available to use to install CoreOS to hard disk. You can burn it to a CD, point to it from a VM installation application (such as Virtual Machine Manager in Linux), or copy to a PXE server and boot it from a network interface card.

3. **Boot install medium**: If you are installing to a virtual machine on a local system or cloud environment, identify the amount of disk space you want the new CoreOS system to have available. When CoreOS boots up, the disk should be available as a device such as /dev/sda or /dev/sdb.

4. **Use live CoreOS**: CoreOS boots up directly to a shell prompt as the username core (which has sudo privilege). CoreOS comes with two user accounts configured by default: root and core. The CoreOS system is running live (not yet installed) at this point. Do the following to prepare for installation.

5. **Create encrypted password**: Create an encrypted password to use with the core user account. For example, you can use the openssl command to create an md5crypt password (that tool comes with CoreOS). When prompted, type the password you want to encrypt (twice):

   ```
   # openssl passwd -1
   Password: ********
   Verifying - Password: ********
   $1$f6e4jyo9$lbch8VJ23oU2cW5grkk4s.
   ```

6. **Create a cloud-config file**: Create a cloud-config file to add user password and other configuration information to CoreOS. See "Using Cloud-Config" (https://github.com/coreos/coreos-cloudinit/blob/master/Documentation/cloud-config.md) for details about the contents of a cloud-config file. For this example, create a file called cloud-config.yaml that contains the following content (replace the passwd string with the one you generated in the previous step):

```
#cloud-config
users:
  - name: core
    passwd: $1$f6e4jyo9$1bch8VJ23oU2cW5grkk4s.
    groups:
      - sudo
      - docker
```

7. **Run the coreos-install script**: Run the following command to install the CoreOS image to the disk device you identified earlier (here I use `/dev/sda` as the disk drive):

```
$ sudo coreos-install -d /dev/sda -c cloud-config.yaml
Checking availability of "local-file"
Fetching user-data from datasource of type "local-file"
Downloading the signature for http://stable.release.core-os.net...
...
Downloading, writing and verifying coreos_production_image.bin.bz2...
...
Success! CoreOS stable 647.0.0 is installed on /dev/sda
```

8. **Reboot**: After the image has completed installing reboot the system:

```
$ sudo reboot
```

9. **Log in**: After CoreOS reboots, log in using `core` as the user name along with the password you encrypted and assigned to that user earlier.

At this point, you can set up a Docker registry in Chapter 3 or start using docker commands, as shown in Chapter 4.

SUMMARY

Docker is available with a variety of different Linux systems. Besides using standard Linux systems, such as Ubuntu, Fedora, Red Hat Enterprise Linux, or CentOS, for running Docker, specialty Linux systems tuned specifically for container deployments are also available. By running those systems as virtual machines, you can start using Docker on Microsoft Windows or Mac OS X systems as well.

This chapter described how to configure Ubuntu, Fedora, and Red Hat Enterprise Linux systems to be ready to run Docker. It also described how to get and configure specialty Linux distributions such as the Atomic Project and CoreOS so you can use them to deploy Docker.

Setting Up a Private Docker Registry

One of the foundations of Docker is the ability to request to use an existing container image and then, if it is not already on your system, grab it from somewhere and download it to your system. By default, "somewhere" is the Docker Hub Registry (`https://hub.docker.com`). However, there are ways to configure other locations from which you can pull docker images. These locations are referred to as *registries*.

By setting up your own private registry, you can keep your private images to yourself. You can also save time by pushing and pulling your images locally, instead of having them go out over the Internet.

Setting up a private registry is simple. It requires getting the service (by installing a package or using the `registry` Docker container image), starting the service, and making sure the proper port is open so the service is accessible. Using registries requires a bit more explanation than setting up one, especially when you consider that features are added to Docker every day that are changing how Docker uses and searches registries for images.

In particular, the way that Docker uses the image namespace is changing to be more adaptable. If your location is disconnected from the Internet, with the Docker hub inaccessible, features are being developed to allow you to use a different default registry. Likewise, new features let you add registries to your search order, much the same way you can have an Internet browser look at different DNS servers.

This chapter describes how to set up a private Docker registry on several different Linux systems. The first examples are simply to help you get a Docker registry up and running quickly to begin testing or learning how to use registries. After that, I describe some techniques for making a Docker registry more production ready.

Later in the chapter, I tell you how to adapt the way your local Docker service uses Docker registries, including how to replace Docker.io as the default registry and add other registries to the search path.

NOTE

Having a local registry in place is not required to use Docker. However, as you build, save, and reuse images throughout this book, you may find it handy to have a way to store your images (especially private ones) without pushing them out to the public Docker Hub Registry. That said, you can skip this chapter for now if you want to learn more about using containers before you jump into setting up a Docker registry.

GETTING AND STARTING A PRIVATE DOCKER REGISTRY

You can run a Docker registry on your Linux system in a number of different ways to store your own Docker images. For Linux distributions that include a docker-registry package (such as Fedora and Red Hat Enterprise Linux), you can install that package and start up the service. For other distributions, you can run the official `registry` container image from Docker.io to provide the service.

See the section later in the chapter that corresponds to the Linux system you are using for instructions on installing and running a Docker registry on that system. For Fedora, I illustrate how to use the docker-registry package, while for Ubuntu I show how to use the `registry` container.

Here are a few general things you should know about setting up a Docker registry:

- **Install anywhere**: Like most servers, the Docker registry does not need to be installed on client systems (that is, where you run your `docker` commands). You can install it on any Linux system that your clients can reach over a network. That way, multiple Docker clients can access your Docker registry.

- **Open port**: If your Docker registry is not on the client, you must be sure that TCP port 5000 is not being blocked by the firewall where the Docker registry is running.

- **Provide space**: If you push a lot of images to your registry, space can fill up quickly. For the docker-registry package, stored images are contained in the `/var/lib/docker-registry` directory. Make sure you configure enough space in that directory to meet your needs, or you can configure a different directory, if you want.

Setting Up a Docker Registry in Fedora

Follow these instructions to install and start up a Docker registry on a Fedora system. At the moment, this procedure creates a version 1 Docker registry from the docker-registry RPM package. Although this procedure was tested on Fedora, the same basic procedures should work for the following Linux distributions:

- Fedora 22 or later
- Red Hat Enterprise Linux 7.1 or later
- CentOS 7.1 or later

The docker-registry package is not included in the Atomic project Fedora, RHEL, and CentOS distributions. So you must use the `registry` container, described later for setting up a Docker registry in Ubuntu, to get that feature on an Atomic Linux system.

 NOTE

During the following procedure, you are going to use image tags to identify the registry where you intend an image to be stored. For a more in-depth look at tags, refer to Chapter 6, "Tagging Images." To get `docker-registry` to work, you may need to edit the `usr/lib/system/docker-registry. service` and remove `--debug`.

1. **Install docker-registry**: When you install the docker-registry package in Fedora, it pulls in more than a dozen dependent packages as well. To install those packages, type the following:

```
# yum install docker-registry
...
Transaction Summary
================================================
```

```
Install  1 Package (+15 Dependent packages)
Total download size: 6.8 M
Installed size: 39 M
Is this ok [y/d/N]: y
```

2. **List docker-registry contents**: Use the rpm command to list the contents of the docker-registry file in Fedora. There are nearly 200 files (mostly python code in the package). This command shows you only documentation and configuration files (I describe how to configure them later):

```
# rpm -ql docker-registry | grep -E "(/etc)|(/usr/share)|(systemd)"
/etc/docker-registry.yml
/etc/sysconfig/docker-registry
/usr/lib/systemd/system/docker-registry.service
/usr/share/doc/docker-registry
/usr/share/doc/docker-registry/AUTHORS
/usr/share/doc/docker-registry/CHANGELOG.md
/usr/share/doc/docker-registry/LICENSE
/usr/share/doc/docker-registry/README.md
```

3. **Open firewall**: If your Fedora system is running a firewall that blocks incoming connections, you may need to open TCP port 5000 to allow access to the Docker registry service. Assuming you are using the firewall service in Fedora, run these commands to open the port on the firewall (immediately and permanently) and see that the port has been opened:

```
# firewall-cmd --zone=public --add-port=5000/tcp
# firewall-cmd --zone=public --add-port=5000/tcp --permanent
# firewall-cmd --zone=public --list-ports
5000/tcp
```

4. **Start the docker-registry service**: If you want to do any special configuration for your Docker registry, refer to the next sections before starting the service. For a simple docker-registry installation, however, you can simply start the service and begin using it, as follows (as the status shows, the docker-registry service is active and enabled):

```
# systemctl start docker-registry
# systemctl enable docker-registry
Created symlink from
   /etc/systemd/system/multi-user.target.wants/docker-registry.
service
   to /usr/lib/systemd/system/docker-registry.service.
# systemctl status docker-registry
docker-registry.service - Registry server for Docker
 Loaded: loaded (/usr/lib/systemd/system/docker-registry.
service;enabled)
 Active: active (running) since Mon 2015-05-25 12:02:14 EDT; 42s ago
```

```
Main PID: 5728 (gunicorn)
   CGroup: /system.slice/docker-registry.service
          ├─5728 /usr/bin/python /usr/bin/gunicorn --access-logfile
               - --max-requests 100 --graceful-timeout 3600-t 36...
   ...
```

5. **Get an image**: A common image used to test Docker is the hello-world image available from the Docker Hub Registry. Run that image as follows (which pulls that image to the local system and runs it):

```
# docker run --name myhello hello-world
Unable to find image 'hello-world:latest' locally
latest: Pulling from docker.io/hello-world
91c95931e552: Download complete
a8219747be10: Download complete
Hello from Docker.
docker.io/hello-world:latest: The image you are pulling has been
verified.
...
```

6. **Allow access to registry**: The docker clients in Fedora and Red Hat Enterprise Linux require that you either obtain a certificate from the registry or you identify the registry as insecure. For this example, you can identify the registry as insecure by editing the /etc/sysconfig/docker file and creating the following lines in that file:

```
ADD_REGISTRY='--add-registry localhost:5000'
INSECURE_REGISTRY='--insecure-registry localhost:5000'
```

After that, restart the local Docker service:

```
# systemctl restart docker
```

7. **Tag the image**: Use docker tag to give the image a name that you can use to push it to the Docker registry on the local system:

```
# docker tag hello-world localhost:5000/hello-me:latest
```

8. **Push the image**: To push the hello-world to the local Docker registry, type the following:

```
# docker push localhost:5000/hello-me:latest
The push refers to a repository [localhost:5000/hello-me] (1 tags)
...
Pushing tag for rev [91c95931e552] on
     {http://localhost:5000/v1/repositories/hello-me/tags/latest}
```

9. **Pull the image**: To make sure you can retrieve the image from the registry, in the second Terminal, remove the image from your system, then try to retrieve it from your local registry:

```
# docker rm myhello
# docker rmi hello-world localhost:5000/hello-me:latest
# docker pull localhost:5000/hello-me:latest
Pulling repository localhost:5000/hello-me
91c95931e552: Download complete
a8219747be10: Download complete
# docker images
REPOSITORY                TAG    IMAGE ID      CREATED      VIRTUAL SIZE
localhost:5000/hello-me latest 91c95931e552 5 weeks ago 910 B
```

In the example just shown, the image was successfully pushed to and pulled from the local repository. At this point, you have these choices:

- If you want to learn more about how the Docker registry works and possibly modify its behavior, skip to the "Configuring a Private Docker Registry" section later in this chapter.

- If you are ready to start using Docker containers, skip ahead to Chapter 4, "Running Container Images."

The next section describes how to set up a Docker registry in Ubuntu.

Setting Up a Docker Registry in Ubuntu

Instead of installing a Docker registry from a software package, you can download the `registry` container from the Docker Hub Registry and use that to provide the Docker registry service. This is a quick and easy way to try out a Docker registry, although the default registry doesn't scale well for a production environment and is more difficult to configure.

> **NOTE**
>
> Several versions of the registry are available. For this example, I use `registry:latest`, which results in an image of a version 1 Docker registry. By the time you try this, there may be a stable version 2 available. I recommend you refer here for information on running the version 2 Docker registry: `https://docs.docker.com/registry/`.

Although this procedure was tested on Ubuntu 14.04, the same basic procedure should work on any Linux system running the Docker service.

To get started here, install Docker as described in Chapter 2, "Setting Up a Container Run-Time Environment," and start up the Docker service. I suggest you open two Terminal windows (shells) to do this procedure. Open one where you plan to run the registry service, so you can watch it in progress as you start up and test it. Open another Terminal, from which you can push and pull images.

1. **Get the registry image:** Run the `docker pull` command as follows to pull the `registry` image from the Docker Hub Registry (see Chapter 5, "Finding, Pulling, Saving, and Loading Container Images," for a description of `docker pull`):

```
$ sudo docker pull registry:latest
Pulling repository registry
204704ce3137: Download complete
e9e06b06e14c: Download complete
...
```

2. **Run the registry image:** To try out the Docker registry, run the image in the foreground so you can watch messages produced as the container image is running (see Chapter 4 for a description of `docker run`). This command starts the latest `registry` image, exposes TCP port 5000 on the system so clients outside the container can use it, and runs it as a foreground process in the first terminal:

```
$ sudo docker run -p 5000:5000 registry:latest
[2015-05-25 21:33:35 +0000] [1] [INFO] Starting gunicorn 19.1.1
[2015-05-25 21:33:35 +0000] [1] [INFO] Listening at:
http://0.0.0.0:5000 (1)
[2015-05-25 21:33:35 +0000] [1] [INFO] Using worker: gevent
...
```

3. **Get an image:** To test that you can push and pull images, open a second Terminal window. A common image used to test Docker is the hello-world image available from the Docker Hub Registry. Run that image as follows (which pulls that image to the local system and runs it):

```
$ sudo docker run --name myhello hello-world
Pulling repository hello-world
91c95931e552: Download complete
a8219747be10: Download complete
Hello from Docker.
This message shows that your installation appears to be working
correctly.
...
```

4. **Tag the image:** Use `docker tag` to give the image a name that you can use to push it to the Docker registry on the local system:

```
$ sudo docker tag hello-world localhost:5000/hello-me:latest
```

5. **Push the image**: To push the hello-world to the local Docker registry, type the following:

```
$ sudo docker push localhost:5000/hello-me:latest
The push refers to a repository [localhost:5000/hello-me] (len: 1)
...
Pushing tag for rev [91c95931e552] on
    {http://localhost:5000/v1/repositories/hello-me/tags/latest}
```

6. **Check the Docker registry log messages**: If the image was pushed to the registry successfully, in the first Terminal you should see messages showing PUT commands succeeding. For example:

```
172.17.42.1 - - [25/May/2015:22:12:37 +0000] "PUT
/v1/repositories/hello-me/images HTTP/1.1" 204 - "-" "docker/1.0.1
go/go1.2.1 git-commit/990021a kernel/3.13.0-24-generic os/linux
arch/amd64"
```

7. **Pull the image**: To make sure you can retrieve the image from the registry, in the second Terminal remove the image from your system, and then try to retrieve it from your local registry:

```
$ sudo docker rm myhello
$ sudo docker rmi hello-world localhost:5000/hello-me:latest
$ sudo docker pull localhost:5000/hello-me:latest
Pulling repository localhost:5000/hello-me
91c95931e552: Download complete
a8219747be10: Download complete
# docker images
REPOSITORY                TAG      IMAGE ID      CREATED      VIRTUAL SIZE
localhost:5000/hello-me  latest  91c95931e552  5 weeks ago  910 B
```

8. **Run the docker registry again**: Instead of running the `registry` image in the foreground, holding the Terminal open, you can have it run more permanently in the background (`-d`). To do that, close the running registry container and start a new image as follows:

```
$ sudo docker run -d -p 5000:5000 registry:latest
```

The Docker registry is running in the background now, ready to use. At this point, you have these choices:

- If you want to learn more about how the Docker registry works and possibly modify its behavior, skip to the "Configuring a Private Docker Registry" section later in this chapter.

- If you are ready to start using Docker containers, skip ahead to Chapter 4.

The next section describes how to set up a Docker registry in other Linux distributions.

CONFIGURING A PRIVATE DOCKER REGISTRY

The default registries that come in the docker-registry package or the `registry` container are fine if you just want to try out a Docker registry. If you want to use a registry in a production environment, however, you need a deeper understanding of how to configure your Docker registry to better suit your needs.

The following sections describe how to modify the Docker registry software for both the docker-registry package and using the registry container.

Configuring the docker-registry Package

To better understand how the docker-registry package software works, start with how the registry is set to run by default. When the docker-registry service starts up in Fedora or Red Hat Enterprise Linux, it runs the `gunicorn` process. There is one main `gunicorn` process and four additional `gunicorn` workers running, by default, to provide the service.

From a full `ps` output the `gunicorn` processes; you can see the options set for them:

```
# ps -ef | grep gunicorn
00:00:00 /usr/bin/python /usr/bin/gunicorn --access-logfile -
 --max-requests 100 --graceful-timeout 3600 -t 3600 -k gevent -b
0.0.0.0:5000 -w 4 docker_registry.wsgi:application
```

Here's what you can learn from this command line:

- **--access-logfile**: Access to the docker-registry service is logged to any file you set. In this case, however, the log file is set to a single hyphen (-), so access messages are simply sent to standard output (where they are picked up by the `systemd` journal and can be viewed by the `journalctl` command).

- **--max-requests 100**: Sets the maximum number of requests that a `gunicorn` daemon can accept to 100. After that, the worker is restarted.

- **--graceful-timeout 3600**: Gives the `gunicorn` worker 3600 seconds (6 minutes) to finish handling a request once it has been sent a restart signal. If it has not completed what it is doing by that time, it is killed.

- **-t 3600**: If the `gunicorn` worker is silent for more than 3600 seconds (6 minutes), it is killed and restarted.

- **-k gevent**: Sets the type of `gunicorn` worker to gevent (an asynchronous type of worker based on Greenlets).

- **-b 0.0.0.0:5000**: Sets the worker to bind on all IP addresses on the system (0.0.0.0) on port 5000. This allows docker clients to connect to the Docker registry through any external network interface on the system via TCP port 5000.
- **-w 4**: Sets the number of worker processes to 4 (above the original gunicorn process).
- **docker_registry.wsgi:application**: Runs the process with the Docker registry wsgi application.

To change the behavior of the docker-registry service, you can edit the /etc/sysconfig/docker-registry file. Here is how that file is set by default in Fedora:

```
# The Docker registry configuration file
DOCKER_REGISTRY_CONFIG=/etc/docker-registry.yml

# The configuration to use from DOCKER_REGISTRY_CONFIG file
SETTINGS_FLAVOR=local

# Address to bind the registry to
REGISTRY_ADDRESS=0.0.0.0

# Port to bind the registry to
REGISTRY_PORT=5000

# Number of workers to handle the connections
GUNICORN_WORKERS=4
```

In the docker-registry file, you can do such things as have the Docker registry listen only on a particular IP address (by default, REGISTRY_ADDRESS=0.0.0.0 listens on all addresses). You can change the port of the service to something other than TCP port 5000 or set the number of gunicorn workers to something other than 4.

The /etc/docker-registry.yml file is set as the Docker registry config file. SETTINGS_FLAVOR=local tells the config file to include common variables and then set the directory /var/lib/docker-registry for local storage use. In the /etc/sysconfig/docker-registry file, the common variables you can set include the following:

- **LOGLEVEL**: By default, the log level is set to info. This can also be set to debug, notice, warning, warn, err, error, crit, alert, emerg, or panic.
- **DEBUG**: Set to either true or false to have debugging turned on or off.
- **STANDALONE**: If set to true (the default), the registry acts as a standalone registry and doesn't query the Docker index.

- **INDEX_ENDPOINT**: If the local registry is not set to run in standalone, the default, the index endpoint is set to `https://index.docker.io`.
- **STORAGE_REDIRECT**: By default, this is disabled.
- **DISABLE_TOKEN_AUTH**: If the service is not in standalone, this variable is enabled to allow token authentication.
- **PRIVILEGED_KEY**: By default, no privileged key is set.
- **SEARCH_BACKEND**: By default, there is no search backend.
- **SQLALCHEMY_INDEX_DATABASE**: By default, the SQLite search backend database is set to: `sqlite:////tmp/docker-registry.db`.

If you want to use a setting flavor other than local, look in the `/etc/docker-registry.yml` file. Different setting flavors can be used for Ceph Object Gateway configuration, Google Cloud Storage configuration, OpenStack Swift Storage, and others.

Other variables you can set that can be picked up by the gunicorn process, include the following. Notice that some of these values show up on the `gunicorn` command line:

- **GUNICORN_GRACEFUL_TIMEOUT**: Sets the timeout for gracefully restarting workers (in seconds).
- **GUNICORN_SILENT_TIMEOUT**: Sets the timeout for restarting workers that have gone silent (in seconds).
- **GUNICORN_USER**: Runs the gunicorn process as the user set here, instead of running it with root user privileges.
- **GUNICORN_GROUP**: Runs the gunicorn process as the group set here, instead of running it with root group privileges.
- **GUNICORN_ACCESS_LOG_FILE**: Sets the name of the log file to direct messages to those that are related to clients trying to access the service. By default, messages are sent to the systemd journal through standard output.
- **GUNICORN_ERROR_LOG_FILE**: Sets the name of the log file to direct messages to those that are related to error conditions. By default, messages are sent to the systemd journal through standard output.
- **GUNICORN_OPTS**: Identifies any extra options you want to pass to the gunicorn process.

After you set or change `/etc/sysconfig/docker-registry` file variables, restart the `docker-registry` service for these features to take effect.

Configuring the `registry` Container

Instead of trying to configure the `registry` container image by modifying the contents of the running container, the creators of that container image suggest you rebuild the registry container image yourself. In particular, you probably want to add security measures to your registry and more flexible storage features.

So far, this book has not yet introduced you to the concepts you need to build your own containers. However, after you have become familiar with the process, if you decide you want to build a custom version 1 registry container, I recommend you refer to the `docker-registry` GitHub page:

```
https://github.com/docker/docker-registry
```

From the `docker-registry` GitHub page, you can find information on how to build a version 1 registry image and links to the Dockerfile used to build it (`https://github.com/docker/docker-registry/blob/master/Dockerfile`).

By the time you read this, Docker registry version 2 may be ready to use. Refer to the Docker registry 2.0 page (`https://docs.docker.com/registry`) for details on how to deploy and configure this newer version of the Docker registry.

UNDERSTANDING THE DOCKER IMAGE NAMESPACE

Similar to the way that the Internet uses the Domain Name System (DNS) to have a unique set of names refer to all the host computers in the world, Docker set out to make a namespace to allow a unique way to name every container image in the world. In that vision, a `docker run` *someimage* would result in the exact same *someimage* being pulled to the local system and run, no matter where your location or what type of Linux system you run it on.

For some potential Docker users, this presents problems. Some Docker installations are disconnected from the Internet. Security requirements of others allow them to search and pull images only from registries that they own themselves. These issues would prevent a pure Docker system from being installed in their environments.

There has been pressure to change some aspects of how the Docker image namespace works, so you can expect that story to evolve over time. As things stand today, however, you should know that a system running Docker purely from the upstream Docker Project code has the following attributes:

- **Search**: An unpatched Docker system today only searches the Docker Hub Registry when you run a `docker search` command.

- **Blocking registries**: Docker does not have a feature to block the Docker Hub Registry. So pulling an image without identifying a specific registry causes Docker to search for that image on the Docker Hub Registry (if it's not already on the local system).

- **Changing the default registry**: Docker doesn't have a feature for changing your default registry to anything other than the Docker Hub Registry.

- **Push confirmation**: Docker does not ask you to confirm a push request before it begins pushing an image.

Changes to some of these features are being discussed in the Docker community. Patches to change how some of these features work are included in Red Hat Enterprise Linux, Fedora, Atomic project, and related Linux distributions. For example, the current version of the docker package in RHEL Atomic (docker-1.8) includes some of those features just mentioned.

For example, here are some settings from the `/etc/sysconfig/docker` file on an RHEL Atomic system that represent features that have not yet been added to the upstream Docker Project:

```
ADD_REGISTRY='--add-registry registry.access.redhat.com'
# BLOCK_REGISTRY='--block-registry'
# INSECURE_REGISTRY='--insecure-registry'
```

The ADD_REGISTRY variable lets you add a registry to use for `docker search` and `docker pull` commands. For users of Red Hat distributions, this puts Red Hat's own registry (`registry.access.redhat.com`) before the Docker Hub Registry, so the user can know he is searching and pulling from that registry first. A user could also replace that registry with his own registries or simply add his own registry in front of Red Hat's registry.

Using the ADD_REGISTRY variable to this file puts any registry you add at the front of the list searched. However, if a requested image is not found in any of the registries you add, the Docker Hub Registry still is searched next. To change that behavior, you need to use the BLOCK_REGISTRY variable.

By setting the BLOCK_REGISTRY variable, you can block access to any registry you choose. Of course, at the moment only the Docker Hub Registry is searched by default. So, to block the Docker Hub Registry from search and pull requests, you could use the following line:

```
BLOCK_REGISTRY='--block-registry docker.io'
```

With that set, any requests for images that could not be found in registries set with ADD_REGISTRY variables would fail to be found, even if they existed at the

Docker Hub Registry. In this way, only registries that you specifically included are searched for images by the users of this particular docker installation.

The INSECURE_REGISTRY='--insecure-registry' variable does not explicitly allow or disallow a registry. This is a specific case where someone wants to use the local Docker client to pull an image from a registry that provides HTTPS communication, but the client doesn't have a certificate from that registry to verify its authenticity. Uncommenting the variable and adding the name of the insecure registry to that line allows the `docker` command to pull from that registry without full authorization. For example:

```
INSECURE_REGISTRY='--insecure-registry myreg.example.com'
```

Again, this and other features just described are not part of the upstream Docker Project. But if you need these features for your installation, you can change how access to registries works by default in Docker using these features that are currently in Fedora, RHEL, CentOS, and related Atomic project systems.

SUMMARY

Setting up a private Docker registry gives you the ability to push and pull images without using the public Docker Hub Registry. This chapter described two different ways of setting up a Docker registry for yourself.

For Linux distributions that have a docker-registry package available (such as Fedora and Red Hat Enterprise Linux), you can install that package and start up the docker-registry service using the `systemctl` command. As an alternative, any system running the Docker service can pull and run the `registry` image, available from the Docker Hub Registry, to offer a private Docker registry.

Besides describing how to set up your own Docker registry, the chapter included a description of how the Docker image namespace works, with the Docker Hub Registry as its centerpiece. Proposed modifications to that model have been implemented in Fedora and other Red Hat sponsored operating systems and are being discussed in the Docker community. These modifications give users the ability to change which registries are set up to be used with search and pull requests from the Docker service.

Part II

Working with Individual Containers

## CHAPTER 4

Running Container Images

IN THIS CHAPTER:

- Run interactive commands from containers
- Run administrative commands inside a container
- Run services from within a container
- Run privileged containers

Once you have the Docker service installed and running on your local Linux system, running your first container is simple. To start, you don't have to have any Docker formatted images installed on your system. The `docker run` command goes out and finds the image for you. For the example, as I'm about to show, you just need a couple hundred megabytes of disk space and a bit of time to wait for the image to download.

 NOTE

Every time you run a container image or commit a container to an image, it consumes disk space. If after running a bunch of containers you begin to get failures from running out of disk space, use the commands `docker rm` (to remove containers) and `docker rmi` (to remove images) to free some space. See Chapter 11, "Cleaning Up Containers," for more information.

Assuming you have an Internet connection, you could run your first container as follows:

```
# docker run fedora cat /etc/os-release
Unable to find image 'fedora:latest' locally
00a0c78eeb6d: Pull complete
Status: Downloaded newer image...

NAME=Fedora
VERSION="22 (Twenty Two)"
ID=fedora
...
```

Several interesting things are going on with this `docker run` command. For example:

- **Identify image and command to run:** The `docker` command line says to find the container image named `fedora`, download it to the local system, and then run the `cat /etc/os-release` command within that container (to check the operating system release of the software in the container). Because no tag is added to the end of the image name, `:latest` is assumed.

- **Find the image:** First, Docker looks on the local system for the `fedora:latest` image. Since it isn't there, Docker searches the docker.io registry, where it finds and downloads the `fedora` image. If you were using Red Hat Enterprise Linux, the `docker` command would check the Red Hat registry before checking the docker.io registry (the Docker Hub Registry).

- **Run the command:** In this example, the `cat` command displays the contents of the `/etc/os-release` file on your screen. Keep in mind that the container has its own file system, so the output tells us that the container was built from a Fedora 22 system. If this container were run on an Ubuntu or Red Hat Enterprise Linux system it would yield the same results.

At this point, you have the `fedora` image on your local system, so the next time you start a `docker run` command for that image, you won't need to download it again. The command runs from the image you stored locally.

Before going on to try out other `docker run` commands, keep in mind these distinctions between images and containers:

- **image:** This is a permanently stored instance of a container. The `docker images` command shows you the images on your system. The `docker rmi image` command lets you delete an image. You can assign multiple aliases (including names and tags) to the same image whenever it is useful. Use the `docker run` command to run an image.

- **container:** A container is created by running an image. If a container runs in the background (detached mode), it can keep running after the `docker run` command exits. You can see running containers with the `docker ps` command. Once a container exits (unless you explicitly remove it), the state of that container will be saved. You can see saved containers that are no longer running with the `docker ps -a` command. You can start a container again (which consists of the image plus any changes you made to that running instance) using the `docker start` *container* command. You can stop a running container with `docker stop` *container*. Replace *container* with the name or container ID of the container created when the image was run.

At this point, run a few commands to get a sense of the results of the container image you just ran:

```
# docker images
REPOSITORY   TAG        IMAGE ID       CREATED        VIRTUAL SIZE
fedora       latest     834629358fe2   3 months ago   241.3 MB
# docker ps
CONTAINER ID  IMAGE    COMMAND    CREATED    STATUS   PORTS     NAMES
# docker ps -a
CONTAINER ID  IMAGE           COMMAND                  CREATED
   STATUS                    PORTS     NAMES
a068cd24ab4b  fedora:latest   cat /etc/os-release a minute ago
   Exited (0) a minute ago              stoic_carson
```

The `docker images` command shows that the `fedora` image stayed on your system and is available to run again. Because the container ran and exited after displaying the output of the `cat` command, the `docker ps` command shows that no containers are currently running. However, `docker ps -a` shows that the container is still available to be started again.

Because no name was assigned to the container, Docker randomly assigned a name (stoic_carson, in this case). To run the container again (which includes the image, any content you may have added to the container, and any options), you run the `docker start` command with either the container ID or name:

```
# docker start -i a068cd24ab4b
...
NAME=Fedora
VERSION="22 (Twenty Two)"
ID=fedora
VERSION_ID=22
...
```

Notice that the `docker start` command took the state that the container was in when it exited (either by being stopped or, as in this case, having completed its task) and essentially reran the previous `docker run` command, including the `cat` command option. I only added the `-i` option, which causes the output from the container to be directed to the local shell (STDOUT).

Many options are available with the `docker run` command. Continuing with the `fedora` image, the next sections of this chapter illustrate many of the options available with the `docker run` command.

RUNNING CONTAINER IMAGES INTERACTIVELY

When you run a container image, it executes the command you supply (or the one that is built in) and then exits. If you want the command to continue to run in the background (as you would for an ongoing service, such as a web server or print server), you can detach it (`-d` option) to have it run in the background. If you want it to run in the foreground, you run it interactively (`-i` option) and typically open a terminal session as well (`-t` option).

Examples of running container images in detached mode are covered in the "Running Containerized Services" section later in the chapter. The next section shows examples of running container images interactively.

Starting an Interactive Bash Shell

A common example of an interactive container is one where you open a shell to work directly inside the container. Running an interactive container image gives you the opportunity to look around inside the container and change the contents.

 NOTE

The contents of basic container images, such as the `fedora` image illustrated here, have changed several times in the process of writing this book. If the `ps` command isn't in the latest version of the `fedora` image, type `yum install procps`, from within the container, to install it.

In the following example, I run the `/bin/bash` command to open a shell in the `fedora` image. I add the `-i` and `-t` options so I can interact with the shell inside the container from my current terminal session:

```
# docker run -it fedora /bin/bash
bash-4.3#
```

Now you have a bash prompt for a shell inside the container. How can you tell that you are inside the container? If the ps command is included in the container (as it is here), run it as follows to see what processes are running:

```
bash-4.3# ps -e
  PID TTY          TIME CMD
    1 ?        00:00:00 bash
    7 ?        00:00:00 ps
```

The output from ps -e (which lists all processes in the process table) tells you a few things. Process ID 1, which is normally init or systemd on a running Linux system, is the bash command. The only other process currently running in the container is the ps command itself. This tells you that you cannot, by default, see the process table from the host system (which could have hundreds of processes running). The container has its own process table.

If you are interested in what else is in the container, here are a few other commands you can run:

```
bash-4.3# rpm -qa | more      View list of installed packages
bash-4.3# rpm -ql curl        See contents of an installed package
bash-4.3# man curl            No way to show man pages
bash: man: command not found
bash-4.3# ip addr show        No way to see network interfaces
bash: ip: command not found
```

So, depending on what the creator of the container image includes, you may not be able to run all the commands you want to run inside the container. However, keep in mind that a container is meant to be lean and include only those components it needs to run. Otherwise, you might as well just use a whole virtual machine.

But don't despair. Most base container images from major Linux distributions include ways to add software to a running container. The fedora base image is no exception. Assuming the host system has an Internet connection and that Docker was configured (as it is by default) to provide a private IP address to each container, you can use the yum or dnf (Fedora and RHEL) or apt-get (Ubuntu and Debian) commands inside a container to add software.

Continuing from within the running fedora image, you can run yum commands to add more software to the container. Typically, you should add software when you first build your images. But to be able to try out the docker run commands in the rest of this chapter, run this yum command to add the software we use later:

```
bash-4.3# yum install iproute net-tools bsd-games words \
          vsftpd httpd httpd-manual -y
Resolving Dependencies
--> Running transaction check
```

```
...
Complete!
bash-4.3# exit
```

Type `exit` to end the shell session and leave the container. At this point, I want to save the container as an image so I can reuse it with other run commands in this chapter. Here's what I do:

```
# docker ps -a
CONTAINER ID    IMAGE            COMMAND         CREATED
   STATUS                       PORTS    NAMES
88f6c09523b5    fedora:latest    "/bin/bash"  3 hours ago
   Exited (0) 7 seconds ago              trusting_heisenberg
# docker commit -a "Chris Negus" 88f6c09523b5 testrun
# docker images
REPOSITORY    TAG      IMAGE ID        CREATED         VIRTUAL SIZE
fedora        latest   834629358fe2    1 month ago     422.2 MB
testrun       latest   226f7543f12a    3 minutes ago   431.6 MB
```

The image named `testrun` is now available on the local system and ready to be used in `docker run` examples that follow.

Playing Some Character-Based Games

I installed the bsd-games package in the `testrun` image created in the previous section. The package contains character-based games used on early UNIX systems. These games provide a fun way to try running some screen-oriented games from a Docker container.

Because we want the container to run, then go away when the game is over, I add the `--rm` option to the command line. This is a good habit to get into, so you don't have a lot of unwanted containers filling up disk space after you are done with them.

Here's how to play `hangman` in an interactive terminal from within a container:

```
# docker run -it --rm testrun /bin/hangman
```

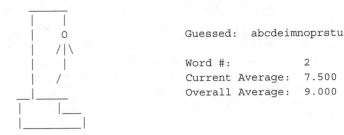

```
Word:   cambodian
Guess:
You got it!
Another word?
```

Here's how to start `snake`, where you use arrow keys to try to grab dollar signs and exit before the snake eats you:

```
# docker run -it --rm testrun /usr/bin/snake
|---------------------------------------------|
| $150                                        |
|                              $              |
|                    I                        |
|                  ss                         |
|        #       s ss                         |
|                 s                           |
|---------------------------------------------|
```

Here's how to start `adventure` to explore the Colossal Cave:

```
# docker run -it --rm testrun /usr/bin/adventure
Welcome to Adventure!!  Would you like instructions?
n
You are standing at the end of a road before a small brick building.
Around you is a forest.  A small stream flows out of the building and
down a gully.
building
You are inside a building, a well house for a large spring.
There is a shiny brass lamp nearby.
...
take lamp
OK
xyzzy
It is now pitch dark. If you proceed you will likely fall into a pit.
light
Your lamp is now on.
quit
```

If you want to play adventure for a bit, type compass directions, up, down, or room names to move around the caves. Pick up items that you find and bring them back to the building to score points.

Running Administrative Commands Inside a Container

Adding the ip-route and net-tools packages to the testrun image makes commands such as `ip` and `route` available to run inside the container. Here are examples of running those commands inside that container and what it tells us about that container's network interfaces:

```
# docker run -it --rm testrun /usr/sbin/ip addr show eth0
165: eth0: <NO-CARRIER,BROADCAST,UP,LOWER_UP> mtu 1500 qdisc noqueue
state DOWN group default
    link/ether 02:42:ac:11:00:24 brd ff:ff:ff:ff:ff:ff
    inet 172.17.0.36/16 scope global eth0
...
# docker run -it --rm testrun /usr/sbin/route
Kernel IP routing table
Destination  Gateway       Genmask      Flags Metric Ref  Use Iface
default      172.17.42.1   0.0.0.0      UG    0      0      0 eth0
172.17.0.0   0.0.0.0       255.255.0.0  U     0      0      0 eth0
# ip addr show docker0
5: docker0: <BROADCAST,MULTICAST,UP,LOWER_UP> mtu 1500 qdisc noqueue
state UP group default
    link/ether 56:84:7a:fe:97:99 brd ff:ff:ff:ff:ff:ff
    inet 172.17.42.1/16 scope global docker0
       valid_lft forever preferred_lft forever
```

The first two `docker` commands shown in the preceding example tell us information about networking within the container, while the `ip` command that follows shows the docker0 network interface on the host. Notice that the host's docker0 interface has an IP address of 172.17.42.1/16. By default, the host hands out addresses via DHCP to containers as they start up. The first `ip` command run from testrun has an IP address of 172.17.0.36/16. Each time you run the `ip` command in this way you see a new IP address because each image starts a new container.

Notice that the `route` command shows that the default gateway is 172.17.42.1. From the `ip` command run on the host, you can see that 172.17.42.1 is the IP address of the docker0 interface on the host. Routing through the host computer's docker0 interface is how containers are able to access network resources outside the local host.

You can add any packages you want in a container, using the `yum` or `apt-get` commands, to extend what commands you can run inside that container. In Chapter 7, "Investigating Containers," I add more commands and run specific `docker` options to further explore inside containers.

While it is nice to be able to run commands interactively from a container, the real value of containers comes from containerizing more complex applications that provide one or more services. Many of the more interesting options to `docker run` are used when you containerize a persistent service, such as a web server or a file server. The next section describes how to use `docker run` to run a service.

RUNNING CONTAINERIZED SERVICES

Running a service from within a container offers many advantages over just running the service directly on the host computer. Some of these advantages include

- **Configuration:** By putting a service inside a container, you can preconfigure all the executables, libraries, configuration files, and other elements needed to provide the service, so you don't have to worry about whether the host system provides those components. Also, you should be able to easily move the container to another host if you need to.
- **Separation:** Because each container has its own separate file system and network interfaces, you can run as many of the same service containers as you want. So, in theory, a host could run 100 separate web server containers, and as long as each container exposed its service on a separate IP address and/or port, those services wouldn't conflict with each other.

Options to `docker run` for starting individual service containers do such things as tell the command run by the container to run in the background (detached), attach to storage volumes on the local host system, and open ports on the host to make services available to the outside world.

To illustrate `docker run` options that are useful for running services, the next sections show how to run a basic web server from within a container. This example is done by running a `fedora` container on a Fedora Linux distribution.

> ## NOTE
>
> While in theory, Docker containers are meant to run anywhere, you will find that not every container runs the same on every system running Docker. Also, know that the `fedora` container I ran when I tried this might be different when you try running it. To have the best chance of getting the same results I do, you could use the same Linux distribution with the same release of Docker (at least docker 1.7 in Fedora 22) and specifically the same container (`fedora:22`).

Running a Containerized Web Server

The Apache web server is the world's most popular web server. By default, it serves web content from the `/var/www/` directory and listens on the default TCP ports 80 (HTTP) and 443 (HTTPS). In this example, I want to have the Apache web server serve content from the `/var/www/html` directory on the host. So, I create that directory on the host and set the proper SELinux context (needed for a Fedora or RHEL system). After that, I add an `index.html` file to have some content to display:

```
# mkdir -p /var/www/html
# chcon -R -t httpd_sys_content_t /var/www/
# echo "Is the Web Server running: YES" > /var/www/html/index.html
```

Using the `testrun` image built earlier in this chapter, here is an example of a `docker run` command for running the httpd service from that image (before you do this, make sure no httpd service or other services on the host are listening on ports 80 or 443):

```
# docker run -d -p 80:80 -p 443:443 --name=MyWebServer \
    -v /var/www/:/var/www testrun \
    /usr/sbin/httpd -DFOREGROUND
```

Let's break down the options used in this example (see Table 4.1).

TABLE 4.1 Options Used with *docker run* Example

`-d`	**Detached**: Tells the containerized command to run the container in the background.
`-p 80:80` `-p 443:443`	**Publish port**: Publishes a container port to a host port. The number to the left of the colon is the host port; the one to the right is the container port. Here we are exposing TCP ports 80 (HTTP) and 443 (HTTPS) to the same port number on the host.
`--name=MyWebServer`	**Container name**: Assigning a name to the container is a good idea if you want to keep it around for a while. Later, you can stop and start the container using that name instead of having to use the container ID.
`-v /var/www/:/var/www/`	**Bind mount volume**: This option mounts a directory from the host (left of the colon) to a directory on the container (right of the colon). In this case, I use `-v` to share the default directory used by Apache to hold shared web content (`/var/www`).
`testrun`	**Image**: In our example, the image name is testrun, which we created from a base fedora image with added httpd and other packages.
`/usr/sbin/httpd -DFOREGROUND`	**Command**: In this case, I ran the httpd daemon with the `-DFOREGROUND` option.

Unlike the commands run earlier in this chapter, where we just ran a command and exited, this web server example keeps running in the background (-d option) and begins to draw on resources from the host computer. To test that the MyWebServer container is running, do the following:

```
# docker ps
CONTAINER ID      IMAGE          COMMAND                  CREATED
   STATUS       PORTS                                     NAMES
a8019984ae79      testrun:latest  "/usr/sbin/httpd -DF  1 hour ago
   Up 1 hour  0.0.0.0:80->80/tcp, 0.0.0.0:443->443/tcp   MyWebServer
```

From the output, you can see that a container ID was assigned (a8019984ae79), the image name is testrun:latest, and that the command run is httpd. The container was run one hour ago, and it has been up for an hour. For all IPV4 network interfaces on the host (0.0.0.0), TCP ports 80 and 443 forward requests to their respective ports within the container.

The last bit of information shows the container name as MyWebServer. I can use that name if I want to start, stop, or remove the container. I could also use that name if I want to run another command in the running container, such as a bash shell to look around inside it (type exit when you are done to return to the host). For example:

```
# docker exec -it MyWebServer /bin/bash
bash-4.3# exit
```

To check that the container can share the text that I added earlier on the host to the /var/www/html/index.html file, I use the curl command from the host to get that file's contents:

```
# curl http://localhost/index.html
Is the Web Server running: YES
```

Because TCP port 80 from the container is exposed to the same port on the localhost, that success message should be displayed.

You may remember that I installed the httpd-manual manual package earlier (which has content stored in /usr/share/httpd/manual inside the container). You could open a web browser to httpd://localhost/manual on the local host to see that content. With that and the mounted /var/www/html directory, httpd service can share a mix of data from inside and outside the container. The result appears as shown in Figure 4.1.

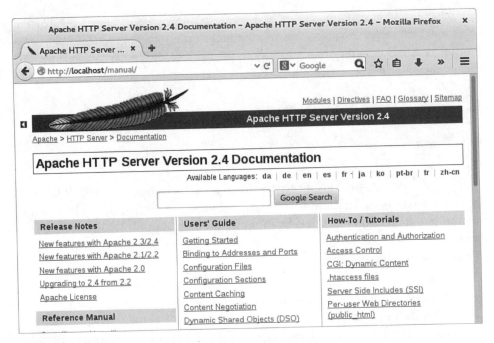

FIGURE 4.1 Display the Apache manual (httpd-manual package) served from inside the httpd container.

Limiting Resources When Running Services in Containers

Containers have no special access to memory or multiple CPUs by default when they are run. You can set specific memory limits or request a certain number of CPUs when you run a container using the `--memory`, `--memory-swap`, `--cpu-shares`, and `--cpuset-cpus` options. Here is an example of how to limit memory and CPU shares when doing a `docker run`.

```
# docker run -d -p 80:80 -p 443:443 --name=LimitedWebServer \
    -v /var/www/:/var/www --memory=10m --memory-swap=-1  \
    --cpu-shares=256 testrun /usr/sbin/httpd -DFOREGROUND
```

Using `--memory=10m` limits the amount of RAM the container can use to 10MB. The `--memory-swap=-1` indicates that an unlimited amount of swap can be used, however (provided the operating system has swap space configured). Here are other examples of how you can limit the amount of memory available to a container:

`--memory=10m`	Container can use 10MB of RAM. If memory-swap not set, container can use 2x memory of swap space (20m) too
`--memory=10m --memory-swap=30m`	Container can use 10MB of RAM. Swap plus memory is limited to 30MB

To limit CPU access for a container, you can use the `--cpu-shares` and `--cpuset-cpus` options. If `--cpu-shares` is not set, all containers have equal access to CPU shares. You can set `--cpu-shares` based on a 1024 scale. The default `--cpu-shares=0` gives a container the full 1024 shares. The preceding example (`--cpu-shares=256`) indicates that only 25% of the available 1024 shares should be allocated to the container while other containers on the system could use 100% of the available shares.

The `--cpuset-cpus` option limits which set of CPUs on the computer can be allocated. The value of `--cpuset-cpus` can be a specific CPU set, a comma-separated list of CPU sets or a range of CPU sets. For example:

`--cpuset-cpus=0,1`	Use CPU set 0 or 1
`--cpuset-cpus=3`	Use the fourth CPU set
`--cpuset-cpus=1-3`	Use CPU set 1, 2, or 3

RUNNING PRIVILEGED CONTAINERS

In most cases, when you use `docker run` to run a container, you want to limit the access that container has to the host system the container is running on. Likewise, you want to keep other containers on the local system from being able to get access to the container you are running. There are, however, cases where you want to allow a container to have greater access to the host system. These containers are called *privileged* containers or *super privileged* containers.

The idea behind privileged containers is that there are times when a container is specifically designed to act on the host system itself. Without opening privileges, the container would not be able to access namespaces on the host (such as the process table, IPC namespace, and D-bus interface).

Host namespaces that can be accessed from a privileged container, and reasons for opening up those namespaces are described in Chapter 13, "Using Super Privileged Containers." Examples of super privileged containers are also included in Chapter 13. For the moment, however, while we are on the subject of the `docker run` command, Table 4.2 presents some options available to the `docker run` command for opening up host privileges to a container.

TABLE 4.2 Host Privileges Options

`--ipc`	**IPC:** Opens access to inter-process communications facilities on the host computer. By default, each container has a private IPC facility.
`--net=host`	**Network interfaces:** Opens direct access to host network interfaces to the container. By default, each container has its own network interfaces.
`--pid=host`	**Process table:** Grants access to the host process table from the container. By default, each container maintains its own process table.
`-e HOST=/host`	**Host file system:** If set, the HOST environment variable tells the container to mount the host's root file system under a particular directory in the container. The recommended location for that is /host.
`--privileged`	**Security separation:** This option turns off the security separation of the command run from the container. So, for example, a process run as the root user would have the same privileges that any process run as root would have on the system.

Again, see Chapter 13 for examples of these options in action.

SUMMARY

The `docker run` command is the way that you turn a stored Docker-formatted container image into a running container instance. Many options are available to the `docker run` command. For example, you can use the interactive (`-i`) and terminal (`-t`) options to run a container that you can interact with from the shell.

Although some containers are meant to be run interactively, more often a container will be run in the background to provide continuous services to users. The `-d` option to `docker run` lets you detach a container process so it runs in the background (typically as a service daemon process). You can expose TCP ports that provide services from the container to the host, so users accessing the host can gain access to a container's services.

Now that you know how to run a container, the next chapter helps you understand how to work with container images. Working with images includes knowing how to pull, save, and load container images.

## CHAPTER 5

Finding, Pulling, Saving, and Loading Container Images

IN THIS CHAPTER:

- Find images with `docker search`
- Pull images from registries
- Save and load images

You don't really need to know much about Docker to start running Docker-formatted containers. As I showed in the previous chapter, if you know an image name, a simple `docker run` command downloads and runs the image of your choosing. Now that you have done a few `docker run` commands, you are ready to dig deeper into managing your images.

This chapter covers how to manage Docker-formatted images in many different ways. Using `docker search`, you can find out what images are available from the Docker Hub Registry (docker.io) and possibly other locations. Using `docker pull`, you can choose specific images to download to your system. With `docker save`, you can save an image from your local system to a tar file, and then add that tar file to another system using the `docker load` command.

In searching for, saving, and loading images, you see the words "registry" and "repository" used. A *registry* is a location where images associated with many repositories may be found. Docker uses *repository* to describe a name that may represent multiple images. For example, the name `docker.io/ubuntu` represents a repository within the Docker.io registry. Within that repository, there may be multiple images that represent containers for different releases of Ubuntu. Typically, an action like `docker pull ubuntu` results in a single image being pulled from a registry to your system (`docker.io/ubuntu:latest`). However, if you run `docker pull -a ubuntu` instead, you get all images associated with the `docker.io/ubuntu` repository.

SEARCHING FOR IMAGES

The Docker Project set up the Docker Hub Registry (`https://registry.hub.docker.com/`) to be the central point of access to thousands of Docker-formatted containers. From a system running the Docker service, you could search the Docker Hub with the `docker search` command for any images made publicly available. Using your own login to the Docker Hub, you can store and keep your own images private, if you choose.

For organizations behind a firewall or whose security considerations require that their own images be stored on their own premises, there are implementations of Docker that allow you to configure your own registries or block users from accessing the Docker Hub. The Docker service implemented in Red Hat Enterprise Linux is an example where you can choose the registries from which you search and pull images.

The following section describes how to search the Docker Hub Registry from the `docker` command line as well as through a web browser. After that, you can learn how to configure your system to allow the `docker` command to search and pull images from registries other than the Docker Hub.

Searching for Images with the `docker` Command

Most implementations of the Docker service are configured to search for images from the Docker Hub. On Ubuntu, Fedora, and other Linux distributions, you can use the `docker search` command to search for images from the Docker Hub. Because some distributions are configured to search their own registries as well (such as Red Hat Enterprise Linux), results from `docker search` commands can differ on different implementations of the Docker service.

Here are some examples of using the `docker search` command to find images from the Docker Hub:

```
# docker search ubuntu
INDEX      NAME                    DESCRIPTION      STARS OFFICIAL
AUTOMATED
docker.io docker.io/ubuntu         Ubuntu is a...    1988 [OK]
docker.io docker.io/ubuntu-upstart Upstart is an...    28 [OK]
...
```

```
# docker search centos
INDEX       NAME                            DESCRIPTION      STARS OFFICIAL AUTOMATED
docker.io   docker.io/centos                The official...  1149 [OK]
docker.io   docker.io/blalor/centos  Bare-bones...          9            [OK]
...
# docker search fedora
INDEX       NAME                  DESCRIPTION      STARS OFFICIAL AUTOMATED
docker.io docker.io/fedora        Official Fed...   180 [OK]
docker.io docker.io/fedora/ssh                       19 [OK]
...
```

The output of `docker search` is sorted by the number of stars associated with an image. Users with accounts to the Docker Hub site can assign a star to images they like. Besides a description of the image, which is truncated by default, the output also shows whether the image is officially created by the project that bears its name (Fedora, Ubuntu, CentOS, and so on) and whether the image is created with automated builds.

If you are creating your own container image, I recommend you start with an official base image from a Linux distribution you trust. If it doesn't have every software package you want in it, you can always add more packages (`apt-get` or `yum` commands). Base container images for Fedora, Ubuntu, and CentOS are preconfigured to access those projects' software repositories (for deb or rpm packages). For Red Hat Enterprise Linux, rhel base container images draw on Red Hat software repositories that are enabled on the host (assuming you are running the container on an RHEL system that has a valid subscription).

Besides Linux base images, container images are available from the Docker Hub that are preconfigured to run particular applications. Sometimes you need to download and modify other software to get the applications to work as you want them to.

```
# docker search mysql
INDEX       NAME                      DESCRIPTION STARS OFFICIAL AUTOMATED
docker.io docker.io/mysql             MySQL is... 868   [OK]
docker.io docker.io/orchardup/mysql               40             [OK]
...
# docker search wordpress
INDEX       NAME                      DESCRIPTION STARS OFFICIAL AUTOMATED
docker.io docker.io/wordpress         The Word... 395   [OK]
docker.io docker.io/ctlc/wordpress                 5             [OK]

...
```

The mysql and wordpress repositories offer images from Docker Hub that are officially available from those projects. They provide container images that are ready to run MySQL database and WordPress rich content management system services, respectively.

Another type of container you can get from the Docker Hub is in between a base operating system container and a configured application. There are container images designed to provide a base environment for developing and/or running applications of a certain type. Here are a few examples:

```
# docker search rails
INDEX       NAME                     DESCRIPTION       STARS OFFICIAL AUTOMATED
docker.io   docker.io/rails          Rails is...       239   [OK]
docker.io   docker.io/lucio/rails    Latest Ruby       2                [OK]
...
# docker search java
INDEX       NAME                     DESCRIPTION       STARS OFFICIAL AUTOMATED
docker.io docker.io/java             Java is...        257   [OK]
docker.io docker.io/develar/java                       9                [OK]...
# docker search golang
INDEX       NAME                     DESCRIPTION STARS OFFICIAL AUTOMATED
docker.io docker.io/golang           Go...             282   [OK]
docker.io docker.io/google/golang                      93               [OK]

...
```

The rails image can be used to create a Dockerfile for a Ruby on Rails application project. For running JavaScript applications, the node image provides an official container image named node. The java image is an official container image that can be used to provide both a run-time and a build environment for Java applications. The golang image offers an environment for running applications written in Google's Go Language.

If you want to refine your searches, you can add options to the docker search command. For example:

```
# docker search -s 10 fedora
INDEX       NAME                DESCRIPTION      STARS OFFICIAL AUTOMATED
docker.io docker.io/fedora      Official Fed...  180 [OK]
docker.io docker.io/fedora/ssh                   19 [OK]
# docker search --no-trunc=true mysql
INDEX       NAME                DESCRIPTION
                                                 STARS    OFFICIAL   AUTOMATED
docker.io docker.io/mysql MySQL is a widely used, open-source
                          relational database management system (RDBMS)..
                                 868      [OK]

...
```

```
# docker search --automated=true centos
INDEX      NAME                    DESCRIPTION     STARS OFFICIAL AUTOMATED
docker.io  docker.io/blalor/centos Bare-bones...      9            [OK]
```

In the examples just shown, the `-s` option is used to find only images that have at least a specified number of stars (in this case, at least 10 stars). The `--no-trunc` option tells `docker search` not to truncate the description field. The `automated=true` option asks `docker search` to only display images that are automatically rebuilt periodically.

The `docker search` command lines shown in this section are useful for finding images and their descriptions for the system from which you are running docker. However, you often need more information to make those images useful. The next section describes how to find more information on images available through the Docker Hub.

Searching for Images on Docker Hub

Just the name and a short description won't tell you everything you need to know about most container images. Some images need to be run in a certain way to provide a running image with data or to turn on special privileges. For images stored on the Docker Hub, you can search the Docker Hub from your web browser and often find more information about an image.

Here are some ways you can search the Docker Hub Registry for images (`https://registry.hub.docker.com/`) from your web browser:

- **Search Registry Box**: Type a search term into the Search Registry box. You see a list of images that have that term in the image name or description. You can sort the results in various ways, including relevance, date created, last updated, number of stars, and so on. As when you search with the `docker search` command, you can also choose to see only images that are Official or created with Automated Builds. Select the image you want for more information about it. Figure 5.1 shows an example for the Docker Hub Registry search for Fedora.

- **Official Repositories**: Select from a handful of official repositories from the Docker Hub Registry page. This is a good way to get images sanctioned by specific Linux distributions (such as CentOS or Ubuntu) or open source project (such as WordPress or mongoDB).

FIGURE 5.1 Search the Docker Hub Registry for images by keyword.

Once you have found an image that interests you, select it to see more details about the image. For example, information on how to use the official WordPress image is available from the WordPress page on the Docker Hub Registry (`https://registry.hub.docker.com/_/wordpress/`). Without that information, it would be difficult to guess all that you could do with an image. Figure 5.2 shows the official WordPress (wordpress) image page:

Continuing with the wordpress image example, the information you can find about the image from its Docker Hub Registry page includes the following:

Supported versions of the image

- A basic `docker run` command line for running the image
- Environment variables to use with `docker run` to change image settings
- Links to the official GitHub page for this container image (`https://github.com/docker-library/wordpress`)
- Dockerfile files used to build the image

If you are looking for documentation on several images, you can go directly to the Docker Library (`https://github.com/docker-library/docs`) and select the name of the image to see its documentation.

Searching Other Repositories for Images

Some implementations of Docker search registries in addition to the Docker Hub Registry also allow you to choose where you look for images with `docker search`. For some of the developers of Docker, this has become a contentious issue.

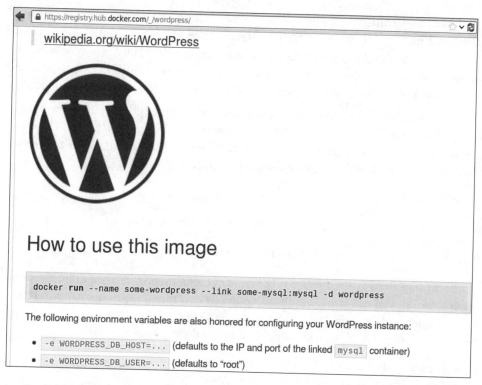

FIGURE 5.2 Get details for an image from the image's Docker Hub Registry page.

The original intention of the Docker Project was that the Docker Hub Registry namespace would be the same, no matter where you ran a Docker-formatted container. So `docker search rhel` and `docker pull rhel` would provide the same results if they were run on Fedora, Ubuntu, or any other system supporting Docker. The first location searched would always be the Docker.io Hub Registry. The argument is that it should be like the Internet, where if you type `www.google.com` into a web browser, you would always get the same site.

The counter argument is that large enterprise companies that want to use Docker don't want to be connected to public registries. They want to completely control their own images and they don't want to risk the possibility of ever having unknown images pulled into their environment. Some on this side of the argument have pointed to DNS server software, such as the bind package, that can be set up to create private DNS server namespaces and never connect to the Internet or can allow their own DNS hostnames to be searched for names before DNS servers from the Internet at large or other DNS servers.

As of this writing, the issue has not yet been completely resolved. Currently, in Red Hat Enterprise Linux and RHEL Atomic Host systems, the `docker` command is configured to point to a container repository on the Red Hat Customer portal for images first, then search the Docker Hub Registry next. The RHEL version of the docker service can also be configured to point to any Docker registry you choose.

For example, if you use the `docker search` command to search for images named rhel7, docker searches both the container registry on the Red Hat Customer portal (`registry.access.redhat.com`) and the Docker Hub Registry, in that order. Here's what that search looks like from a RHEL Atomic system:

```
# docker search rhel7
NAME           DESCRIPTION                             STARS  OFFICIAL AUTOMATED
redhat.com     registry.access.redhat.com/rhel    This... 0
redhat.com     registry.access.redhat.com/rhel6   This... 0
redhat.com     registry.access.redhat.com/rhel7   This... 0
```

By tailing the systemd journal (`journalctl` command) in a separate Terminal window before you run your search, you can see that the `docker` command in RHEL Atomic queries both the Red Hat Customer Portal (`access.redhat.com`) registry and, after that, the docker.io registry. For example:

```
# journalctl -f -u docker
time="2015-04-14T23:09:22-04:00" level="info"
    msg="GET /v1.17/images/search?term=rhel7"
time="2015-04-14T23:09:22-04:00" level="info"
    msg="+job search(rhel7)"
time="2015-04-14T23:09:22-04:00" level="info"
    msg="+job resolve_repository(rhel7)"
time="2015-04-14T23:09:22-04:00" level="info"
    msg="-job resolve_repository(rhel7) = OK (0)"
endpoint.newEndpoint: starting with
    address=registry.access.redhat.com, secure=false
endpoint.newEndpoint: address after prefixing:
    registry.access.redhat.com
endpoint.newEndpoint:
    trimmedAddress=http://registry.access.redhat.com, version=
time="2015-04-14T23:09:23-04:00" level="info"
    msg="+job resolve_repository(docker.io/rhel7)"
time="2015-04-14T23:09:23-04:00" level="info"
    msg="-job resolve_repository(docker.io/rhel7) = OK (0)"
endpoint.newEndpoint: starting with
    address=https://index.docker.io/v1/, secure=true
endpoint.newEndpoint: address after prefixing:
    https://index.docker.io/v1/
endpoint.newEndpoint: trimmedAddress=https://index.docker.io,
    version=v1
endpoint.newEndpoint: terminating
```

I cut date/time stamps and hostnames from each journal message. You can see that both addresses (`registry.access.redhat.com` and `docker.io`) are searched for rhel7. As a result, the search returns rhel7 images from both registries.

In Red Hat Enterprise Linux, which registries are searched for images is determined from information in the `/etc/sysconfig/docker` file. When the `docker` service starts up, it looks for ADD_REGISTRY and BLOCK_REGISTRY options in this file. By default, they are set as follows:

```
ADD_REGISTRY='--add-registry registry.access.redhat.com'
# BLOCK_REGISTRY='--block-registry'
```

The ADD_REGISTRY option sets `registry.access.redhat.com` as the location to be searched first by `docker search` commands. The BLOCK_REGISTRY line is commented out. So the only other registry that is enabled by default, docker.io, remains enabled and will return search results after any results found from the Red Hat site.

Here are examples for changing options in the `/etc/sysconfig/docker` file that would modify search results returned from the local Docker service in Red Hat Enterprise Linux. In this first example, if you don't want to search the Red Hat registry first, simply comment out the line and restart the Docker service:

```
# ADD_REGISTRY='--add-registry registry.access.redhat.com'
```

If you want to block search or download of images from the docker.io Registry Hub, you could uncomment and modify the BLOCK_REGISTRY option as follows:

```
BLOCK_REGISTRY='--block-registry docker.io'
```

To configure the Docker service so a selected Docker registry is searched, you can add an ADD_REGISTRY line. For example, this is what you add to be able to search a Docker registry located at myregistry.example.com listening on port 5000:

```
ADD_REGISTRY='--add-registry myregistry.example.com:5000'
```

Pulling Images from Registries

To download an image from a Docker registry so it is available on a system running the Docker service, you can use the `docker pull` command. Although a `docker pull` is done automatically when you do a `docker run` command and the image is not already present on the local system, some prefer to pull an image first before using it. One reason is that an image can sometimes take a while to download and you may not want to wait for that to occur at run time.

You can refer to an image you want to pull simply by its short name (such as ubuntu or fedora). But other elements can be added to an image's short name. For example, given an image named hangman, when you go to pull that image, you might need to identify other information to get the specific image you want, such as

- **Registry name:** This could be the name and port number of the image location. For example, myregistry.example.com:5000/hangman identifies an image named hangman and tries to pull it from port number 5000 on the system named myregistry.example.com.

- **User name:** Adding a user name from the Docker Hub Registry identifies the user that pushed the image to the registry. Essentially, the user name is like a subdirectory of the Docker Hub. So, to pull an image named hangman from a repository of a user named cricket, you could pull the name cricket/hangman.

- **Tag:** Tags are a way of adding multiple names to the same image. When you ask to pull an image name and don't add a tag, the tag latest is implied. So, if you pull cricket/hangman, it downloads cricket/hangman:latest. That image might appear on your local system as cricket/hangman:latest, cricket/hangman:1.7, and possibly other names. If other versions of an image name exist, you have to ask specifically for the one you want when you pull the image (for example, cricket/hangman:1.5). This is important to understand if, for example, you want to work with a specific container image version of Fedora or Ubuntu. (See Chapter 6, "Tagging Images," for more information on using image tags.)

Here are some examples of command lines for pulling images:

```
# docker pull cricket/hangman:1.7
Pulling repository cricket/hangman
be9a1bc2da8f: Download complete
1403322a81c5: Download complete
511136ea3c5a: Download complete
00a0c78eeb6d: Download complete
834629358fe2: Download complete

# docker pull cricket/hangman
Pulling repository cricket/hangman
1403322a81c5: Download complete
511136ea3c5a: Download complete
00a0c78eeb6d: Download complete
834629358fe2: Download complete
```

```
# docker images | grep hangman
cricket/hangman    1.7       be9a1bc2da8f    2 weeks ago      427.3 MB
cricket/hangman    latest    1403322a81c5    44 minutes ago   427.3 MB
cricket/hangman    1.9       1403322a81c5    44 minutes ago   427.3 MB
```

From the output, you see two images (be9a1bc2da8f and 1403322a81c5). One image is tagged 1.7, and the other is tagged both latest and 1.9. If you had just pulled the latest image, you would not have gotten the 1.7 image (be9a1bc2da8f).

To pull an image from a registry other than the Docker Hub, you can identify either the IP address or hostname as part of the image name. In this example, the hangman image is stored on a system at address 192.168.0.118 that has a docker-registry service running on TCP port 5000:

```
# docker pull 192.168.0.118:5000/hangman
Pulling repository 192.168.0.118:5000/hangman
1403322a81c5: Download complete
511136ea3c5a: Download complete
00a0c78eeb6d: Download complete
834629358fe2: Download complete
```

Because with `docker pull`, the first part of the registry name is used to identify where to find the image, you could have substituted the same system's hostname and pulled the image as well:

```
# docker pull myregistry.example.com:5000/hangman
Pulling repository myregistry.example.com:5000/hangman
...
Status: Image is up to date for myregistry.example.com:5000/hangman
```

As noted earlier, pulling a short name implies that you want the image tagged as latest from the Docker Hub. So, for example, running `docker pull ubuntu` results in pulling a set of images that gets the latest image, with that image possibly containing multiple tags:

```
# docker pull ubuntu
...
# docker images | grep ubuntu
ubuntu  14.04.2            d0955f21bf24    4 weeks ago    188.3 MB
ubuntu  latest             d0955f21bf24    4 weeks ago    188.3 MB
ubuntu  trusty             d0955f21bf24    4 weeks ago    188.3 MB
ubuntu  trusty-20150320    d0955f21bf24    4 weeks ago    188.3 MB
ubuntu  14.04              d0955f21bf24    4 weeks ago    188.3 MB
```

If you want to test Ubuntu containers for all available releases, you can add the -a option. Keep in mind, this could download multiple gigabytes of images. For example:

```
# docker pull -a ubuntu
Pulling repository ubuntu
...
# docker images | grep ubuntu
ubuntu  14.04.2        d0955f21bf24  4 weeks ago    188.3 MB
```

Using -a in this case results in 17 different Ubuntu container image versions being pulled to the local system. With tags, about 32 different image names are identified.

SAVING AND LOADING IMAGES

Pulling isn't the only way to get images put onto a system so they can be used by Docker. You can save an image from your local system to a tar file. Then you can copy and somehow transport the image to another system, where it can be loaded.

The docker save command lets you save all images associated with a particular repository. By simply giving a repository name to docker save, all versions of the repository name, the tags, and parent layers are streamed in tar format to standard output. As an alternative, you can save that output to a file.

After downloading all images from the CentOS repository on the Docker Hub, here's an example of saving all those images to a single tar file, and then using the scp command to copy the tar file to another system:

```
# docker save -o allcentos.tar centos
# du -sh allcentos.tar
1.6G   allcentos.tar
# scp allcentos.tar host2:/tmp
```

At this point the allcentos.tar file has been copied to the /tmp directory on host2. Now you can log in to the host2 system and load the allcentos.tar file as follows:

```
# docker load -i /tmp/allcentos.tar
# docker images | grep centos
REPOSITORY TAG             IMAGE ID      CREATED      VIRTUAL SIZE
centos     7               0114405f9ff1  3 days ago   215.7 MB
centos     centos7         0114405f9ff1  3 days ago   215.7 MB
centos     latest          0114405f9ff1  3 days ago   215.7 MB
centos     7.1.1503        b58de3b24eb7  2 weeks ago  212.1 MB
centos     centos7.1.1503  b58de3b24eb7  2 weeks ago  212.1 MB
centos     5.11            2e4a66ce2189  6 weeks ago  284.2 MB
centos     centos5.11      2e4a66ce2189  6 weeks ago  284.2 MB
centos     6.6             0bc55ae673f7  6 weeks ago  202.6 MB
...
```

From the output of `docker images`, you can see that all the images from the `centos` repository are now on the new system. So, if you wanted to try to containerize an application with different versions of `centos`, there are now multiple versions of `centos` container images on your system.

If you want to save and load a single image, instead of using the short image name, you can use a specific image ID or a full image name. The longer name might include the full repository name, user name, and a tag associated with the specific image. Here are some examples:

```
# docker save -o myhangman_1.7.tar cricket/hangman:1.7
# docker save -o myhangman_1.9.tar 1403322a81c5
```

At this point, each tarball contains all the layers needed to make the image you saved. After transporting either of the tar files to another system running the Docker service, you can load it using the `docker load` command and look at the results as follows:

```
# docker load -i myhangman_1.7.tar
# docker images | grep hangman
REPOSITORY        TAG     IMAGE ID      CREATED         VIRTUAL SIZE
cricket/hangman   1.7     be9a1bc2da8f  22 hours ago    427.3 MB
```

Notice that only the specific image was saved and loaded into the other system running Docker. That image is now ready to use.

SUMMARY

The Docker Hub Registry offers access to thousands of Docker-formatted images. Using the `docker search` command, you can find images from the Docker Hub Registry. Once you know the name of an image repository that holds an image you want, you can use the `docker pull` command to pull one or more images from that repository to your local system.

When you have an image on your local system that you want to copy to another system, you can use the `docker save` command to save a single image or a repository full of images to a tarball. You can then copy that tarball to another system and load it so it is available to Docker using the `docker load` command. The next chapter goes into detail on how to work with image tagging.

Tagging Images

After you have created an image using `docker build` or by committing a container to an image with `docker commit`, you can add additional tags to the image using `docker tag`. Using images named `ubuntu` and `fedora` from the Docker Hub to illustrate, here are some reasons that you might want to add tags at the end of an image name to further identify that image:

- **Version number**: A version number can help identify which version of a product was used to build the image. For example, an `ubuntu` image might be tagged 15.04 (to indicate the Ubuntu release) and also 15.04.2 (to identify a specific point release). Likewise, the Fedora project tags its base `fedora` images 20, 21, 22, and so forth, to match its releases.

- **Version name**: A name is sometimes assigned to a particular version of an image. For example, Ubuntu version 15.04 is also named vivid (for the release name Vivid Vervet). Fedora 20 also includes the tag name heisenbug on the `fedora:20` image.

- **latest**: When someone runs an image without specifically identifying a tag, the `docker` command looks for the image of that name with the `:latest` tag. For example, running `docker run ubuntu` pulls and runs the `ubuntu:latest` image. So setting the `latest` tag on an image identifies that image as the one to use when only the basic part of the image name is requested.

By attaching text to the beginning part of an image name, you can identify the registry where the image can be found (when running a `docker pull`) or into which the image will be put (when running a `docker push`). Here are a couple of types of images you can apply to the front part of an image name:

- **Registry name and port**: One of the most important uses of image tagging is to add a name of a registry. With a registry name (and optionally a port number) added to the first part of an image name (separated by a slash), a `docker pull` or `docker push` knows exactly where to put or get the image you are looking for. When a user name is identified as the registry name, Docker looks to the registry on the docker.io hub associated with the user account.

- **User name**: When a user account is created on the docker.io registry, that account's user name can be added to the front of an image name to identify that the image should be part of that user's registry on docker.io. For example, if I pushed an image named `docker.io/cricket/hangman`, the `hangman` image would be directed to the personal storage area for the user named `cricket` at the `docker.io` registry (Docker Hub).

This chapter teaches you to use the `docker tag` command to add tags to existing images, essentially enabling the images to be identified by different names.

Assigning Names to Images

An image name is assigned to a Docker image when that image is first created. There are several ways of creating an image. These include the following:

- **Building an image**: When you first build an image from a Dockerfile file, you can assign a name to it. Here's an example of building an image from a Dockerfile file in the current directory and assigning it the name `fedweb`:

```
# docker build -t fedweb .
```

- **Committing a container**: After you have run a container and changed it in some way that you want to keep, you can commit those changes back to a container image using `docker commit`. In this example, I ran the `fedweb` image and called the container `newfedweb`. Then I committed `newfedweb` to a new image called `myfedweb`:

```
# docker run -d -p 80:80 --name=newfedweb fedweb
# docker stop newfedweb
# docker commit -m "Web server with extra data" \
  -a "Chris Negus" newfedweb myfedweb
```

- **Exporting and Importing an image**: You can save an image as a tarball to your file system using `docker export`. You can name an image when you import it from a previously exported tarball to your system. For example, my friend Joe exports his own container (`joefedweb`) to a tarball and sends it to me. Then I import the container image.

```
# docker export joefedweb > joefedweb.tar
# cat joefedweb.tar | docker import - joefedweb
```

At this point, I have three new images on my system. Notice that without adding a tag to the image name, each image is assigned "latest" as its tag. For example:

```
# docker images *web
REPOSITORY   TAG      IMAGE ID       CREATED          VIRTUAL SIZE
joefedweb    latest   88abf604cfcc   12 minutes ago   526.6 MB
myfedweb     latest   8340292d5467   3 hours ago      706.5 MB
fedweb       latest   f583b458b447   4 hours ago      696.7 MB
```

Using these three images, the next sections illustrate how the `docker tag` command can add tags and additional repository information to an image name in ways that make the images more usable.

ASSIGNING TAGS TO IMAGES

By adding tags to images you can be more specific about what an image contains. The most common use of tags is to add version information to an image. As a new version of an image becomes available, it can replace the "latest" instance of an image and still retain tags (which act as aliases to the same image) to other defining information on the image.

Say that you want to add tags to images you created earlier to identify version names and numbers for those images. Here are examples of how you might do that:

```
# docker tag fedweb fedweb:1.5
# docker tag fedweb fedweb:monkey
# docker images fedweb
```

```
REPOSITORY      TAG         IMAGE ID        CREATED         VIRTUAL SIZE
fedweb          1.5         f583b458b447    12 hours ago    696.7 MB
fedweb          latest      f583b458b447    12 hours ago    696.7 MB
fedweb          monkey      f583b458b447    12 hours ago    696.7 MB
```

You can tell that the three fedweb images are actually the same image by the fact that the image IDs for all three are the same (f583b458b447). Next, say that you want to use `myfedweb` as a later release of `fedweb`. You could tag `myfedweb` to indicate that the image is also known by the name `fedweb:1.7` and `fedweb:giraffe`, along with being the latest version of `fedweb`. Because `fedweb:latest` already exists, you need to force the name (`-f`).

```
# docker tag myfedweb fedweb:1.7
# docker tag myfedweb fedweb:giraffe
# docker images *fedweb
REPOSITORY      TAG         IMAGE ID        CREATED         VIRTUAL SIZE
fedweb          1.5         f583b458b447    13 hours ago    696.7 MB
fedweb          latest      f583b458b447    13 hours ago    696.7 MB
fedweb          monkey      f583b458b447    13 hours ago    696.7 MB
fedweb          giraffe     8340292d5467    12 hours ago    706.5 MB
fedweb          1.7         8340292d5467    12 hours ago    706.5 MB
# docker tag myfedweb fedweb:latest
FATA[0000] Error response from daemon: Conflict: Tag latest is already
set to image f583b458b447..., if you want to replace it, please use -f
option
# docker tag -f myfedweb fedweb:latest
# docker images *fedweb
REPOSITORY      TAG         IMAGE ID        CREATED         VIRTUAL SIZE
fedweb          latest      8340292d5467    12 hours ago    706.5 MB
fedweb          1.5         f583b458b447    13 hours ago    696.7 MB
fedweb          monkey      f583b458b447    13 hours ago    696.7 MB
fedweb          giraffe     8340292d5467    12 hours ago    706.5 MB
fedweb          1.7         8340292d5467    12 hours ago    706.5 MB
```

Notice that forcing (`-f`) the `fedweb:latest` image name and tag on the `myfedweb` image not only makes that image the default when someone requests `fedweb` but also removes the `latest` designation from the original image (f583b458b447). As an alternative, you can remove the tag for any image with multiple names without removing the image itself. For example:

```
# docker rmi fedora:latest
Untagged: fedora:latest
```

ASSIGNING REPOSITORY NAMES TO IMAGES

While the `image_name:tag` portion of an image name identifies what the image is, information attached to the front of that name can identify the repository that stores the image. While no repository information is required when you name a container image, the syntax for adding that information is as follows:

```
[repository]:[port#]/[username]/image_name:tag
```

The `username` can be replaced with the name of a user account name on the Docker Hub (docker.io). Identifying a user name makes it easy to push an image to the repository under your user account at the Docker Hub. You can skip the user name and instead identify the location of a private repository (either by IP address or hostname), along with an optional port number, if you want to push an image to a registry located on a particular host and, optionally, a specific port on that host.

Attaching a User Name to an Image

If you have a user account at the Docker Hub, you can replace `username` with the user account name that you choose. For example, if I had a user account at docker.io named cricket, I could add that user name to an image that I want to push to docker.io. I might do the following to indicate that an image named `fedweb:latest` is destined for that domain:

```
# docker tag fedweb:latest cricket/fedweb:latest
# docker images *fedweb
REPOSITORY          TAG       IMAGE ID        CREATED         VIRTUAL SIZE
cricket/fedweb      latest    8340292d5467    12 hours ago    706.5 MB
fedweb              latest    8340292d5467    12 hours ago    706.5 MB
```

Notice that now two names are associated with the same Image ID. With the user name attached to the image, you can push that image to the docker.io repository. Assuming the user name cricket again, here's how to authenticate to docker.io as you push an image up to that account on the docker.io repository:

```
# docker push cricket/fedweb
The push refers to a repository [cricket/fedweb] (len: 1)
Sending image list
Pushing repository cricket/fedweb (1 tags)
...
Pushing tag for rev [8340292d5467] on {https://cdn-registry-1.
docker.io/v1/repositories/cricket/fedweb/tags/1.5}
```

Because only the user name is added to the image and not a separate repository name, the image is pushed to the repository associated with the cricket user account on docker.io. If you were to log in as cricket at `https://hub.docker.com/`, you could see the pushed image as shown in Figure 6.1.

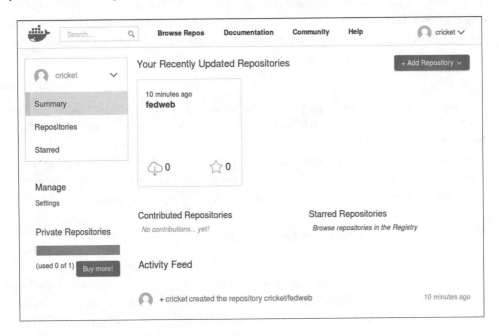

FIGURE 6.1 Log in to docker.io to see the images you have pushed.

If you want the image to be available from another tag name, you can tag the image again and push it. In this example, I add the tag `cricket/fedweb:monkey` to the existing image. Notice that when I push the name with the new tag to the docker registry for cricket at docker.io it shows that the layers that make up the image have already been pushed to docker.io:

```
# docker push cricket/fedweb:monkey
The push refers to a repository [cricket/fedweb] (len: 1)
Sending image list
Pushing repository cricket/fedweb (1 tags)
511136ea3c5a: Image already pushed, skipping
00a0c78eeb6d: Image already pushed, skipping
...
```

Upon returning to cricket's account, clicking on the Tag tab lets you see all the images and aliases (tags) to each image available within the user account. In Figure 6.2 you can see that the `cricket/fedweb` image has two tags on it (1.5 and monkey).

FIGURE 6.2 See the tags assigned to each image from your docker.io account.

At this point, because I have not restricted the image, anyone who wanted to use my cricket/fedweb image could do so using the `docker pull cricket/fedweb` command, as shown in the Pull this repository box in Figure 6.2. Anyone can also find that image by searching for `cricket/fedweb` on the docker.io hub.

```
# docker search cricket/fedweb
NAME                DESCRIPTION     STARS     OFFICIAL    AUTOMATED
cricket/fedweb                      0
```

With the container entry displayed on docker.io, you can add a description of the image. Select the edit icon on the Information tab and you can add a short description and full description of the image. After you save that information, the short description is displayed when someone searches for the image. For example:

```
# docker search cricket/fedweb
NAME                DESCRIPTION                         STARS   OFFICIAL...
cricket/fedweb      Test apache web server container    0
```

Attaching a Repository Name to an Image

By attaching a repository name to an image, you can use `docker push` on that image to direct it to be pushed to a docker registry you identify. You can set up your own private docker registry by installing the docker-registry package, starting up the docker-registry service, and making that service available on a particular port on an accessible system.

If you had the docker-registry service set up at a host named `myregistry.`
`example.com`, listening on the default port (TCP 5000), you could tag an image so
you could push it to that registry. For example, here's how to tag the `fedweb:1.5`
image we were working with earlier so it could be pushed to `myregistry.example.`
`com`:

```
# docker tag fedweb:1.5 myregistry.example.com:5000/fedweb:1.5
# docker images myregistry.example.com:5000/fedweb
REPOSITORY                    TAG IMAGE ID    CREATED    VIRTUAL SIZE
myreg.example.com:5000/fedweb 1.5 f583b458b447 1 day ago 696.7 MB
```

To actually push the image to the registry, you could type the following:

```
# docker push myregistry.example.com:5000/fedweb:1.5
The push refers to a repository [myregistry.example.com:5000/fedweb]
   (len: 1)
Sending image list
Pushing repository myregistry.example.com:5000/fedweb (1 tags)
511136ea3c5a: Image successfully pushed
...
f583b458b447: Image successfully pushed
Pushing tag for rev [f583b458b447] on {http://myregistry.example.
com:5000/v1/repositories/fedweb/tags/1.5}
```

In fact, you could apply multiple image names and tags to the same image so
that the same image (identified by the image ID) could be pushed to different registries. Returning to the previous example, at this point, anyone with access to your
docker-registry system can pull the image to their local system. For example:

```
# docker pull myregistry.example.com:5000/fedweb:1.5
Pulling repository myregistry.example.com:5000/fedweb
f583b458b447: Download complete
511136ea3c5a: Download complete
...
Status: Downloaded newer image for myregistry.example.com:5000/fedweb:1.5
```

SUMMARY

By tagging a Docker formatted container image you can identify not only what an
image contains, but also where it should be stored and possibly which user account
repository is associated with it. It is typical to add tags that identify version number
and version names of the software in the image. Images can also be tagged with
hostnames and IP addresses, so the images can be pushed to and pulled from a
docker-registry service running on a host.

## CHAPTER 7

Investigating Containers

IN THIS CHAPTER:

- Inspect images and containers for configuration data
- View the history of an image
- Attach to a container process to follow what it's doing
- Execute a new process in a running container
- Look at log messages from a container process
- Copy files from a running container

So far, you have run, pulled, pushed, saved, loaded, and searched for containers. At this point, it may all look a bit like magic. If you are ready to dig deeper into the processing going on with a particular container, many tools are available with Docker, and with the Linux systems they run on, to look more closely at a running container.

This chapter teaches you how to use `docker inspect` to look at an image before you run it to see how that image is configured. The same `docker inspect` command can be used on containers to see run-time information (such as the container's process ID, network interfaces, and mounted volumes) along with other information about the container.

After your images and containers have been inspected, you can use other commands to look into them further. There are `docker` command options to attach to a container's process, execute a new process, view log files, copy files, and list processes inside the container.

INSPECTING IMAGES AND CONTAINERS

Each image carries information with it that includes default configuration settings, information about who created it, and details about when and how it was created. After you have run a container, additional information is included with that container, such as container network settings, whether the container is still running, and information on mounted volumes.

By running the `docker inspect` command on an image or a container, you can see the low-level data associated with it. This can help you in using or debugging problems with the image or container. For example, seeing a container's IP address can tell you where a client application (such as a web browser) can find the service running in the container.

To view output in a way that is easy to read, `docker inspect` displays information in JSON format. This makes it easier to see each individual key and value pair and how it fits in the structure of information associated with the image or container.

To see how `docker inspect` works, the following sections illustrate how to look at the low-level data associated with a `fedora` image running a simple web server using the `python` command and SimpleHTTPServer module.

INSPECTING AN IMAGE

Chapter 5, "Finding, Pulling, Saving, and Loading Container Images," describes how you can find and get information about a Docker-formatted container image before you pull it to your local system. These methods include

- **Finding images with `docker search`:** With this command, you can search the Docker Hub and possibly other registries by keyword to find images that meet your needs. From those results, you can see available images and repositories, whether an image is official or created with automated builds, and how many stars have been voted for an image.

- **Browsing Docker Hub for images:** Besides allowing you to search for images, the Docker Hub site (`hub.docker.com`) lets you browse for and sort available images. This registry also often shows information about how images are created and how to use those images.

- **Listing local images with `docker`:** Once an image is on your system, the `docker images` command lets you see basic information about that image. For example, you can see the repository the image came from, the image name and tag, the image ID, when it was created, and its virtual size.

Once you have chosen an image and pulled it to your local system and before running the image, you might want to inspect low-level information for it. You can use the `docker inspect` command to find details about the image and how it was created.

Inspecting Base Images with `docker inspect`

Inspecting an image can give you some insight into when it was created, the Docker version used to build it, ports it exposes, and other information. Here are examples of `docker inspect` commands. This command inspects the latest `ubuntu` container. If the `ubuntu:latest` image has not already been pulled to your system, this action pulls the image and also inspects it. Note that each time you pull an image, the output from `docker inspect` and the image itself could change. I trimmed the output to highlight selected information:

```
# docker inspect ubuntu:latest | less
[{
    "Architecture": "amd64",
    "Author": "",
    "Comment": "",
    "Config": {
        "AttachStderr": false,
        "AttachStdin": false,
        "AttachStdout": false,
        "Cmd": [
            "/bin/bash"
        ],
...
        "Env": [
        "PATH=/usr/local/sbin:/usr/local/bin:/usr/sbin:/usr/bin:/sbin:/bin"
        ],
...
        "NetworkDisabled": false,
...
    "Created": "2015-03-20T06:16:47.003636554Z",
    "DockerVersion": "1.4.1",
    "Id":
"d0955f21bf24f5bfffd32d2d0bb669d0564701c271bc3dfc64cfc5adfdec2d07",
    "Os": "linux",
...
}
]
```

From the output, you can see that the architecture of the container is amd64 (64-bit PC compatible). The Comment and Author lines were not defined when this image was created. The Config section sets up the environment in which the container runs.

The `/bin/bash` command is run by default, if no other command is identified at run time. Because attaching standard input, output, and error are set to false, you need to specify options on the command line when you run this container's default bash command (something like, `docker run -it ubuntu`). In the Env section, only the PATH variable is set to define which directories are searched for commands run. NetworkDisabled set to false indicates that the network interface should be started within the container.

The last section shows basic information about how the container was created. You can see the date the container image was created, the version of Docker used to create it (1.4.1), the long form of the container's ID, and the operating system (Linux).

Information you can find about the `fedora` image is similar. Here are some of the highlights when inspecting the latest `fedora` image:

```
# docker inspect fedora:latest | less
[{
    "Architecture": "amd64",
    "Author": "Lokesh Mandvekar \u003clsm5@fedoraproject.org\u003e",
...
    "Created": "2014-12-31T22:33:27.395254797Z",
    "DockerVersion": "1.4.1",
    "Id":
"834629358fe214f210b0ed606fba2c17827d7a46dd74bd3309afc2a103ad0e89",
    "Os": "linux",
}
]
```

Because the `fedora` image is a base image, like the `ubuntu` image, there is little specialized configuration. For example, like the `ubuntu` base image the `fedora` image doesn't set a MacAddress for network cards, it simply sets a network interface to start automatically ("NetworkDisabled": false). No special requirements are set for memory use or swap space required. These base images are meant to be generic, so you can tune them yourself when you create your own containers and images from them.

Inspecting Application Images with `docker inspect`

While base images are meant to be generic, images built to run specific applications tend to include more low-level configuration settings. An example of a Docker-formatted container image that includes more customization is the `wordpress` image (available from the Docker Hub). Here's an example of what that image's low-level data looks like:

```
# docker inspect wordpress:latest | less
...
"Config": {
...
    "Cmd": [
        "apache2-foreground"
    ],
...
    "Entrypoint": [
        "/entrypoint.sh"
    ],
    "Env": [
"PATH=/usr/local/sbin:/usr/local/bin:/usr/sbin:/usr/bin:/sbin:/bin",
        "PHP_INI_DIR=/usr/local/etc/php",
        "PHP_EXTRA_BUILD_DEPS=apache2-dev",
        "PHP_EXTRA_CONFIGURE_ARGS=--with-apxs2",
        "GPG_KEYS=6E4F6AB321FDC07F2C332E3AC2BF0BC433CFC8B3
➥0BD78B5F97500D450838F95DFE857D9A90D90EC1",
        "PHP_VERSION=5.6.8",
        "WORDPRESS_VERSION=4.2.1",
        "WORDPRESS_UPSTREAM_VERSION=4.2.1",
        "WORDPRESS_SHA1=c93a39be9911591b19a94743014be3585df0512f"
    ],
    "ExposedPorts": {
        "80/tcp": {}
    },
...
"Volumes": {
        "/var/www/html": {}
    },
    "WorkingDir": "/var/www/html"
},
"Created": "2015-04-30T05:58:47.912933967Z",
"DockerVersion": "1.6.0",
...
```

The `docker inspect` command reveals that more container-specific information was added into the `wordpress` image than in the base images illustrated earlier. In the Config section, the entrypoint.sh script in the container's root directory is set to start when you run the container. The apache2-foreground script is defined as an option to entrypoint.sh when it is run.

A set of environment variables are defined in the `wordpress` container. These variables set such things as directories in the shell's path, the directory containing

PHP ini scripts, and version information. The ExposedPorts variable exposes TCP port 80 (HTTP content) from the container to the host. The Volumes variable tells Docker to mount /var/www/html from the host inside the container. Then it sets WorkingDir to that directory, to be used as the working directory for the container.

As with the other images, the Created line tells when the image was created. The DockerVersion variable tells which version of Docker the container is designed for.

Looking at the History of an Image

Images are created by building a base image. Each time a new command is run on the image, a new container layer is created. If those layers are saved with the image, you can see that information later using the docker command.

There are good reasons for saving an image in layers instead of compressing those layers into a single image. If, for example, you are running several different containers on the same computer, if they all have the same base image (identified by an image ID), it can save on storage space. On top of the base image, you may add a certain set of development libraries. Then you might add a standard set of services. The more you can duplicate each layer, the more space you can save.

To see the history of an image, run docker history on that image. Here is an example:

```
# docker history ubuntu
IMAGE          CREATED        CREATED BY                       SIZE
d0955f21bf24   6 weeks ago    /bin/sh -c #(nop) CMD [/bin/bash]  0 B
9fec74352904   6 weeks ago    /bin/sh -c sed -i 's/^#\s*...     1.895 kB
a1a958a24818   6 weeks ago    /bin/sh -c echo '#!/bin/sh...    194.5 kB
f3c84ac3a053   6 weeks ago    /bin/sh -c #(nop) ADD file:...   192.5 MB
511136ea3c5a   23 months ago
```

You can see that after the original image was created 23 months ago, six weeks ago the image was changed four times. You can see that someone ran shell commands to create the image. Any future container that uses any of the image's layers listed by name in the IMAGE column would not have to pull that particular layer, but can simply use the one that is already on the system.

INSPECTING RUNNING CONTAINERS

Once you have run a container, you can query that container to find much of the same information you found querying the original image. On top of the image information, you can also see a lot of data that was set from the `docker run` command and otherwise added to the configuration settings on the container at run time.

The `docker inspect` information you uncover can help you troubleshoot problems with a running container or simply understand how the container is working. You can run `docker inspect` on either a running container or one that is no longer running, but has not been deleted. In other words, any container you can see with `docker ps` or `docker ps -a` commands.

Although there are times when you just want to dump out all low-level configuration settings for a container, other times you might want to select particular pieces of information. The `docker inspect` command also allows you to provide a value name and display just that value, if you choose.

Start a Container to Inspect

To practice inspecting a container, start with one on which you can use a few `docker run` options. For this example, I start up a `fedora` base image and run the SimpleHTTPServer module. This launches a simple web server.

To create some data for the web server to share, I run an `echo` command to put some words into an `index.html` file. Then I start up the web server. This is what the two command lines look like:

```
# echo "Web Server Test: Successful" > /var/www/html/index.html
# docker run -d -p 8080:8080 --name="fed_web"    \
    --restart="on-failure:5"  -w /var/www/html    \
    -v /var/www/html:/var/www/html                 \
    fedora python -m SimpleHTTPServer 8080
8f77610d10f2af42b158859ab7c689caf43829ebefda6ea7ac9bc5dce3890b6f
```

The web server runs in the background as a daemon process (`-d`). The TCP port 8080 is exposed from the container to the host. The container is named `fed_web`. By setting `--restart="on-failure:5"` if this container fails, `docker` tries up to five failed attempts to restart the container. (By default, the container would not try to restart on failure.)

The working directory for the web server is `/var/www/html`. To provide data to that directory in the container, I bind mount the `/var/www/html` directory on the host to that same directory in the container.

The name of the image used is `fedora` (which calls `fedora:latest` by default). After that, the `python` command runs with the SimpleHTTPServer module to serve data on TCP port 8080. To check that the container is running, type the following from the host system:

```
# curl -L localhost:8080
Web Server Test: Successful
# docker ps
CONTAINER ID   IMAGE          COMMAND                CREATED
    STATUS         PORTS                   NAMES
8f77610d10f2  fedora:latest  "python -m SimpleHTT  5 minutes ago
    Up 5 minutes  0.0.0.0:8080->8080/tcp    fed_web
```

The curl command queries the local TCP port 8080 and returns the value I echoed into the host's index.html file (Web Server Test: Successful). The docker ps command shows that the container is still running and that data requested from port 8080 on the host is directed to that same port in the container.

With the container up and running and serving data, it's time to start inspecting that container.

Inspect an Entire Container Configuration

If you want, you can just output all the running container's information to your screen (STDOUT). As with images, to output low-level configuration information from a container, use the docker inspect command. I suggest you either pipe the output through the more command or direct it into a file to view the contents.

I break up the output from docker inspect and highlight some of the attribute/value pairs in the following example:

```
# docker inspect fed_web
...
    "Args": [
        "-m",
        "SimpleHTTPServer",
        "8080"
    ],
    "Config": {
        "AttachStderr": false,
        "AttachStdin": false,
        "AttachStdout": false,
        "Cmd": [
            "python",
            "-m",
            "SimpleHTTPServer",
            "8080"
        ],
```

The three arguments given to the python command when the container is run are stored in the Args attribute.

The Config section starts out showing that standard error (AttachStdErr), standard input (AttachStdin), and standard output (AttachStdout) are not attached to the terminal session that started the container. Those settings would be set to true instead of false if, for example, you were running a bash shell to interact directly with the container from your console.

The Cmd attribute of the Config section holds the command (python) and all the arguments passed to it (-m, SimpleHTTPServer, and 8080). The output continues:

```
    "CpuShares": 0,
    "CpusetCpus": "",
    ...
    "Env": [
"PATH=/usr/local/sbin:/usr/local/bin:/usr/sbin:/usr/bin:/sbin:/bin"
    ],
    "ExposedPorts": {
        "8080/tcp": {}
    },
    "Hostname": "8f77610d10f2",
```

If there were a lot of containers on the system, you might want to assign CPU shares to each container to ensure that the containers that were most important got the highest percentage of CPU time (CpuShares get no CPU priority here). If CPUsetCpus were defined here (it is not), the container could only run on selected CPUs. Those two values could have been set on the docker run command line with the -c and --cpuset-cpus="" options, respectively.

The Env section includes the PATH setting, which defines the directories to look in when a command is run in the container. ExposedPorts shows that TCP port 8080 is exposed on the same port number on the host. Because no hostname was defined on the command line, the first 12 characters of the container ID are used as the hostname. (To assign a hostname inside a container you could use the -h hostname option to docker run.) The output continues:

```
    "Image": "fedora",
...
    "NetworkDisabled": false,
...
    "User": "",
...
    "WorkingDir": "/var/www/html"
},
```

The image attribute shows the name of the image used (fedora, in this case). The default NetworkDisabled value of false enables networking from within the container. The User is not set here, but if it were, the command run from the container would run as the user identified. For example, by setting -u apache from the docker run command line, the web server could have run as the user apache instead of as root. As noted earlier, the working directory (the directory from which the command is run) is set to /var/www/html. In this case the web server serves out content from there. The output continues:

```
"HostConfig": {
...
    "PortBindings": {
        "8080/tcp": [
            {
                "HostIp": "",
                "HostPort": "8080"
            }
        ]
    },
    "Privileged": false,
    "PublishAllPorts": false,
    "ReadonlyRootfs": false,
    "RestartPolicy": {
        "MaximumRetryCount": 5,
        "Name": "on-failure"
...
```

The PortBindings attribute sets TCP port 8080 to be exposed on port 8080 for all IP addresses (HostIp) on the host. The Privileged attribute (false) indicates that the container has no privileges to access other containers or the host itself, except in limited ways that are otherwise specified (such as explicitly mounting a volume from the host). With PublishAllPorts set to false, only ports from the container that are explicitly indicated (TCP port 8080 in this case) will be accessible from the same port on the host.

With ReadonlyRootfs set to false, the root file system can be written to. By default, the RestartPolicy attribute is set to not restart the container if it fails. In this example, however, the MaximumRetryCount is set to 5. So five retries must fail after the container fails before Docker gives up trying to start it again. The output continues:

```
"HostnamePath": "/var/lib/docker/containers/8f77610.../hostname",
"HostsPath": "/var/lib/docker/containers/8f77610.../hosts",
"Id": "8f77610d10...",
"Image": "834629358f...",
"LogPath": "/var/lib/docker/containers/8f776.../8f776...-json.log",
"MountLabel": "system_u:object_r:svirt_sandbox_file_t:s0:c157,c580",
"Name": "/fed_web",
```

Some standard Linux files destined to be used in the container are stored on the host and bind mounted into the container. That and other information are stored in the `/var/lib/docker/containers` directory on the host, in a directory named after the container's ID. I truncated the container IDs in the preceding example.

The HostnamePath attribute sets the location of the hostname file, where the container's `/etc/hostname` file is stored. The hostname is set to the first 12 characters of the container's ID, if it is not explicitly set in `docker run`. HostsPath sets the location of the `/etc/hosts` file, which attaches the container's hostname to its IP address, as well as setting the IP address for the localhost and for IPV6-specific addresses.

The LogPath defines the location of the log file associated with this container. Under the `/var/lib/docker/containers` directory is a subdirectory for each container. That subdirectory holds the log file for that container under the name that begins with the container ID and ends with -json.log. To see log messages in that log file, type `docker logs fed_web`.

MountLabel sets the SELinux context that must be on a file on the host before that file can be bind mounted into the container. If you typed `ls -lZ` on the `/var/lib/docker/container/container_id/` directory, you would see that the hostname, hosts, and `resolv.conf` files all have the same SELinux file context that is set in the MountLabel attribute (svirt_sandbox_file_t).

The Name attribute contains the name of the container preceded by a slash (/fed_web). The output continues:

```
"NetworkSettings": {
    "Bridge": "docker0",
    "Gateway": "172.17.42.1",
    "GlobalIPv6Address": "",
    "GlobalIPv6PrefixLen": 0,
    "IPAddress": "172.17.0.9",
    "IPPrefixLen": 16,
    "IPv6Gateway": "",
    "LinkLocalIPv6Address": "fe80::42:acff:fe11:9",
    "LinkLocalIPv6PrefixLen": 64,
    "MacAddress": "02:42:ac:11:00:09",
    "NetNs": "",
    "PortMapping": null,
    "Ports": {
        "8080/tcp": [
            {
                "HostIp": "0.0.0.0",
                "HostPort": "8080"
            }
        ]
    }
},
```

The Bridge defines the name of the network (docker0 by default) that provides connectivity for Docker containers on the host. In this example, the host address on that network is 172.17.42.1, as indicated by the Gateway attribute. After that, several IPV6 attributes are not set (because IPv6 networking is not enabled in Docker by default).

The MacAddress (02:42:ac:11:00:09) indicates the address of the virtual network interface card inside the container. The Ports definition shows the assignment of TCP port 8080 to all IP addresses on the host (HostIp is 0.0.0.0) and the host TCP port 8080. The output continues:

```
    "ProcessLabel": "system_u:system_r:svirt_lxc_net_t:s0:c157,c580",
    "ResolvConfPath": "/var/lib/docker/containers/8f77610d1.../
➥resolv.conf",
    "State": {
        "Error": "",
        "ExitCode": 0,
        "FinishedAt": "0001-01-01T00:00:00Z",
        "OOMKilled": false,
        "Paused": false,
        "Pid": 10750,
        "Restarting": false,
        "Running": true,
        "StartedAt": "2015-05-04T22:23:09.12704039Z"
    },
    "Volumes": {
        "/var/www/html": "/var/www/html"
    },
    "VolumesMode": {
        "/var/www/html": {}
    },
    "VolumesRW": {
        "/var/www/html": true
    }
}
]
```

The ProcessLabel shows the SELinux security context for the process run from the container. If you were to type `ps -efZ | grep c157,c580` on the host, you would see that the `python` command was running with the security context listed in the ProcessLabel attribute. Also notice that the c157,c580 portion of the ProcessLabel matches that part of the security context assigned to the bind mounted files described earlier. This mechanism (if SELinux is in enforcing mode on the system) prevents regular containers from accessing files and other resources from other containers.

The State attributes provide information about the current state of the container. In this case, because the container is currently running, the Running attribute is set to true.

The last set of information has to do with mounting volumes. The Volumes attribute, shows which local directories are mounted inside the container. In this case, it is just /var/www/html. After that, the Volume Modes attribute sets permission on the directory and VolumesRW defines whether the directory is read-only.

Inspect Individual Container Attributes

You can selectively display information from a container, whether that container is running, paused, or stopped. To do that, you pass options to docker inspect that identify specific attributes that interest you with the --format option.

Not only can you pull out particular pieces of information about your container, you can also pass that information to another command to act on that information. For example, to check the IP address set for your container, you could type the following:

```
# docker inspect --format='{{.NetworkSettings.IPAddress}}' fed_web
172.17.0.9
```

To check that the IP address is up and accessible, you could pipe that output to the ping command as follows:

```
# ping -c 2 $(docker inspect \
    --format='{{.NetworkSettings.IPAddress}}' fed_web)
PING 172.17.0.9 (172.17.0.9) 56(84) bytes of data.
64 bytes from 172.17.0.9: icmp_seq=1 ttl=64 time=0.127 ms
64 bytes from 172.17.0.9: icmp_seq=2 ttl=64 time=0.104 ms
--- 172.17.0.9 ping statistics ---
2 packets transmitted, 2 received, 0% packet loss, time 999ms
rtt min/avg/max/mdev = 0.104/0.115/0.127/0.015 ms
```

As the output shows, I was able to query the IP address and then show two packets sent and received from the container. As another example, I could pass that IP address to the curl command to try to get content from the web service. Here, I add port 8080 to the command line because that is the port the web service is listening on:

```
# curl -L $(docker inspect \
    --format='{{.NetworkSettings.IPAddress}}' fed_web):8080
Web Server Test: Successful
```

The following sections show how you can find different types of information about a container and, in some cases, use that information as input to other commands.

Inspect a Container Running a Terminal Session

When you start a container to run a shell terminal session, you can inspect that container from another shell to see that the container has standard input, output, and error (STDIN, STDOUT, STDERR) attached to that shell. Then you can find further ways of investigating that container's shell session.

Open two shell sessions on your Docker host and you can follow along with this procedure. From the first shell, type the following:

```
# docker run -it --name=bashtest fedora /bin/bash
bash-4.3# ls
bin   dev  home  lib64       media  opt   root  sbin  sys  usr
boot  etc  lib   lost+found  mnt    proc  run   srv   tmp  var
```

With the container named `bashtest` open with a bash shell, open a second shell on the same host and inspect settings associated with that shell attaching to the container's standard input, output, and error:

```
# docker inspect --format='{{.Config.AttachStdin}} \
    {{.Config.AttachStdout}} \
    {{.Config.AttachStderr}}' bashtest
true true true
```

If you want to watch and even interact with the bash shell that originally opened the container, you can do that using the `docker attach` command. From the second shell, type the following:

```
# docker attach bashtest
bash-4.3# pwd
/
bash-4.3# ps
  PID TTY          TIME CMD
    1 ?        00:00:00 bash
    8 ?        00:00:00 ps
bash-4.3#
```

At this point, you could type from either the first or second shell session. Anything you type from one shell appears on the other shell. When you are done, type `exit` to close the shell and stop the container. In this case, I typed `pwd` and `ps` in one shell session and any input, output, or error data appears in both shells.

Figure 7.1 shows an example of the two shell sessions, with the first shell in the foreground.

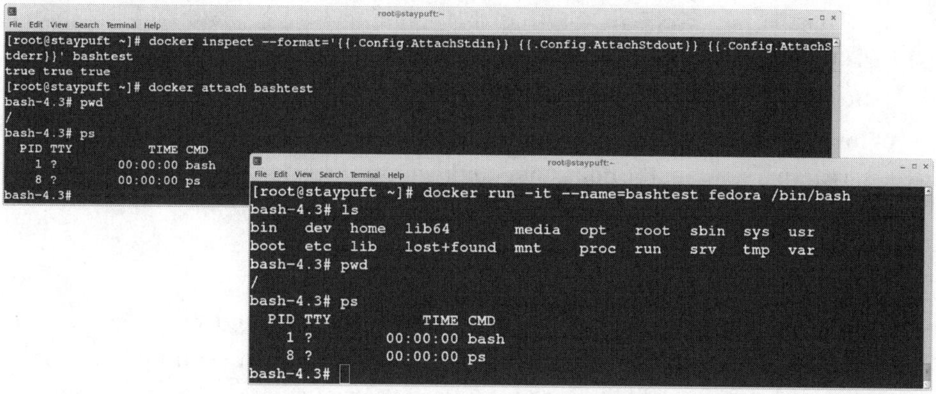

FIGURE 7.1 Inspect a container for attachments to stdin, stdout, and stderr.

Inspect Memory and CPU Limits for a Container

As you begin to grow your use of containers, with multiple containers needing to interact with each other, you may find those containers competing for resources. Using options to `docker run`, you can limit the amount of memory or swap area available to a container. You can also set CPU priorities and restrict CPU usage for containers.

The following examples show how to individually list memory and CPU limitations that are set on containers. Because, by default, these resources are not limited when you run a container, I re-ran the `fed_web` container I ran earlier, adding the following options:

- `--cpuset-cpus=0`: Sets the first CPU on the system to execute commands from the container

- `--cpu-shares=512`: Sets the proportion of CPU cycles the container can get

- `--memory=1G`: Limits the amount of memory the container can use to 1G

- `--memory-swap=2G`: Limits the amount of swap space a container can use to 2G

Here's how you could inspect for each of those pieces of information individually.

```
# docker inspect --format='{{.Config.Cpuset}}' fed_web
0
# docker inspect --format='{{.Config.CpuShares}}' fed_web
512
# docker inspect --format='{{.Config.Memory}}' fed_web
1.073741824e+09
# docker inspect --format='{{.Config.MemorySwap}}' fed_web
2.147483648e+09
```

From the output, you can see that the container is set to use the computer's first CPU (0). The container's CpuShares is set to 512, with the default value being 1024; this container would get a smaller share of CPU availability than the average.

As for memory usage, the container would be limited to 1G (1.073741824e+09) of RAM. In terms of swap, the container could consume up to 2G (2.147483648e+09) of swap space.

Inspect the SELinux Contexts for a Container

In a regular Linux system the root user owns everything and can access everything. When SELinux is implemented on a Linux system (as it is on Fedora, RHEL, and other highly secure systems), SELinux can restrict what a running process can access. This is done by having a process run in a particular SELinux context and by SELinux using that context to restrict what the process can access.

Two SELinux labels are defined in a container's low-level data, on Fedora, Red Hat Enterprise Linux, CentOS, and similar systems, that help restrict a container from being able to access content on the host belonging to other containers. Those labels are MountLabel and ProcessLabel. Here are a few of ways to list that information:

```
# docker inspect fed_web | grep Label
"MountLabel": "system_u:object_r:svirt_sandbox_file_t:s0:c176,c430",
"ProcessLabel": "system_u:system_r:svirt_lxc_net_t:s0:c176,c430",
# docker inspect --format='{{.MountLabel}}' fed_web
system_u:object_r:svirt_sandbox_file_t:s0:c176,c430
# docker inspect --format='{{.ProcessLabel}}' fed_web
system_u:system_r:svirt_lxc_net_t:s0:c176,c430
```

The value of MountLabel represents the SELinux file context that is set on files on the host that can be bind mounted inside this particular container. The ProcessLabel is the SELinux context used on the process running from the container. In the example of the fed_web container, the python command used to run the simple web server uses the ProcessLabel.

With SELinux you can use a ps command with a -z option to see the SELinux context for the process. Using ls with -z lets you see the file context on a file that the process running from the container can bind mount within the container. With the container still running, you can get the process ID of the command running from the container and then pass the PID to the ps command as follows:

```
# docker inspect --format='{{.State.Pid}}' fed_web
32503
# ps -fZp 32503
LABEL                                            UID  PID   PPID  C STIME
```

```
      TTY        TIME      CMD
system_u:system_r:svirt_lxc_net_t:s0:c176,c430 root 32503 1433   0 11:20
    ?          00:00:07 python -m SimpleHTTPServer 8080
# docker ps | grep fed_web
022ac55f6206 fedora:latest "python -m SimpleHTT 1 minute ago 1 minute
      0.0.0.0:8080->8080/tcp   fed_web
# cd /var/lib/docker/containers/022ac55f6206*
# ls -Z hostname hosts resolv.conf | grep sandbox
-rw-r--r--. root root
    system_u:object_r:svirt_sandbox_file_t:s0:c176,c430 hostname
-rw-r--r--. root root
    system_u:object_r:svirt_sandbox_file_t:s0:c176,c430 hosts
-rw-r--r--. root root
    system_u:object_r:svirt_sandbox_file_t:s0:c176,c430 resolv.conf
```

Starting with the preceding docker inspect command, I queried for the process ID of the process running from the container (PID 32503 in this case). Using ps to see a full (-f) listing with SELinux context (-z) for the process ID (-p 32503), you can see that the SELinux context matches the context contained in the Process-Label for the running web server (python process).

Next, look at the container ID for this container (022ac55f6206 is the short form) and change to the container's directory under /var/lib/docker/containers. Using ls to list the SELinux context (-z), you can see that the context on the hostname, hosts, and resolv.conf files is set to the MountLabel value in the container.

One last thing to mention about SELinux contexts: Every file bind mounted from the host to a container has svirt_sandbox_file as part of its file context. Every process run from the container has svirt_lxc_net_t as part of its context. What prevents a process run from a container to access resources belonging to another container is the last part of the SELinux context. In this example, the c176,c430 portion of that context is unique to this container and prevents it from accessing other resources from the host or from other containers.

FINDING MORE WAYS TO LOOK INTO CONTAINERS

Your container is now up and running and you have thoroughly inspected its low-level settings. Using the docker command with a few different subcommands, you can find out more about your running containers.

Using docker top to See Container Processes

A container typically runs one process. However, using docker exec you can open other processes within that container, most notably you can open a shell to look around at what is going on inside a container. With `docker top`, you can see all the processes running in a container. Here is an example (your output will be somewhat different):

```
# docker top fed_web
UID    PID    PPID   C  STIME   TTY     TIME      CMD
root   12882  1433   0  23:17   pts/8   00:00:00  nsenter-exec --nspid
                                                    32503 --console
                                                    /dev/pts/8 -- /bin/bash

root   12883  12882  0  23:17   pts/8   00:00:00  /bin/bash
root   32503  1433   0  11:20   ?       00:00:07  python -m
                                                    SimpleHTTPServer 8080
```

From the output you can see that three processes are running inside the container. When the container started, the `python` command was run. From a second terminal, I opened a `/bin/bash` shell, which starts up `nsenter-exec` on the host to open the required namespaces to the container. So `docker top` shows those three processes on the host, along with their process ID (PID) numbers from the host.

When I run a `ps -ef` command inside the host, I don't see `nsenter-exec`, but only the `python` and `/bin/bash` processes (plus the `ps -ef` command I just ran). Notice that the process IDs inside the container are different because the container has its own process table:

```
# ps -ef
UID    PID  PPID  C STIME TTY     TIME CMD
root     1     0  0 May05 ?   00:00:12 python -m SimpleHTTPServer 8080
root    15     0  0 06:38 ?   00:00:00 /bin/bash
root    20    15  0 06:38 ?   00:00:00 ps -ef
```

Using `docker attach` to Interact with a Service Inside a Container

You can attach to any running container to see the processing going on with it. If the container simply opens a bash shell (as I showed earlier), you can interact directly with that shell by attaching a shell to it from another process. The same thing can be done to interact with a service running in a container.

Using the `fed_web` example created earlier, I can attach to that container as it is running and watch as the web server responds to requests it receives:

```
# docker attach fed_web
172.17.42.1 - - [06/May/2015 06:46:32] "GET / HTTP/1.1" 200 -
172.17.42.1 - - [06/May/2015 06:47:46] "GET / HTTP/1.1" 200 -
172.17.42.1 - - [06/May/2015 06:55:05] code 404, message File not found
172.17.42.1 - - [06/May/2015 06:55:05] "GET /badfile HTTP/1.1" 404 -
```

In the example just shown, I run two `curl localhost:8080` commands, which the first two lines show are able to serve up data (the contents of the default `index.html` file). On the third line, it shows I try to see the file called `badfile`, which isn't on the server. It results in a "file not found" and a code 404 result when looking for `/badfile`.

Using `docker exec` to Start a New Process in a Running Container

Instead of just attaching to a process running in a container, you can actually start a new process to interact with a container. Chapter 4, "Running Container Images," shows an example of how to open a bash shell to work inside a running container (for example, `docker exec -it fed_web /bin/bash`). However, you can run any command you want from within the container (include `yum` or `apt-get` to install more commands to run).

In this example, I run `docker exec` to execute a `yum` command inside my `fed_web` container to install the net-tools package. Then I run a few commands from that package to check out the container's view of its network interfaces:

```
# docker exec -it fed_web yum install net-tools -y
Resolving Dependencies
--> Running transaction check
---> Package net-tools.x86_64 0:2.0-0.31.20141124git.fc21 will be
installed
...
# docker exec -it fed_web route -n
Kernel IP routing table
Destination Gateway      Genmask        Flags Metric Ref  Use Iface
0.0.0.0     172.17.42.1  0.0.0.0        UG    0      0      0 eth0
172.17.0.0  0.0.0.0      255.255.0.0    U     0      0      0 eth0
# docker exec -it fed_web netstat -tupln
Active Internet connections (only servers)
Proto Recv-Q Send-Q Local Address Foreign Address State   PID/Program name
tcp        0      0 0.0.0.0:8080  0.0.0.0:*       LISTEN  1/python
```

After the net-tools package is installed, I run the `route` and `netstat` commands from that package. The output from the `route` command shows that the default gateway from the container is 172.17.42.1 (the IP address of the docker0 network interface on the host). The `netstat` command shows that the python process (which provides the web service) is listening on all local network interfaces on port 8080 (0.0.0.0.:8080).

Using `docker logs` to See Container Process Output

Instead of attaching to a container to watch the output from its processing live, as long as the container is still either running or stopped (not removed) you can go back and look at the output from the container's processing. Running `docker logs` on a container basically dumps all the output from a container's processing to your screen (STDOUT) and exits.

Using the `fed_web` example again, notice that the output is the same as you saw with `docker attach`, but it doesn't continue to watch for output, it simply exits:

```
# docker logs fed_web
172.17.42.1 - - [06/May/2015 06:46:32] "GET / HTTP/1.1" 200 -
172.17.42.1 - - [06/May/2015 06:47:46] "GET / HTTP/1.1" 200 -
172.17.42.1 - - [06/May/2015 06:55:05] code 404, message File not found
172.17.42.1 - - [06/May/2015 06:55:05] "GET /badfile HTTP/1.1" 404 -
#
```

Using `docker diff` to See How a Container Has Changed

Docker keeps track of any changes to the files and directories that occur in a container after it is running. You can view the changes to the container as compared to the original image you run using the `docker diff` command. After making some changes to my `fed_web` container, this is the kind of information that `docker diff` shows about those changes:

```
# docker diff fed_web
A /var/www
A /var/www/html
C /root
C /tmp
D /root/anaconda-ks.cfg
A /tmp/anaconda-ks.cfg
...
```

The output shows that the `/var/www` and `/var/www/html` directories were added (actually, they are mounted from the host). I moved the `anaconda-ks.cfg` file from `/root` to the `/tmp` directory. This caused the `/root` and `/tmp` directories to be changed. It also shows that `/root/anaconda-ks.cfg` was deleted and `/tmp/anaconda-ks.cfg` was added.

It is a good idea to use `docker diff` to check on the changes to a container before you commit that container to a permanent image.

Using `docker cp` to Copy Files from a Container

There may be times when you want to look at a file within a container without interrupting what's going on in the container. One way to do that is to simply copy files from a container with `docker cp`. To copy the `index.html` file from a running `fed_web` container, you could type the following:

```
# docker cp fed_web:/var/www/html/index.html /tmp
# cat /tmp/index.html
Web Server Test: Successful
```

SUMMARY

Looking at low-level data associated with images and containers provides an excellent way to see what is going on with them. Using `docker inspect` on base images, you can see the basics on how that image is intended to run. Inspecting images created to run a specific application can reveal specifics about that container, such as environment variables, entry points, mounted volumes, and working directories.

Investigating low-level data for running containers with `docker inspect` can tell you a lot about what is happening as containers are running. From each container, you can see the process ID of the process running, network interfaces, mounted volumes, and other information.

Once a container is running, there are many other ways to find out information about that container as well. You can use `docker top` to see processes running in a container. With `docker attach`, you can attach to a container's running process. The `docker exec` command lets you execute a new command within a running container. The `docker logs` command lets you see log messages generated from the process running from a container. With `docker cp` you can copy files from a container.

## CHAPTER 8

Starting, Stopping, and Restarting Containers

IN THIS CHAPTER:

- Stop and start containers
- Restart a container
- Send signals to a container
- Pause and unpause a container
- Rename a container
- Create containers

You have gotten some containers running and looked inside them. Now you are ready to start doing more with containers. While a container image is running, you can stop it, pause it, kill it, or restart it. After a container has run (whether you stopped it or it just completed), you can start that container instance again. You can also rename a container and wait to see how it exits.

Using some of the containers run in earlier chapters, I show you how you can use different `docker` command options to work with the containers you have created. After that, I show a quick way to create a container that you can use at a later time.

STOPPING AND STARTING A CONTAINER

When a container is running, it can be exposed to your host system in different ways. Ports from the container can be exposed on the host. The commands run in the container can have standard input, output, and error exposed to a shell session on the host. Once a container is stopped (by either completing its task or having a `docker stop` command run on it), it tends to release those resources and stay on your system in a state where it can be restarted later.

The `docker start` command is simple. When you are starting a container originally run as a detached service, you don't need any additional options. You only need options to `docker start` when you want to run the command from that container interactively.

Instead of stopping and starting a container in two separate steps, you can use `docker restart` to stop the service and then start it right back up again. These commands are shown in the next sections.

Stopping and Starting a Detached Container

I have an image called `testrun` (see Chapter 4, "Running Container Images," for a description of how I created it) that consists of a `fedora` base image with the httpd package installed. I run the following command to start the web server (httpd) in the background with the detached option (`-d`), have it mount the host `/var/www` directory in the container, and expose TCP ports 80 and 443 to the host. (Make sure that no other web server is running and using these ports on the host or the container will fail.)

Here's the `docker run` command to run the httpd server and then a few other commands to check it:

```
# docker run -p 80:80 -p 443:443 -d --name=WebServer \
   -v /var/www/:/var/www/ testrun /usr/sbin/httpd -DFOREGROUND
# docker ps
CONTAINER ID   IMAGE         COMMAND             CREATED
  STATUS          PORTS                                   NAMES
19a2b9483278   testrun:latest "/usr/sbin/httpd -DF  2 hours ago
  Up 2 hours    0.0.0.0:80->80/tcp, 0.0.0.0:443->443/tcp  WebServer
# netstat -tupln | grep -E "(:80)|(:443)"
tcp6  0  0 :::80     :::*     LISTEN    27194/docker-proxy
tcp6  0  0 :::443    :::*     LISTEN    27186/docker-proxy
# echo "The Web Server is Up" > /var/www/html/index.html
# curl http://localhost/
The Web Server is Up
```

The `docker ps` command shows that the `WebServer` container is running. Running `netstat` shows that the docker-proxy processes are listening on TCP ports 80 and 443. After I echo "The Web Server is Up" to the `/var/www/html/index.html` file, running the `curl` command shows that the web server can serve that file from the directory mounted from the host.

Now, if I want to stop the container, I can use the `docker stop` command on either the container ID or container name. For example:

```
# docker stop WebServer
WebServer
# docker ps -a | head -n 2
CONTAINER ID  IMAGE            COMMAND            CREATED
   STATUS                  PORTS
     NAMES
19a2b9483278  testrun:latest "/usr/sbin/httpd -DF  2 hours ago
   Exited (0) 2 minutes ago 0.0.0.0:80->80/tcp, 0.0.0.0:443->443/tcp
     WebServer
# netstat -tupln | grep -E "(:80)|(:443)"
# curl http://localhost/
curl: (7) Failed to connect to localhost port 80: Connection refused
```

After running `docker stop`, the container no longer appears in output from `docker ps`, but it does appear with `docker ps -a`. From that output, you can see that the container exited "2 minutes ago." The `/usr/sbin/httpd` process is no longer running, but the contents of the container should still exist on the local system.

Running `netstat` shows that docker-proxy is no longer listening on ports 80 or 443. The `curl` command shows that the web server is no longer serving the contents of the `index.html` file.

Starting a stopped container that runs detached (`-d`) is easy. The saved container remembers the options it ran with originally (exposed port numbers, bind mounted directories, and so on). Any files added or changed when the container ran are still in the container. So all you have to do is run `docker start` on it. Here's an example of starting the exited WebServer container back up and then checking that it is running properly:

```
# docker start WebServer
WebServer
[root@fedora21 ~]# docker ps
CONTAINER ID IMAGE            COMMAND            CREATED
   STATUS           PORTS                                 NAMES
19a2b9483278 testrun:latest "/usr/sbin/httpd -DF 23 hours ago
   Up 17 seconds  0.0.0.0:80->80/tcp, 0.0.0.0:443->443/tcp  WebServer
[root@fedora21 ~]# netstat -tupln | grep -E "(:80)|(:443)"
tcp6   0   0 :::80   :::*      LISTEN    3976/docker-proxy
tcp6   0   0 :::443  :::*      LISTEN    3968/docker-proxy
[root@fedora21 ~]# curl http://localhost/
The Web Server is Up
```

As you can see, the WebServer container is up and running again.

Starting and Stopping an Interactive Container

You just saw what happens when you stop a container that has a service running in the background. If a process running in a container is running interactively, with standard input, standard output, and standard error coming to the local terminal window, if you run `docker stop` from another window, the session closes rather unceremoniously on the person who opened the session.

For example, open a bash shell from an `ubuntu` container, as follows:

```
# docker run -it --name=bashbuntu ubuntu /bin/bash
root@10716cc23942:/
# pwd
/
```

Next, open another shell on the system and run `docker stop` to stop it. The container exits from the shell in which it was started (the `exit` command pops up on its own in the other shell after the `docker stop` runs, without me typing it).

```
# docker stop bashbuntu
bashbuntu
# docker start -ai bashbuntu
```

After the `docker stop` is run, I start the container again. To have it work interactively again, however, I add the following options:

- **-a:** The attach (`-a`) option attaches your terminal session to the standard output and standard error coming from the bash shell running in the container. This is what allows you to see the output from the container's bash shell.
- **-i:** The interactive (`-i`) option connects your terminal session to the standard input from the bash shell running inside the container. This option lets you type commands into the shell from inside the container.

Figure 8.1 shows an example of the container being run, stopped, and started again from two separate shell sessions.

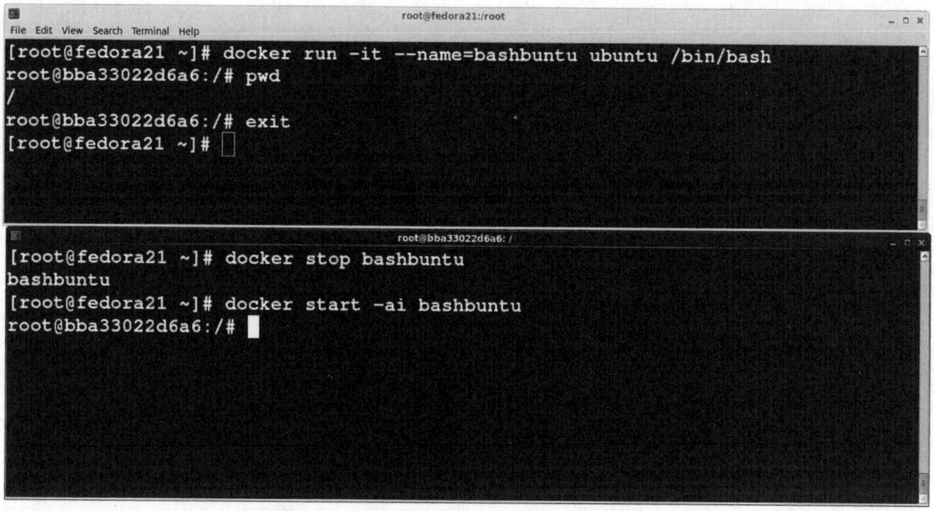

FIGURE 8.1 After stopping an interactive container, restart it with `docker start -ai`.

RESTARTING A CONTAINER

Instead of stopping and starting a container as separate steps, you can do both at once using the `docker restart` command. An advantage to running `docker restart` is that you can try to stop the main process running in the container, and if it doesn't stop cleanly, you can tell `docker restart` to send it a kill signal if it doesn't stop after a set number of seconds.

Try running `docker restart` on the WebServer container to bring it down and back up again. Sometimes this is a good thing to do if your container gets in a weird state or isn't responding. Restarting a container that starts a service typically causes that service to reread its configuration files.

Here's an example of restarting the WebServer container:

```
# docker restart -t 30 WebServer
WebServer
# docker ps
CONTAINER ID   IMAGE           COMMAND              CREATED
   STATUS        PORTS                                 NAMES
19a2b9483278   testrun:latest  "/usr/sbin/httpd -DF 24 hours ago
   Up 3 seconds 0.0.0.0:80->80/tcp, 0.0.0.0:443->443/tcp  WebServer
```

In this case, the container stops immediately and then starts right back up again. Just in case, I added the `-t 30` option. If for some reason the container had not stopped in 30 seconds, a kill signal would have been sent to kill the container's primary process, thereby killing the container.

Although `docker stop` and `docker restart` are two ways to send signals that end the first process running in a container, there are other ways to explicitly send signals to a container as well. The `docker kill` command lets you send any valid signal you choose to a container.

Sending Signals to a Container

The `docker kill` command sends a kill signal (SIGKILL) to the main process running in a container, immediately killing that process, as well as the container itself (and any other processes running in it). Just as with the Linux `kill` command, however, you can use the `docker kill` command to send any signal you choose to a container.

In general, it is best to use the `docker stop` command to stop a container, since it tries to terminate the container cleanly. However, if for some reason the container is hanging and can't be terminated cleanly, `docker kill` is sure to kill the container.

If I found that I was unable to stop the WebServer container, I could kill it with the following command. But be warned that this could make the container unable to start again. For example:

```
# docker kill WebServer
WebServer
# docker start WebServer
WebServer
# docker ps
CONTAINER ID   IMAGE   COMMAND   CREATED   STATUS   PORTS   NAMES
# docker log WebServer
httpd (pid 1) already running
```

Killing the container without shutting it down properly causes the httpd process to stop without properly cleaning up (in this case, removing the PID file). If a container becomes unable to start after you have killed it (or, perhaps, the system has shut down improperly), there are a few things you might do:

- **Remove it**: In most cases, you should just remove an unusable container (`docker rm`) and do a new `docker run` to start the container from scratch.
- **Save and fix it**: In the case where there is something of value inside the container (maybe you manually added data or configuration information), you

can commit the container to an image, export the image as a tarball, untar the tarball, fix the problem (in this case, remove the `run/httpd/httpd.pid` file), pack it back into a tarball, and import it back into your system.

- **Launch from a script**: Instead of starting a service directly from a container, launch it from a script. The script can do any cleanup needed to start the service cleanly before launching the service. In this case, it would first delete the `/run/httpd/httpd.pid` file (if it exists) before starting the httpd daemon.

So, to make the point clear, don't just kill a container if you don't have to, since it could make the container unusable if it does not clean up properly when it exits. That said, you can use `docker kill` to send other signals to a container.

Valid signals are listed on the signal man page (type `man 7 signal`). A `docker stop` sends a terminate (SIGTERM) signal to a container. With no options `docker kill` sends a kill (SIGKILL) signal. So you don't need to specify either of those signals to send them to a container. Here are examples of other signals you might want to send specifically to a container:

```
# docker kill -s SIGHUP WebServer
# docker kill -s SIGINT bashbuntu
```

When some applications, such as the httpd service, receive a SIGHUP signal, they reread their configuration files. This is a good way to change your web server configuration without shutting down the service. The SIGINT signal sends a keyboard interrupt to the container process. If you were running a bash shell from a container in another window when the SIGINT was sent to it, it would be as if you had pressed Ctrl+C. You would see ^C on your screen, and the current line would be interrupted.

The types of signals a process accepts can be different with different applications. Likewise, how it responds to each signal can be different as well. You should check the individual executable you want to signal to see what signals it supports.

PAUSING AND UNPAUSING CONTAINERS

The `docker pause` command lets you suspend all processes running in a container. To bring the container's processes back to life, use `docker unpause`. These features work using the cgroups freezer feature to suspend and unsuspend every process in the selected container.

Here is an example of pausing and unpausing the WebServer container used in earlier examples:

```
# docker pause WebServer
WebServer
# docker ps
CONTAINER ID    IMAGE           COMMAND             CREATED
   STATUS                   PORTS
     NAMES
ad6851772d60    testrun:latest "/usr/sbin/httpd -DF About an hour ago
   Up About an hour (Paused) 0.0.0.0:80->80/tcp, 0.0.0.0:443->443/tcp
     WebServer
# curl localhost
# docker unpause WebServer
WebServer
# curl localhost
The Web Server is Up
```

Notice that you can see that the container is paused from the output of the `docker ps` command. While the WebServer container is paused, it doesn't respond for requests for content on the server. After it is unpaused, it responds as it would normally.

WAITING FOR A CONTAINER'S EXIT CODE

Using `docker wait`, you can identify a running container and then wait until that container exits. When it exits, the `docker wait` itself exits and prints the original container's exit code. To use this feature, first start the `docker wait` command to identify the running container for which you want to see the exit code:

```
# docker wait WebServer
```

Next, open another shell and kill the WebServer container to cause it to return a nonzero (unsuccessful) exit code:

```
# docker kill WebServer
WebServer
```

Back at the `docker wait` command, the exit code should have appeared. In this case, the exit code is 137:

```
# docker wait WebServer
137
```

Exit code 137 indicates that the web server did not exit successfully, but instead was killed.

RENAMING A CONTAINER

If you don't like the name of a container (whether it is running or stopped), you can change it. Nothing complicated here: Just run `docker rename`, followed by the old name of the container and the new name you want to assign. For example:

```
# docker ps
CONTAINER ID     IMAGE         COMMAND              CREATED
  STATUS         PORTS                              NAMES
38178d6e6ff8       testrun:latest "/usr/sbin/httpd -DF  7 minutes ago
  Up 7 minutes   0.0.0.0:80->80/tcp, 0.0.0.0:443->443/tcp  WebServer
# docker rename WebServer HttpdServer
# docker ps
CONTAINER ID     IMAGE         COMMAND              CREATED
  STATUS         PORTS                              NAMES
38178d6e6ff8       testrun:latest "/usr/sbin/httpd -DF  7 minutes ago
  Up 9 minutes   0.0.0.0:80->80/tcp, 0.0.0.0:443->443/tcp  HttpdServer
```

Comparing the two `docker ps` commands, you can see the container named WebServer is now named HttpdServer.

CREATING A CONTAINER

The normal way to create a container (a running instance of an image) is with the `docker run` command. With `docker run`, as long as you don't add the `--rm` option, after the container exits it is saved so you can run it again. Instead of running the container right now, however, if you just want to create a container, you can use `docker create` instead.

With `docker create`, you identify an image you want to use and the command you want to run in it. When you launch `docker create`, instead of running the command inside the container image, it just saves the resulting container.

When it comes to options you can use with `docker create`, they are pretty much the same ones you use with `docker run`. There are a couple of exceptions. For example, you wouldn't use `--rm` with `docker create` because the result of a `docker create` is a container that is saved and ready to run, so removing it would be counterproductive.

Likewise, you don't need the `--detach=true` (or `-d`) option. When you start the container later, it runs detached by default. If you want it to run interactively, you need to add the `-a` option (to run with standard output and standard error directed to the process) and/or the `-i` option (to run with standard input connected to the process).

Because the options you use with `docker create` are otherwise the same as the `docker run` options described in Chapter 4, refer to that chapter for a more exhaustive description of how the different options work. I have, however, provided a few examples of `docker create` here so you can see that command in action.

Say that you want a container to run `boggle` later from the `cricket/hangman` image used in examples earlier in the book, but you want to run it immediately. You could run the following:

```
# docker create --name=mybog -it cricket/hangman boggle
3dd0cdb06b377c020f93d160161d38e8b67cce49161707a6ec46c59d4af31b7f
# docker ps -a | head -n 2
CONTAINER ID          IMAGE            COMMAND    CREATED
    STATUS                      PORTS     NAMES
3dd0cdb06b37  cricket/hangman:1.9   "boggle"   5 minutes ago
    Exited (0) 4 minutes ago              mybog
# docker start -ai mybog
+---+---+---+---+   Type '?' for help
| Y | F | O | X |
+---+---+---+---+   2:51
| W | J | I | W |
+---+---+---+---+
| U | C | T | P |
+---+---+---+---+
| D | E | P | O |
+---+---+---+---+
fox
pit
duct
```

To create the container to run the Boggle game, I add a name (`mybog`), along with the `-it` options (to identify the container as one that runs interactively from a pseudo terminal session). At a later time, I run the container using the `-a` (attach) and `-i` (interactive) options.

SUMMARY

Once a container has been saved to your system (after an exited `docker run` or a new `docker create`), there are many ways of working with that container. To stop a running container, you can use `docker stop`. However, you can also use `docker pause` to pause it or `docker kill` to kill it immediately. The `docker kill` command can also send other signals to a container, such as a SIGINT (to send an interrupt) or SIGHUP (which cause some applications to reread configuration files).

Instead of stopping and then starting a container again, you can use `docker restart` to stop a container and start it again in the same command. Other ways of working with containers include `docker rename` (to rename a container) and `docker wait` (to wait for a container to exit and display its exit code). If you want to create a container, but not run it immediately, the `docker create` command lets you do that.

## CHAPTER 9

Configuring Container Storage

IN THIS CHAPTER:

- Add storage to a container
- Share storage among containers
- Manage host storage

Docker container images are meant to contain reusable applications. To make that happen, it is typical to have a container store data by attaching to storage outside the container. There are two categories of storage to consider when using Docker:

- **Managing storage and volumes for a container**: Adding storage space to a host doesn't automatically make more storage available to containers running on that host. There are, however, ways to mount and use host storage volumes within a container. Volumes mounted on one container can also be made available to other containers.

- **Managing the Docker storage on a host**: Docker itself uses an area from the host's storage to manage Docker images and containers on that host, along with metadata for those images and containers. What are the best practices that an administrator should consider when setting up Docker on a host or on multiple hosts?

The first part of this chapter focuses on managing container storage. The second part of the chapter covers the best way to manage a Docker host's storage.

MANAGING STORAGE FOR A CONTAINER

Docker image creators and consumers want to keep images small. Large images are not desirable for downloading, even in local repositories. Fortunately, Docker images need only contain the packages required for the desired Linux distribution and application running inside the container.

So how does a container maintain data without committing the image changes and therefore changing the image each time there are changes to the data? The solution is to use bind mounts of external volumes. This way the container image used in the application doesn't change. All state changes are persisted in storage external to the container.

Using Volumes from the Host

To bind mount a volume into a container at run time you use the -v option to the docker run command. Arguments that you pass to the -v option include the directory you want to share from the host computer (for example, /tmp/volume), followed by a colon and the mount point for that directory within the container (for example, /data). Here is an example:

```
# docker run -v /tmp/volume:/data -d myappcontainer
```

However, bind mounting a volume into a container can open you up to some potentially dangerous scenarios. Consider the following example:

```
# docker run -v /etc:/data -d badappcontainer # DO NOT DO THIS
```

A Docker container considers itself to have root privilege. Bind mounting /etc, or other critical volumes, into a container is dangerous. Docker and container technology are supposed to provide isolation for containers. But this is a case where the isolation is deliberately broken.

In Linux systems that support Security Enhanced Linux (SELinux), SELinux provides extra protection and isolation when running containers. With SELinux enforcement turned on, bind mounting a file or directory requires a special SELinux label be set for it. In the following example, I make a new directory in /tmp and bind mount it into a container. Inside the container, I try to edit a file in that directory.

```
# setenforce 1
# mkdir /tmp/vol
# docker run -v /tmp/vol:/data -it fedora:latest bash
bash-4.2#
```

From the bash shell open inside the container, when I try to edit or touch the file /data/myfile, SELinux prevents me from writing to the volume.

```
bash-4.2# touch /data/myfile
touch: cannot touch '/data/myfile': Permission denied
bash-4.2# exit
```

To give a container explicit permission to change the contents of a volume being bind mounted, we must change the SELinux label using the :z suffix on the volume. For example:

```
# docker run -v /tmp/vol:/data:z -it fedora:latest bash
```

Inside the container I can make changes to that mounted directory:

```
bash-4.2# touch /data/myfile
bash-4.2# ls /data
myfile
```

It works! SELinux prevents any accidents by forcing us to be explicit about changing the permissions. Inside the container we can see that the new file also has the appropriate SELinux label.

```
bash-4.2# ls -alZ /data/
drwxrwxr-x. 1000 1000 unconfined_u:object_r:svirt_sandbox_file_t:s0 .
drwxr-xr-x. root root system_u:object_r:svirt_sandbox_file_t:s0:c437,c645 ..
-rw-r--r--. root root system_u:object_r:svirt_sandbox_file_t:s0 myfile
```

When I exit and look in /tmp/vol on the host, I see the new file and its data.

```
bash-4.2# exit
$ ls /tmp/vol/
myfile
```

Data Volume Container

One of the advantages of using Docker containers is the ability to see and use volumes from one container in another container. What is commonly called a *data volume container* allows you to share a volume from a source container with one or more target containers. This has some advantages including sharing persistent storage across several containers and providing a layer of abstraction around the bind mount.

When you bind mount the volume into a container, give the container a name and add the :z suffix to the mount point. This container is the data volume container or the source container. Here's an example with a container named datavol.

```
# docker run -v /tmp/vol:/data:z --name=datavol -it fedora:latest bash
```

In another shell, run a new container and use the `--volumes-from=` option to identify the first container name. For example:

```
# docker run --volumes-from=datavol -d fedora:latest touch /data/mydata
```

With a bash shell still open to the container called `datavol` you can see the new file called `mydata` created. Examining the `/tmp/vol` directory on the host you see the new file there too.

```
bash-4.2# ls /data
mydata
bash-4.2# exit
# ls /tmp/vol
mydata
```

Furthermore, the data volume container doesn't even need to remain running. If you exit the data volume container named `datavol`, you can still change the volume. In the target container create a third file called `mynewdata`.

```
# docker run --volumes-from=datavol -d fedora:latest touch /data/mynewdata
```

You see on the host that that `/tmp/vol/mynewdata` has been created. If you start and attach to the data volume container again, you can see the change there too in `/data/mynewfile`.

```
# docker start datavol
datavol
# docker attach datavol
bash-4.2# ls /data
myfile mynewdata mydata
```

Write-Protecting a Bind Mount

I've demonstrated how you can bind mount a volume safely and also shown how to share that volume with another container using `--volumes-from`. But what if I need a volume in a container, but I want to exclude that specific volume from being shared with other containers that try to access my volumes with `--volumes-from`.

For that purpose, Docker lets me use a `:Z` suffix. Note the uppercase Z instead of the lowercase z. This suffix lets me mount a volume for use in a container but protects it from being used in another container.

```
# mkdir /tmp/vol2
# docker run -v /tmp/vol:/data:z -v /tmp/vol2:/data2:Z --name=datavol \
    -it fedora:latest bash
```

```
bash-4.2# exit
# docker run --volumes-from=datavol -d fedora:latest touch /data2/mydata
touch: cannot touch '/data2/mydata': Permission denied
```

In the example just shown, I can write to /data and /data2 directories inside the datavol container (associated with /tmp/vol and /tmp/vol2 on the host, respectively). From within the second container, however, I can write to the volume called data1, but not the one called data2. That's because the :z suffix was used.

Mounting Devices

Sometimes it's useful to be able to mount devices. For example, if I have dozens of Docker containers running, it is efficient to be able to attach into a container to examine log files if something goes wrong.

So I can make a container's logging visible on the host through the system logging device (/dev/log). Here is an example:

```
# docker run -v /dev/log:/dev/log -i -t \
  fedora:latest logger "SYSLOG-TEST This is a test"
# journalctl -b | grep SYSLOG
May 05 18:08:41 myhost logger[3617]: SYSLOG-TEST This is a test
```

In the example just shown, the /dev/log device from the host is mounted inside the container. The container runs a logger command to send a message to the systemd journal (via the /dev/log device). The container exits after sending the log message. After that, running the journalctl command on the host displays the message that logger sent.

Mounting Sockets

There are also use cases where bind mounting a socket is useful. Access to TCP communication inside a container is one such use case.

A specific use case that uses the access to the Docker daemon's socket is running a continuous integration (CI) Docker build agent inside a container. A Dockerfile file appearing in a mounted directory could be a trigger to build a Docker image. The CI tool triggered by the Dockerfile's appearance would run another Docker container on the same host to build the Docker image.

But this Docker container is not running inside the CI Docker container. So bind mounting the /var/run/docker.sock allows a Docker client inside the container to execute docker build and docker run commands from inside the container but on the host. This avoids having to run Docker-in-Docker.

This next example demonstrates several Docker features and ideas:

- Bind mounting a socket
- Using a privileged container
- An interesting use case

Create a simple Dockerfile using any text editor. Here is an example of the contents of a Dockerfile:

```
FROM fedora:latest
MAINTAINER Doc Hand <dhand@thedocks.com>
RUN yum -y update; yum -y install systemd-libs docker; yum clean all
```

To use that Dockerfile to build a container image, assuming the Dockerfile is in the current directory, type the following:

```
# docker build -t myrepo/docker .
```

Now run the myrepo/docker image, remembering that the container needs to be able to see the socket that the Docker daemon is listening on:

```
# docker run -v /var/run/docker.sock:/var/run/docker.sock \
    -it myrepo/docker bash
```

Now inside the container run a docker command. For example, if you try to list the available images at this point, it fails:

```
# docker images
  2014/08/05 16:18:56 Get
  http:///var/run/docker.sock/v1.12/containers/json:
  dial unix /var/run/docker.sock: permission denied
```

The previous command fails because of SELinux permission issues. To access sockets from within a container, you must turn on the privileged option. The :z or :z suffix can't help here. To set privileged mode to true, type the command as follows:

```
# docker run --privileged=true \
    -v /var/run/docker.sock:/var/run/docker.sock -it myrepo/docker bash
```

Now run a few more docker commands from within a container. These should succeed:

```
bash-4.2# docker images
bash-4.2# docker ps
```

For more information on privileged containers and super privileged containers see Chapter 13, "Using Super Privileged Containers."

STORAGE STRATEGIES FOR THE DOCKER HOST

A Docker image is not a single image. It is in fact a set of layered images. A new image can be started from scratch and is often called a *base image*. (Run docker history on an image name to see the layers that make up that image.)

An image can be created by layering on top of a parent. Layers are added by installing new software, by adding new directories or files to the image, or by running commands that change the underlying layer.

There are two ways I can see layers when using Docker. When I run a docker pull of images from a registry, I often see multiple image layers being pulled for the single image I requested. When I run a docker build command, I see various layers being added when I use the ADD, RUN, or EXPOSE Dockerfile commands. Each of these layers has a unique name and can be mounted when needed for running a container. Even so-called temporary layers that are part of a docker build are really kept as part of the final named image layer.

Figure 9.1 shows the multiple layers if I were to install JBoss on a Java image that was itself based on a Fedora base image. When I run a container based on this image, the topmost layer represents the writable layer inside the container. All the other layers are immutable. In this example the container is running on an Atomic Host.

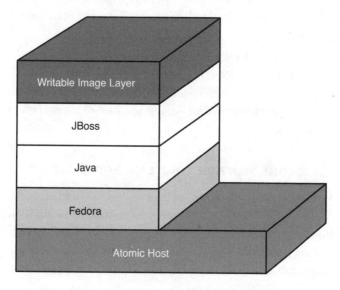

FIGURE 9.1 Docker images are built in layers, with the top layer writable.

Layers make Docker and Linux containers different from virtual machines (VMs). In a VM the entire image is stored on the machine for each type of VM. If common components like Fedora are inside different VM images, each image still has to have the common component inside the image. With Docker there is only one instance of a specific version of the Fedora layer (for example, Fedora 22), and it is shared across the Java and JBoss images, just as the Java and Fedora image layers are shared across the Java and JBoss images.

Docker uses a storage backend abstraction to implement the layered images. This allows you to manage the various layers of a complete image and to share those layers across related images. So if you already have the lower layers of an image on your system and only need the top layer, a `docker pull` only downloads that top layer.

Fedora, Red Hat Enterprise Linux, Fedora Atomic Host, and RHEL Atomic Host use the device-mapper backend. This allows the Docker implementation to use the device-mapper thin provisioning module to implement the layers.

Thin provisioning means that if I have a pool of storage I can overadvertise how much space is in the pool, because I know that the initial image usage will likely be smaller than the allocation request. Unused blocks are not allocated.

However as the image needs more storage, more capacity can be added from the pool to that specific image. However, the pool is limited and as it is likely technically overallocated, an administrator should pay close attention and add more storage to the pool as needed.

There are other storage backend implementations such as vfs, btrfs, and aufs. However, they either are considered immature at the time of this writing (btrfs), unsupported in the upstream kernel at the time of this writing (aufs), or just not practical (vfs, as it doesn't share disk space for use between layers). This could change in the future.

Attaching External Storage to a Docker Host

On the host, Docker uses the `/var/lib/docker` volume to hold all the Docker images and containers. The host's Docker repository is contained in this volume. In most cases, an administrator will not be able to predict precisely how large the local Docker repository will become on the host. As more and more images are added and more and more containers are started, this volume can quickly run out of space.

If you are running the Docker host as a virtual machine (for example, a RHEL Atomic Host), it is prudent to keep RHEL Atomic Host images as small as possible. Base RHEL Atomic Host images are quite small.

If you have a small RHEL Atomic Host image (for example, 8GB), this is hardly enough space to work with many Docker images and containers. Docker will quickly fill up the `/var/lib/docker` directory, where all the Docker images and metadata are stored. It is recommended to provide an external volume and bind mount that volume to the `/var/lib/docker` directory on the Docker host.

On Debian and Ubuntu you can change the `/etc/default/docker` file (add `DOCKER_OPTS="-g /path/to/dir"`). But Fedora and RHEL, which use systemd, don't follow that approach. Furthermore with SELinux labels, it is important to use the `/var/lib/docker` directory.

Expanding Storage with Logical Volume Manager

Starting with a Fedora host that has an Atomic virtual machine running on it, follow these instructions to create an LVM volume on the host, attach it to the Atomic VM, and mount it on the `/var/lib/docker` directory within that VM. The following instructions assume that Docker started cleanly on the Atomic VM. Any important Docker images or containers in `/var/lib/docker` can be copied to the new partition and made available when the new partition is mounted.

To be safe, if there are important images, containers, or other metadata, you should back them up in case something goes wrong in creating the new disk space.

1. **Create LVM partition:** On the Fedora host, for this example there is a storage device of Linux LVM type (8e) represented by `/dev/sdb1`. I create an LVM partition that consumes that entire 130G disk (which I can see using the `fdisk -l` command). The result of the following commands is an LVM partition named `/dev/docker_vg/mydocker`:

```
# fdisk -l /dev/sdb
Device     Boot Start        End     Sectors   Size Id Type
/dev/sdb1        2048 273672191  273670144   130G 8e Linux
# pvcreate /dev/sdb1
  Physical volume "/dev/sdb1" successfully created
# vgcreate docker_vg /dev/sdb1
Volume group "docker_vg" successfully created
# lvcreate -l 100%FREE -n mydocker docker_vg
Logical volume "mydocker" created.
```

2. **Create a file system:** On the Fedora host, add a file system on the new partition:

```
# mkfs.ext4 /dev/docker_vg/mydocker
```

3. **Add the partition to the Atomic VM:** Open Virtual Machine Manager (`virt-manager` command), select the Atomic virtual machine, and select to shut it down. Select the Show Virtual Hardware Details button, select Add

Hardware, select Storage, click Select Managed or Other Existing Storage, and browse to select the new partition (`/dev/docker_vg/mydocker`). Make sure the Bus type is IDE and Device type is Disk Device; then select Finish.

4. **Start the Atomic VM**: Start up the Atomic VM and log in as root user.

5. **Stop the Docker service**: On the Atomic system, stop the Docker service as follows:

```
# systemctl stop docker
```

6. **Copy Docker files**: Mount the new partition temporarily and copy all the files from `/var/lib/docker` there. In this example, the partition is `/dev/sdb`. For example:

```
# mkdir /mnt/tmp
# mount /dev/sdb /mnt/tmp
# cp -r /var/lib/docker/* /mnt/tmp/
# umount /mnt/tmp
```

7. **Get UUID**: On the Atomic system, determine the name of the new storage device (in this example, it shows up as `/dev/sdb`). Then type the following to get the UUID from the device:

```
# blkid /dev/sdb
/dev/sdb: UUID="9d73e64c-9422-459c-9677-27c2e8cbbc30" TYPE="ext4"
```

8. **Set partition to mount**: Add that UUID to the `/etc/fstab` file so the partition automatically mounts on the `/var/lib/docker` directory. For example:

```
UUID=9d73e64c-9422-459c-9… /var/lib/docker ext4 defaults 1 1
```

9. **Mount the partition**: To mount the new partition on `/var/lib/docker`, type the following:

```
# mount -a
```

10. **Restart docker**: To restart the Docker service, type the following:

```
# systemctl start docker
```

The steps for adding storage are complete. You can start using Docker again.

SUMMARY

Being able to add outside storage is an important feature if you want to do more than just run simple containers. Features for mounting storage volumes to containers allow you to keep your containers simple and portable, while making the data accessible outside each container. Because images and containers themselves consume space on the host system, being able to expand disk space on the host is also a consideration.

To add storage to a container when you run an image, you can use the -v option to identify what directory on the host to mount and where to mount it in the container. There are also `docker run` options that allow you to share or limit access to volumes among multiple containers.

On the host system itself, Docker stores images, containers, and other metadata in the `/var/lib/docker` directory. If you are using containers in a host being run as a virtual machine, you can attach storage from the host computer and mount it on the `/var/lib/docker` directory in that virtual machine. In that way, you can grow the Docker content you can store in the virtual machine.

Configuring Container Networking

Docker offers a convenient way to use Linux Containers (LXC). LXC provides process isolation and resource limits for each container. Docker provides an extra layer on this isolation to make containers portable (image format) and easier to use (from an application programming interface or the command line). This isolation extends to the way in which a container's network interfaces can be isolated from the host system as well.

Part of container isolation allows each container to think it is the root process of its own machine. This is why some people consider Docker containers as lightweight virtual machines. The fact that a Docker container does not have its own, separate kernel makes it different from a virtual machine. But Docker containers do have similar behavior to virtual machines.

One way Docker provides this extra illusion of a container being its own machine is the fact that Docker provides the container process with its own IP address. Docker does this by setting up a virtual interface and bridging this to the host machine's network. The bridge on the host side is called `docker0`. Each container managed by this `docker0` bridge is assigned its own IP address. However, Docker still provides container isolation.

For a container to provide a service based on IP to other containers or applications it must expose the port that the service uses. For example, a default Apache web server container should expose ports 80 and 443, as illustrated in the following Dockerfile example:

```
FROM fedora:22
MAINTAINER William Henry email ipbabble @ gmail dot com
# Update the system
RUN yum -y update; yum clean all
# Install httpd
RUN yum -y install httpd
EXPOSE 80 443
ENTRYPOINT /usr/sbin/httpd -DFOREGROUND
```

The preceding Dockerfile uses the EXPOSE keyword to define a port that will be exposed from the container. Using the EXPOSE keyword does not immediately expose the defined port to other containers or to applications on the host system. For those entities to have access to this port, additional steps are needed to link or port map the port outside the container:

- **Exposing ports**: Linking allows a container to access the exposed port of a container on the same machine.
- **Mapping ports**: Mapping provides a mechanism to map an exposed port to the host machine's external ports.

With the Dockerfile just shown in the current directory, the following command builds a container called `myrepo/fedora-httpd` from that file:

```
# docker build -t=myrepo/fedora-httpd .
```

In the next section I describe how to make the exposed port available to another container by linking the containers together. After that, I show how to map container ports to host ports so they are exposed outside the host.

EXPOSE PORTS TO OTHER CONTAINERS

Using the `myrepo/fedora-httpd` image built in the previous section (which exposes its running web server on ports 80 and 443), I link another container to it and use the exposed port 80 from the second container. First I run the `myrepo/fedora-httpd` container and give it the name `link-test`:

```
# docker run -d --name=link-test myrepo/fedora-httpd
```

Notice that I run the container in detached mode with the -d parameter (and not interactively on a TTY with -it).

Next I run a second container that I name `linked` and link it to `link-test`. I'm mapping the link to the name `lt` (short for `link-test`). This is the name I use from inside the second container to access port 80 in the first container.

```
# docker run -it --link=link-test:lt --name=linked fedora:22 bash
```

I don't have to name this second container, but it's good practice to do so. From within this second container, running the `env` (environment) command shows the following:

```
bash-4.2# env
HOSTNAME=d71eb38e62d5
TERM=xterm
LT_PORT_80_TCP=tcp://172.17.0.3:80
LT_PORT_80_TCP_PORT=80
LT_PORT_80_TCP_PROTO=tcp
LT_PORT=tcp://172.17.0.3:80
PATH=/usr/local/sbin:/usr/local/bin:/usr/sbin:/usr/bin:/sbin:/bin
PWD=/
container_uuid=d71eb38e-62d5-0a15-902c-6901a4ed5d26
LT_NAME=/linked/lt
SHLVL=1
HOME=/root
LT_PORT_80_TCP_ADDR=172.17.0.3
_=/usr/bin/env
```

Notice that there are several environment variables starting with `LT`. Those variable names are derived from the `lt` string I assigned to the link name in the `docker run` command. Any port exposed from the first container is accessible from the new container in the same way.

Now I can use the `curl` command to leverage the link between the two containers and display the html page available on port 80 of the container named `lt` or `link-test`. I only show the first few lines here:

```
bash-4.2# curl http://lt
<!DOCTYPE html PUBLIC "-//W3C//DTD XHTML 1.1//EN" "http://www.w3.org/TR/
xhtml11/DTD/xhtml11.dtd">
<html xmlns="http://www.w3.org/1999/xhtml" xml:lang="en">
  <head>
    <title>Test Page for the Apache HTTP Server on Fedora</title>
...
```

Links are a powerful tool for linking containers together. In the next section I build up a scenario.

MAP PORTS OUTSIDE THE HOST

To expose a port from a container so it is available from a port on the host, you use the -p option of docker run. With that option, you can expose the container port to the same port number on the host or to a different port number. If a container is linked to another container, only the ports explicitly mapped to the host are available to clients of that host. In other words, while linking to a container makes ports available to the other container, that action doesn't automatically make the same ports available to the host system.

The following sections illustrate how ports are mapped from containers to the hosts they are running on. They also show how mapping ports affects how some ports within containers are protected from outside access.

Map a Port from Linked Containers

Figure 10.1 illustrates two containers linked together on a host named H1. Host H1 has the default Docker bridge docker0. One port is exposed within the container (port 8080 on container C1), and one port is mapped to a port on the host (port 80 on container C2). The following steps describe a way to create this configuration.

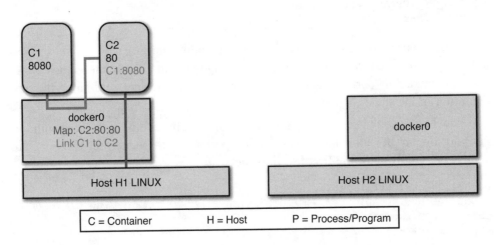

FIGURE 10.1   Linked containers can share exposed ports or map ports to host.

1. **Run C1 container**: This can simply be an application that is exposing its HTTP-based UI over port 8080. For example, it could be a Jenkins container. In this case, I run a simple web server with a python module:

```
# docker run -d --name=C1 -w /var/www/html \
    -v /var/www/html:/var/www/html fedora:22 \
    /bin/python -m SimpleHTTPServer 8080
```

2. **Run C2 container**: Next I run container C2 with exposed port 80 mapped to the host port 80. I also link C2 to the C1 container:

```
# docker run --name=C2 -d --link=C1:C1 -p 80:80 myrepo/fedora-httpd
```

3. **Check access to C1 port from C2**: The `docker0` bridge allows C2 to link to C1 and also maps C2's port 80 to host H1's port 80. If I use the `docker exec` command to enter into C2 using a `bash` shell, I can run `curl` on port 8080 to see any content available in `/var/www/html/` on the host from within C2:

```
# docker exec -i -t C2 bash
bash-4.2# curl http://C1:8080
The server is running.
```

4. **Check access to H1 port from H2**: Now on host H2, I start a normal `bash` shell process P1 that consumes C2's web page exposed on port 80 and mapped to H1's port 80. I can do this simply by running the `curl` command with H1's IP address. And just like the example in the previous section I should see the html page returned. Figure 10.2 illustrates this action.

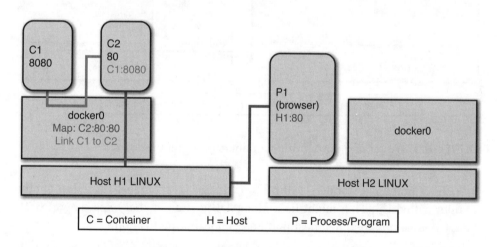

FIGURE 10.2 Access the container port mapped on H1 from a process on H2.

This demonstrates that C2's exposed port is consumable due to the mapping of port 80 to the same port on the host. The browser from H2 cannot access C1's information because I did not map that to the host's port 8080 or any other port. P1 cannot access C1 through C2 as P1 is not a container and is not on the same host.

Connect Containers on Different Hosts

It is possible to have applications from multiple containers that need to work together but happen to be running on different hosts. Using just Docker, without additional tools, you can map container ports to host ports, where you might have just linked the containers together if they were on the same machine.

Building on the configuration described in the previous section, Figure 10.3 shows an example of how connections between applications running in containers on different hosts might be set up using linked containers and ports mapped to their respective hosts:

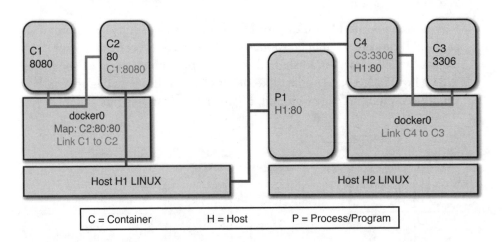

FIGURE 10.3 Accessing ports from containers on different hosts.

With C1 and C2 containers still running on host H1, on host H2 I start another container called C3. This might be a MongoDB container that exposes port 3306. Like C1 it is not mapped to a host port and is not linking to another container.

I can now start another container C4 that is linked to C3. This is a normal fedora container running bash. If I run the env command inside C4, I can see the C3 links in my environment, just like the example in the previous section. I can also use the curl command to display the html page exposed on C2 through the mapped port 80. I cannot connect to C1 because I cannot link to C1 from a different host.

It is important to note from the scenario just described that

- I can link containers on the same host.
- I can connect containers on different hosts by mapping exposed container ports to host ports.

This is useful, but it leaves out one important use case. If I have an application that spans multiple hosts and I want to "contain" that application within a namespace, I'm missing something. For example, suppose I have multiple containers in multiple applications that all expose port 80. Many of these containers may be deployed on the same host. I cannot map them all to port 80 on the same host. I would have to map each container's port 80 to some host port.

However, containers on other hosts that consume information from port 80 of the containers on the first host don't want to be burdened with understanding the dynamic mapping that must occur for all these containers to provide their service. The consumer just wants to consume from port 80. This is a common problem, especially in service providers like Platform as a Service (PaaS) systems where achieving density of application containers across hosts is important for efficiency and cost.

Docker is primarily concerned with managing images and containers on a single host. Currently there is no cross host management in Docker itself. In other words, Docker provides no out-of-the-box solution for linking containers on multiple hosts. Something else is required that allows applications to interact "naturally" within the same namespace across multiple hosts.

Kubernetes, covered later in Chapter 15, "Orchestrating Containers with Kubernetes," and Chapter 16, "Creating a Kubernetes Cluster," is the Docker-based technology used to orchestrate the deployment of multicontainer applications across multiple hosts. Kubernetes provides the mechanism that manages the dynamic mapping of hosts and ports between the containers.

ALTERNATIVES TO THE DOCKER0 BRIDGE

Although Docker provides the `docker0` bridge to provide network access to containers on a system running Docker, you don't have to use that bridge. In this section we consider two use cases:

- A container uses an alternative to the `docker0` bridge.
- A host's Docker daemon uses an alternative to `docker0`.

Changing Network Mode for a Container

It is possible to change the network mode for a single container using the `--net` parameter. With `--net`, you can use the default bridge (`docker0`), a different bridge, or provide no network access at all. Here are examples of ways to use the `--net` option:

- **Default network bridge**: Specifying `--net=bridge` creates a new network stack for the container on the Docker bridge called `docker0`. This is the default behavior.
- **No networking**: Specifying `--net=none` informs Docker to run the container with no networking at all. The container is isolated from the network. This could be useful for running some sort of interactive utility, such as a calculator or a game.
- **Another container's network**: Specifying `--net=mycontainer` informs Docker to start the container and have that container reuse the network stack of the container called `mycontainer` on the same host system.
- **Bypass bridge**: Specifying `--net=host` means the container uses the host network stack directly from inside the container, bypassing the bridge.

To understand how these `--net` options work, the next section shows a series of examples that explore the different arguments you can give to the `--net` option.

Examining Network Options

To examine some `--net` options, I create an image from a Dockerfile by using the `fedora` base image and installing the net-tools package. Here are the contents of the Dockerfile:

```
FROM fedora:22
MAINTAINER William Henry email ipbabble @ gmail.com
# Update the system
RUN yum -y update; yum clean all; yum -y install net-tools
ENTRYPOINT /bin/bash
```

With the Dockerfile in the current directory, here's how to build the image:

```
# docker build -t=nettools .
```

Before running a container I look at the host's IP stack with the `docker0` bridge and see the bridge and the host's network interfaces. I am only showing the important interfaces and have left off loopback and the network interface to virtual machines running on the system.

```
# ifconfig
docker0: flags=4163<UP,BROADCAST,RUNNING,MULTICAST> mtu 1500
 inet 172.17.42.1 netmask 255.255.0.0 broadcast 0.0.0.0
 inet6 fe80::382b:6bff:fefb:9d8 prefixlen 64 scopeid 0x20<link>
 ether 5a:85:58:d1:ac:f3 txqueuelen 0 (Ethernet)
 RX packets 19427 bytes 1057038 (1.0 MiB)
 RX errors 0 dropped 0 overruns 0 frame 0
 TX packets 21384 bytes 266330243 (253.9 MiB)
 TX errors 0 dropped 0 overruns 0 carrier 0 collisions 0
eth0: flags=4163<UP,BROADCAST,RUNNING,MULTICAST> mtu 1500
 inet 162.xxx.yyy.zzz netmask 255.255.255.0 broadcast 162.xxx.yyy.255
 inet6 fe80::aaaa:55ff:ccc:1 prefixlen 64 scopeid 0x20<link>
 ether 04:01:55:56:00:01 txqueuelen 1000 (Ethernet)
 RX packets 51651 bytes 512011975 (488.2 MiB)
 RX errors 0 dropped 0 overruns 0 frame 0
 TX packets 41427 bytes 3509038 (3.3 MiB)
 TX errors 0 dropped 0 overruns 0 carrier 0 collisions 0
```

Now I run the new `nettools` image without the `--net` option, so the container is assigned an IP address from the default pool of IP addresses (`172.17.0.0/16`). In this case, it is assigned an IP address of `172.17.0.8`:

```
# docker run -ti nettools
```

The `ifconfig` command here shows the normal IP stack using the bridge from the container's own contained network interfaces:

```
# ifconfig
eth0: flags=67<UP,BROADCAST,RUNNING> mtu 1500
 inet 172.17.0.8 netmask 255.255.0.0 broadcast 0.0.0.0
 inet6 fe80::42:acff:fe11:8 prefixlen 64 scopeid 0x20<link>
 ether 02:42:ac:11:00:08 txqueuelen 0 (Ethernet)
 RX packets 6 bytes 508 (508.0 B)
 RX errors 0 dropped 0 overruns 0 frame 0
 TX packets 6 bytes 508 (508.0 B)
 TX errors 0 dropped 0 overruns 0 carrier 0 collisions 0
lo: flags=73<UP,LOOPBACK,RUNNING> mtu 65536
 inet 127.0.0.1 netmask 255.0.0.0
 inet6 ::1 prefixlen 128 scopeid 0x10<host>
 loop txqueuelen 0 (Local Loopback)
 RX packets 0 bytes 0 (0.0 B)
 RX errors 0 dropped 0 overruns 0 frame 0
 TX packets 0 bytes 0 (0.0 B)
 TX errors 0 dropped 0 overruns 0 carrier 0 collisions 0
```

Notice that the `eth0` interface is using an address on the `docker0` bridge. This is the default behavior: `--net=bridge`.

Now I run the same container with the `--net=host` option:

```
# docker run -it --net=host nettools
```

Inside the container, I run `ifconfig`, which shows the host's network interfaces, instead of the separate network interfaces normally assigned, by default, in the container:

```
# ifconfig
docker0: flags=4163<UP,BROADCAST,RUNNING,MULTICAST> mtu 1500
 inet 172.17.42.1 netmask 255.255.0.0 broadcast 0.0.0.0
 inet6 fe80::382b:6bff:fefb:9d8 prefixlen 64 scopeid 0x20<link>
 ether 5a:85:58:d1:ac:f3 txqueuelen 0 (Ethernet)
 RX packets 19435 bytes 1057574 (1.0 MiB)
 RX errors 0 dropped 0 overruns 0 frame 0
 TX packets 21384 bytes 266330243 (253.9 MiB)
 TX errors 0 dropped 0 overruns 0 carrier 0 collisions 0
eth0: flags=4163<UP,BROADCAST,RUNNING,MULTICAST> mtu 1500
 inet 162.243.151.77 netmask 255.255.255.0 broadcast 162.243.151.255
 inet6 fe80::601:55ff:fe56:1 prefixlen 64 scopeid 0x20<link>
 ether 04:01:55:56:00:01 txqueuelen 1000 (Ethernet)
 RX packets 51829 bytes 512026047 (488.3 MiB)
 RX errors 0 dropped 0 overruns 0 frame 0
 TX packets 41539 bytes 3524564 (3.3 MiB)
 TX errors 0 dropped 0 overruns 0 carrier 0 collisions 0
...
```

Notice all the host's interfaces are present (as before I am only showing the bridge `docker0` and the `eth0` interfaces). So setting `--net=host` removes the bridging layer normally present and can be useful for increasing performance. However, when I use this on all my containers on the host I need to be careful of clashing exposed ports.

This is also a good demonstration of how Docker is really nothing more than an abstraction layer on top of a host's kernel. It mainly just provides a layer on top of the container technology built into Linux.

CHANGING THE DOCKER NETWORK BRIDGE

If the default `docker0` bridge doesn't fit the organization's network topology, there is a mechanism to change the bridge that the Docker daemon uses. The Docker daemon can be started and attached to a preexisting bridge. The following command attaches the Docker daemon to a bridge named `mybridge` on the host:

```
# /usr/bin/docker -d --selinux-enabled -b=mybridge
```

It is also possible to switch off networking for all containers on a host. For example:

```
# /usr/bin/docker -d --selinux-enabled -b=none
```

You don't typically run the Docker daemon manually. On systems that start Docker using the systemd service (Fedora, RHEL, CentOS, and others), change the options passed to the Docker daemon in the /etc/sysconfig/docker file. By default, those systems only have --selinux-enabled set by default. To add the mybridge example shown earlier, edit the OPTIONS line in /etc/sysconfig/docker so it appears as follows:

```
OPTIONS='--selinux-enabled -b=mybridge'
```

The next time you restart the Docker service, it picks up the new option. For example:

```
# systemctl restart docker
# ps -ef | grep /usr/bin/docker

root 18540  1  0 13:06 ?    00:00:00 /usr/bin/docker -d
    --selinux-enabled -b=mybridge --insecure-registry localhost:5000
# docker run -ti nettools ifconfig eth0
[root@0f8e98ce321d /]# ifconfig eth0
eth0: flags=67<UP,BROADCAST,RUNNING>  mtu 1500
      inet 192.168.122.3  netmask 255.255.255.0  broadcast 0.0.0.0
```

In this case, you can see that the nettools container picks up an IP address in the 192.168.122.0/24 range instead of the default 172.17.0.0/16 range.

SUMMARY

Networking for applications running in Docker containers is different from networking applications that run directly on the host. Because containers have network interfaces that, by default, are different from those on the host, extra effort is needed to expose network ports to other containers or to the outside world (via host ports).

When you build a Docker container, you can identify ports as being exposed. A container that links to another container with an exposed port can communicate to the exposed port. To make a port accessible outside the container (or other containers it is linked to), you can map a container port to a port on the host.

The default network bridge on the host that is used to provide connectivity for Docker containers on the system is named docker0. For an individual container, you can identify a different network bridge to use (or none at all). Likewise, you can identify a different bridge to use by default when you start up the Docker service.

While networking is one feature of Docker containers that can be separate from network interfaces on the host, containers also include other features to restrict access to host privileges. Chapter 11, "Cleaning Up Containers," describes how to remove old Docker containers and images from your system, as well as how to check that Docker is not running out of disk space.

Cleaning Up Containers

IN THIS CHAPTER:

- Check and allocate disk space
- Remove images
- Remove containers
- Clean up containers before saving

Every time you pull down a new image or run a container, you consume space on your system. If you are not paying attention, you could gobble up all your disk space and make Docker (and possibly your entire system) temporarily unusable. That said, Docker offers ways of minimizing the amount of space you consume and tools for erasing unneeded containers when you are ready to clean house.

Of course, saving computer resources is at the heart of containerization. So while Docker makes it easy for you to create and extend containers, it also makes it easy to remove unneeded images and containers.

This chapter takes you through `docker` commands for removing images and containers you no longer need. It also tells you where Docker stores its data so you can be sure that enough space is allocated there to meet your needs. After that, you can read about ways of cleaning up containers so you can save them more efficiently as images or run containers in a way that has them clean up when they exit (`--rm` option to `docker run`).

MAKING SPACE FOR IMAGES AND CONTAINERS

Docker saves its data in the `/var/lib/docker` directory structure. If Docker commands begin to fail because you have run out of disk space, you need to make sure there is enough disk space in that directory to handle your needs. You can use the standard `df` command to do that:

```
# df -h /var/lib/docker
Filesystem              Size  Used Avail Use% Mounted on
/dev/mapper/rah-root    3.0G  2.3G 791M   26% /var
```

The example just shown is for an RHEL Atomic host. As you can see, there is only 3.0G of space available in total for the `/var` directory that could potentially be used in `/var/lib/docker`. Because `/dev/mapper/rah-root` is a logical volume, you could add more space to that logical volume if you need to. Chapter 9, "Configuring Container Storage," describes how to add more disk space to a system using logical volume management (LVM).

The focus of this chapter, however, is on cleaning up your existing disk space. The way to do that is to list the images and containers on your system and remove the ones you don't need.

REMOVING IMAGES

Images that have been pulled or saved to your system remain there until you remove them. There's no automatic clean-up for images you stop using. So, particularly if you have limited disk space, you occasionally need to remove ones you no longer want.

To remove an image, you can use the `docker rmi` command with the name of the local image (or images) you want to remove. There really isn't anything tricky about removing containers. There are just a few things to consider:

- Trying to remove an image that is in use (whether the container is running or paused) will fail. You can override that and force a removal with the `-f` option. In general, however, it's best to stop any container running from that image before removing the image.

- Be explicit about the image you want to remove. If you don't indicate a tag with the image name you want to delete, it assumes you mean the `:latest` tag.

- If there are multiple names (aliases or just extra tags) on a container image, `docker rmi` only removes the tag and not the image itself. If there are no other names when you ask to remove it, the image is physically removed from your system.

- The surest way to remove a physical image is to identify it by image ID when you run the `docker rmi` command. When you do that, you see all the tags related to that image being removed before the image itself is deleted.

- You can remove multiple images at once by adding several image names to a single `docker rmi` command line or by feeding image names or image IDs to that command from another command.

The next section describes how to delete individual images from your system.

Removing Individual Images

The following examples illustrate how to remove images from your local system, including how to deal with some of the issues described in the previous section. For these examples, I pulled all Ubuntu images from the Docker Hub to the local system (`docker pull -a ubuntu`). The result is more than 30 separate images, most of which are represented by multiple names. I display them using the `docker images` command:

```
# docker images | grep ubuntu
REPOSITORY        TAG              IMAGE ID      CREATED      VIRTUAL SIZE
docker.io/ubuntu  14.10            d191563ad36b  7 days ago   194.4 MB
docker.io/ubuntu  utopic           d191563ad36b  7 days ago   194.4 MB
docker.io/ubuntu  utopic-20150427  d191563ad36b  7 days ago   194.4 MB
docker.io/ubuntu  latest           07f8e8c5e660  7 days ago   188.3 MB
docker.io/ubuntu  trusty           07f8e8c5e660  7 days ago   188.3 MB
docker.io/ubuntu  trusty-20150427  07f8e8c5e660  7 days ago   188.3 MB
docker.io/ubuntu  14.04            07f8e8c5e660  7 days ago   188.3 MB
docker.io/ubuntu  14.04.2          07f8e8c5e660  7 days ago   188.3 MB
docker.io/ubuntu  trusty-20150320  b7cf8f0d9e82  2 weeks ago  188.3 MB
```

The `docker rmi` command can have two different effects on images. If I remove an image name and there are more names associated with the image, the name is removed (untagged), but the image is still there. If I remove an image by name and it is the last name representing the image or by image ID, the image is deleted from the system. Here is what happens when I try to remove these `ubuntu` images in different ways:

```
# docker rmi ubuntu
Untagged: ubuntu:latest
# docker rmi ubuntu
Error response from daemon: No such image: ubuntu:latest
# docker rmi ubuntu:utopic
```

```
Untagged: ubuntu:utopic
# docker rmi docker.io/ubuntu:utopic-20150427
Untagged: docker.io/ubuntu:utopic-20150427
# docker rmi 07f8e8c5e660
Untagged: docker.io/ubuntu:14.04
Untagged: docker.io/ubuntu:14.04.2
Untagged: docker.io/ubuntu:trusty
Untagged: docker.io/ubuntu:trusty-20150427
Deleted: 07f8e8c5e66084bef8f84887785...
Deleted: 37bea4ee0c816e3a3fa025f3612...
Deleted: a82efea989f94b1d9fac76e26e3...
Deleted: e9e06b06e14c2f7d8df0251e3bb...
```

Multiple aliases are associated with the image name `ubuntu`. By not adding a tag, in the first example, `docker rmi` assumes you mean `ubuntu:latest` and removes only that tag. Notice that running the same command again doesn't touch any of the other `ubuntu` images (it still assumes you mean `ubuntu:latest`). In the next example, you can add any tag to the base image name to remove that specific image name (`ubuntu:utopic`). Although not needed, you can add the registry name as well to untag that name from the image (`docker.io/ubuntu:utopic-20150427`).

With all those examples so far, because the name does not represent the last existing name for the image on the local system, the image is only untagged and not physically removed. The easiest way to physically remove the image is to remove it by image ID (as I did with `docker rmi 07f8e8c5e660`). However, here is an example where removing the last name associated with an image also removes the image itself:

```
# docker rmi docker.io/ubuntu:14.10
Untagged: docker.io/ubuntu:14.10
Deleted: d191563ad36befdc3322d27...
Deleted: 8d07608668f6d6265fc0d4b...
Deleted: 14975cc0f2bcfc529f862ef...
Deleted: 9802b3b654ece46f8e09379...
```

Keep in mind that images often consist of multiple layers (each of which is seen as an image itself to Docker). So even though you only asked to delete one image, multiple layers are shown as being deleted.

Removing Multiple Images

If you just want to clear out all the images on your local system, you can do that by listing all the existing image IDs and feeding that list to the `docker rmi` command. The easiest way to get a list of image IDs to feed to the command is with the `docker images -q` command:

```
# docker images -q
b7cf8f0d9e82
1403322a81c5
1403322a81c5
9a8ad4567c27
9a8ad4567c27
1a97a9cc4d1b
1a97a9cc4d1b
10acc31def5d
10acc31def5d
f5f0b338bbd6
f5f0b338bbd6
```

To feed that list of image IDs to a `docker rmi` command, you could type the following:

```
# docker rmi $(docker images -q)
Untagged: docker.io/ubuntu:trusty-20150320
Deleted: b7cf8f0d9e82c9d96bd7afd22...
Deleted: 2c014f14d3d95811df672ddae...
Deleted: a62a42e77c9c3626118dc4110...
Deleted: 706766fe101906a1a6628173c...
Untagged: docker.io/cricket/hangman:1.9
Untagged: docker.io/cricket/hangman:latest
Deleted: 1403322a81c5362762f84a26b...
Deleted: 834629358fe214f210b0ed606...
Deleted: 00a0c78eeb6d81442efcd1d7c...
Deleted: 511136ea3c5a64f264b78b543...
Error response from daemon: No such image: 1403322a81c5
Untagged: registry.access.redhat.com/rhel7/rhel-tools:7.1-9
Untagged: registry.access.redhat.com/rhel7/rhel-tools:latest
```

You can watch as each name is untagged and each image is removed. Removing images in this way can result in the same image name being requested to be removed multiple times. In the example just shown, notice that there is a message about an image starting with 1403322a... stating that there is no such image. If you look up a bit higher, you can see that it was already removed, so that is not really an error.

Instead of feeding images one at a time from a list to the `docker rmi` command, that command also allows you to put multiple image names or image IDs on the same command line. So another way to delete multiple images would be something like this:

```
# docker rmi 1403322a81c5 0114405f9ff1 53b6894a9c8a
Untagged: cricket/hangman:1.9
Untagged: cricket/hangman:latest
Deleted: 1403322a81c5362762f84a26b2c818fcc0c9f...
```

```
Untagged: centos:7
Untagged: centos:centos7
Untagged: centos:latest
Deleted: 0114405f9ff12fb7b012d0f7eb2f958c6ab86...
Deleted: 3d3c8202a57465ab6a24852559d21ca72a4af...
Deleted: b6718650e87e3706c52682c87ecfd7a7e1fc1...
Untagged: redis:latest
Deleted: 53b6894a9c8af40f9f12b722518b570cfb791...
Deleted: ef119c54808b9a791d89076b9d795d4cd157d...
Deleted: f94bd3b706e967987a9a433c1b3a909b7db60...
...
```

REMOVING CONTAINERS

Each time a container is run, a new layer is added to it, essentially creating a new container. Unless you explicitly have that new container removed (using the `--rm` option of `docker run`), it remains on your system, ready to be restarted or saved as an image.

Removing a container is only a bit trickier than removing an image. The main thing to remember is that, by default, you can't remove a running container. So you either need to stop it first or remove it with the force option (`-f`).

As with images, you can remove containers either individually or by passing a list of containers to the `docker rm` command. Before you remove containers, you can check how much space each container is consuming using the `-s` option to the `docker ps` command. When you do that, you may notice that the containers are actually small. This is because the size of the container is only the size in addition to what is in the image that the container started from.

Removing Individual Containers

To remove an individual container all you need to do is use the name or image ID of the container on a `docker rm` command line. The following examples show ways to remove containers that are in different states.

Removing a Running or Paused Container

In the following examples, of the running containers on this system, one is paused and the other is running. Use the `docker ps` command to see what is running:

```
# docker ps
CONTAINER ID   IMAGE                           COMMAND          CREATED
   STATUS                      PORTS           NAMES
705c1a4e30e0   rhel7/rhel-tools:latest  "/usr/bin/bash"  9 seconds ago
   Up 51 seconds (Paused)                      rhel-tools
```

```
eaddcc59bc86   cricket/hangman:latest   "go-fish"      4 hours ago
     Up 4 hours                          grave_pare
```

Notice that when you try to remove these containers, the command fails the same way, whether the container is running or paused:

```
# docker rm eaddcc59bc86
Error response from daemon: Conflict, You cannot remove a running
container. Stop the container before attempting removal or use -f
FATA[0000] Error: failed to remove one or more containers
# docker rm rhel-tools
Error response from daemon: Conflict, You cannot remove a running
container. Stop the container before attempting removal or use -f
FATA[0000] Error: failed to remove one or more containers
```

Also notice that in one case, I use the name of the container and in the other I use the container ID. A container that is paused cannot be removed, even with the force option. So, I unpause it, stop it, and then remove it. For the other one, I remove it with the force option while it is still running:

```
# docker unpause myrhel-tools
myrhel-tools
# docker stop myrhel-tools
myrhel-tools
# docker rm myrhel-tools
myrhel-tools
# docker rm -f eaddcc59bc86
eaddcc59bc86
# docker ps
CONTAINER ID  IMAGE  COMMAND  CREATED  STATUS  PORTS  NAMES
#
```

As you can see, both containers are no longer running. Both containers have also been removed.

Removing a Container That Has Stopped

After a container has stopped (assuming you didn't run it with the --rm option), the new container remains on the system. You can start it again (using docker start), save it as an image, or remove it when you no longer need it. To see the containers that were run on your system but have exited, type the following:

```
# docker ps -a
CONTAINER ID  IMAGE          COMMAND           CREATED
     STATUS                  PORTS     NAMES
d70cfe9cc624  ubuntu:latest  "/bin/bash"       16 seconds ago
     Exited (0) 9 seconds ago          reverent_poitras
5f785798faae  fedora:latest  "python -m SimpleHTT  2 minutes ago
```

```
            Exited (137) 4 seconds ago            MyWebServer
4b043f61e00    hangman:latest "go-fish"                6 hours ago
            Exited (0) 6 hours ago            agitated_mcclintock
...
```

When you remove a container, use the `docker rm` command with either the container ID or its name. Here are some examples:

```
# docker rm reverent_poitras
reverent_poitras
# docker rm 5f785798faae
5f785798faae
```

Removing Multiple Containers

Just as you did with images, you can remove multiple containers by directing a list of container names to the `docker rm` command. You can use the `docker ps -a -q` command to get a list of all containers still on your system but no longer running. For example:

```
# docker ps -a -q
16a6a35759cb
55a35f0736ac
04b043f61e00
8f94e788d173
9f43d1f6e699
176feb8ee722
0cd1ee87a368
cf1e1242b5a3
...
```

Now, to delete those containers, just pass the standard output of that command to the standard input of the `docker rm` command as follows:

```
# docker rm $(docker ps -a -q)
16a6a35759cb
55a35f0736ac
04b043f61e00
8f94e788d173
9f43d1f6e699
176feb8ee722
0cd1ee87a368
cf1e1242b5a3
...
```

Although the output looks the same (a listing of container names), the command line just shown results in all the local containers that are no longer running being removed from your system.

CLEANING UP AND SAVING CONTAINERS

If you add some software and save some data to a container, you may decide that you want to keep that container in a more permanent way and store it as an image. In Chapter 5, "Finding, Pulling, Saving, and Loading Container Images," I describe how to save and commit containers to images. Here I talk about what you can do to clean up and reduce the containers before you save them as images.

I create two containers for this example: One from a `fedora` base image and one from an `ubuntu` base image. The two Linux systems have different tools for managing software packages. So you need to go about cleaning up those containers in different ways.

> **NOTE**
>
> Although the tools for saving a container as an image are readily available, this is not necessarily the most efficient way to create the images you want. A better approach is to use `docker build` to build the container image you want from a base image, including any clean-up commands in it that you see fit. The `docker build` command is described in Chapter 12, "Building Docker Images."

Cleaning Up and Saving an Ubuntu Container

I execute a `docker run` on an `ubuntu` base image, open a shell, and install several server packages with `apt-get install`. After stopping the container I attach to it again and run the following commands to clean it up and reduce its size:

```
# docker start -ai 369f25938d44
root@369f25938d44:/# apt-get remove unneeded_packages
root@369f25938d44:/# apt-get clean
root@369f25938d44:/# rm unneeded_files
root@369f25938d44:/# exit
# docker export 369f25938d44 > myubuntu.tar
# docker rm 369f25938d44
# cat myubuntu.tar | docker import - mynewubuntu:latest
699c4def6a4cc14e75417bdf5c9d2e1769745845fd905cb989522bc166cafa3c
# docker images
REPOSITORY      TAG       IMAGE ID       CREATED            VIRTUAL SIZE
mynewubuntu     latest    699c4def6a4c   About a minute ago  257.4 MB
```

The `apt-get remove` and `rm` commands are just to remind you to remove any packages and files you no longer feel you need. After exiting the shell running in the container, I export the container to a tarball file named `myubuntu.tar`. I can then remove the old container since I no longer need it.

Next, I pipe the contents of the tarball to the `docker import` command, which saves it as an image to the local system under the name `mynewubuntu:latest`. After that, the image appears in the list displayed from `docker images` and it is ready to use.

Cleaning Up and Saving a Fedora Container

Starting with a `fedora` base image this time, I execute a `docker run` to open a shell and install several server packages with `yum install`. After stopping the container I attach to it again and run the following commands to clean it up and reduce its size:

```
# docker start -ai 6d64eb633e02
bash-4.3# yum remove unneeded_packages
bash-4.3# rm unneeded_files
bash-4.3# yum clean all
Cleaning repos: fedora updates
Cleaning up everything
bash-4.3# exit
# docker export 6d64eb633e02 > myfedora.tar
# docker rm 6d64eb633e02
# cat myfedora.tar | docker import - mynewfedora:latest
7a0b47e65b1f028bec94420a234c45beb48f02c0a8d7c222ac999a5913b16d3b
# docker images
REPOSITORY    TAG      IMAGE ID      CREATED            VIRTUAL SIZE
mynewfedora   latest   7a0b47e65b1f  About a minute ago  245.7 MB
```

As with the `ubuntu` container example earlier, I remove unneeded packages and files, clean metadata left around after installing packages, and exit the shell. With the container stopped, but still on the system, I export the container to a tarball and remove the old container. To bring the tarball back into the system as an image, I direct the contents of the `myfedora.tar` file to standard output (using the `cat` command) and pipe it to a `docker import` command, giving the new image the name `mynewfedora:latest`.

SUMMARY

Docker keeps images and containers around after they have been pulled or run. If you are not careful, this can consume a lot of your system's storage space in ways that you may not be aware of. As a rule, keep an eye on the amount of disk space available in the `/var/log/docker` directory, since that is where Docker stores its images and containers.

Every once in a while, check the images and containers stored on your system and clean out any that you don't need. Run `docker images` to see what images are stored on your system and `docker rmi` to remove them. For containers, run `docker ps` and `docker ps -a` to see the containers on your system and `docker rm` to remove them.

To save the contents of a container more permanently, you can use `docker export` and `docker import` on a container to save it out to a tarball and then bring it back into the system as an image. Before you do that, however, it's a good idea to clean it up by removing unneeded cached data, packages, and files.

## CHAPTER 12

Building Docker Images

IN THIS CHAPTER:

- Build a simple Docker container image
- Use `Dockerfile` instructions
- Learn tips to build images more efficiently

Although you can create Docker images by adding software to a running container and committing it to an image (`docker commit`), the preferred way to create Docker images is with the `docker build` command. The file you create to hold the instructions for building a Docker image is literally named `Dockerfile`.

There are several reasons why building Docker images from a `Dockerfile` is preferred to manual changes and commits:

- **Reproducible**: If you add software to a running container and commit it to an image, there's no record of exactly what you did to create that image. With a `Dockerfile`, you can see exactly what was added to a base image and simply build the image again from that file to reproduce it.

- **Correctable**: If you make a mistake building the image, you can just fix the `Dockerfile` and run `docker build` again. In fact, because `docker build` creates a new container layer at each step, a later build starts after the most recent successful step. This can save a lot of time in the build process if only one or two steps need to be corrected near the end of the build.

- **Portable**: While Docker images can be relatively small, the size of even a large `Dockerfile` is trivial. If you give a `Dockerfile` to someone who has access to the base image you are building from (which could be in a public registry) and any other files needed in the build, they could rebuild your container image and reuse it on their own system, without having to transport the whole image.

- **Verifiable**: Given a known base image and a `Dockerfile`, someone can verify what is pulled into the container they build. If someone just hands you a finished container, you would have to open it up and look around to see what is inside it.

- **Updatable**: If a `Dockerfile` does a `yum` (or `dnf`) or `apt-get` command to install software packages, unless you ask for specific versions of those packages, the build grabs the latest versions of the packages you request. So a simple rebuild results in a Docker image that contains the latest software available from the software repositories you have configured.

This chapter takes you through the process of building your own images from `Dockerfile` files. Along the way, I describe tips for using Docker effectively to build images that can be stored and run efficiently.

Once you understand the process and components for building Docker images, see Chapter 18, "Exploring Sample Dockerfile Files," for some complex and interesting `Dockerfile` examples to get ideas for all kinds of Docker images you can build.

DOING A SIMPLE DOCKER BUILD

Assuming the Docker service is up and running on your system, to build your own Docker image all you need is a `Dockerfile` file, access to the base image you want to start with, and any other files you want to add to that image. On the `docker build` command line all you need is an indication of where the `Dockerfile` file is to build from, which is often indicated with a dot (.) for the current directory.

There are other options you can set with `docker build` as well that I describe later. For now, here are steps for creating your first simple Docker image:

1. **Make a directory for the Dockerfile**: Create a directory to hold your `Dockerfile` file. For example:

   ```
   # mkdir ~/Imagedir
   # cd ~/Imagedir
   ```

2. **Create a Dockerfile file**: Using any text editor, create a `Dockerfile` file with the following contents (replacing your name on the MAINTAINER line):

   ```
   # Character-based games container image
   FROM fedora:latest
   ```

```
MAINTAINER John W. Jones
RUN dnf install -y bsd-games words
# Start the application
ENTRYPOINT ["/usr/bin/hangman"]
```

3. **Build the image**: Type the following command (with the `Dockerfile` in the current directory) to build an image. The `-t` option is used to name the image `myhangman`:

```
# docker build -t myhangman .
Sending build context to Docker daemon 2.048 kB
Sending build context to Docker daemon
Step 0 : FROM fedora:latest
 ---> ded7cd95e059
Step 1 : MAINTAINER John W. Jones
 ---> Running in 7b56400206f3
 ---> 58f0c53fc128
Removing intermediate container 7b56400206f3
Step 2 : RUN dnf install -y bsd-games words
 ---> Running in 706da0a49bdf
...
Installed:
  bsd-games.x86_64 2.17-46.fc22          words.noarch 3.0-23.fc21
Complete!
 ---> c889372d5ed1
Removing intermediate container 706da0a49bdf
Step 3 : ENTRYPOINT /usr/bin/hangman
 ---> Running in 9a9bcb54cee4
 ---> 934e99e33296
Removing intermediate container 9a9bcb54cee4
Successfully built 934e99e33296
```

4. **Run the image**: Use the `docker run` command to run the image. This launches the `hangman` game in your current shell. The `-it` option runs the container interactively:

```
# docker run -it myhangman

     _____
    |     |
    |     O
    |
    |
    |
   _|_____                        Guessed:  acdeiorstu
  |     |__                       Word #:          3
  |        |                      Current Average:  4.667
  |_____|                      Overall Average:  6.500

 Word:  directdiscourse
Guess:
You got it!
Another word? n
```

5. **Check the image**: Use the following commands to see that the new image and the previously run container are on your system:

```
# docker images
REPOSITORY          TAG        IMAGE ID       CREATED         VIRTUAL SIZE
myhangman           latest     934e99e33296   9 minutes ago   319.9 MB
docker.io/fedora    latest     ded7cd95e059   5 weeks ago     186.5 MB
# docker ps -a
CONTAINER ID   IMAGE             COMMAND              CREATED
  STATUS                         PORTS     NAMES
6a507de124ff   myhangman:latest  "/usr/bin/hangman"   9 minutes ago
  Exited (0) 6 minutes ago                 jolly_darwin
```

If all goes well, you should be able to play a game of hangman from the container. Here are a few things to help you think about what happens during a build:

- **Docker daemon does the build**: The docker build command doesn't actually build the container. That command passes information needed to do the build to the Docker daemon.

- **Restrict build directory**: Put your Dockerfile file in a directory that only contains files needed for the build. That's because any files in the current directory or its subdirectories are sent to the Docker daemon and are available to be used in the container by ADD commands. So, for example, if you were to put your Dockerfile in the /var directory, every file and directory under /var would be sent to the Docker daemon for possible inclusion in the container. This would significantly slow the build process and consume too much disk space unnecessarily.

- **Intermediate containers**: Each instruction adds a new layer to the existing image and commits an intermediate container image. With this approach, each time you run docker build on the same Dockerfile the build can start from the most recent successful instruction and continue from there.

- **Build options**: Use at least the -t option when building an image, to assign a name to that image. If you plan to push the image to a registry, you can include a user name (such as cricket/myhangman) or a hostname (such as registry.example.com:5000/myhangman). Other build options are described later in this chapter.

- **Base image (FROM)**: If your system is connected to the Internet, the fedora:latest base image (on the FROM line) is pulled from the Docker Hub Registry. If it has already been pulled, the image is used from the local system. FROM must be the first instruction in the Dockerfile, aside from comments. The :latest tag is actually not required, because :latest is assumed if no tag is entered. However, if you want a specific version of a base image, be sure to add that tag (for example, fedora:22).

- **MAINTAINER**: This identifies the author of the image. This information is stored inside the image. It is typically to add your full name and email address.

- **RUN**: Commands put on RUN lines are run during the build process (not when the container itself runs later). The `fedora` base image is enabled to install packages from the Fedora repository (using `yum` or `dnf` install commands). In this case, I installed the bsd-games and words packages on a RUN line. I can use the RUN instruction with any command I want from a `Dockerfile` to change the image at build time.

- **ENTRYPOINT**: This line identifies the command to be executed when you use `docker run` to start the container—in this case, `/usr/bin/hangman`. The ENTRYPOINT essentially identifies the intention of the container image. You can override the ENTRYPOINT command when you run the container using the `--entrypoint=""` option. However, an easier way to be able to allow someone running an image to override the default command is to use CMD instead of ENTRYPOINT (as described later).

The example shown here illustrates the basic process for building a simple container. However, there are more instructions you can add to your `Dockerfile` to customize your container. Many of these instructions are illustrated in the next sections of this chapter.

SETTING A COMMAND TO EXECUTE FROM A DOCKERFILE

The CMD and ENTRYPOINT instructions identify what command is started when you run the container image. Commands set by the RUN instruction, however, are only used when you build the image, while CMD and ENTRYPOINT are used at the time you execute `docker run`. Those three instructions have different meanings, as illustrated in the following Dockerfile examples.

Using the CMD Instruction

With CMD, you can identify the default command to run from the image, along with options you want to pass to it. If there is no ENTRYPOINT in the `Dockerfile`, the value of CMD is the command run by default when you start the container image. If there is an ENTRYPOINT in the `Dockerfile`, the ENTRYPOINT value is run as the command instead, with the value of CMD used as options to the ENTRYPOINT command.

You can only have one CMD line in a `Dockerfile`. Here's an example of a `Dockerfile` that includes a CMD instruction to run the `cat` command to list a couple of files:

```
FROM fedora:latest
MAINTAINER John Jones
CMD ["cat","/etc/hosts","/etc/os-release"]
```

In this example if you build an image called `mycmd`, `docker run mycmd` results in `hosts` and `os-release` files being output to the shell. The CMD arguments in this case are the command (`cat`) followed by two file names (`/etc/hosts` and `/etc/os-release`). The arguments are in JSON format (square brackets and double-quotes in a comma-separated list). The CMD line could have simply been `CMD cat /etc/hosts /etc/os-release`, which would cause the command to be run by a shell (`sh -c`) instead of being executed directly.

The CMD instruction can be overridden when you run the image. So, notice the different results from running `mycmd` in two different ways:

```
# docker build -t mycmd .
# docker run mycmd              Runs cat to list hosts, os-release files
# docker run -it mycmd bash     Runs bash, ignoring cat command
```

Any time you add an argument to the end of a `docker run` command, the CMD instruction inside the container is ignored. So the second example opens a `bash` shell instead of running the `cat` command. If you want to assign a command that is not overridden by options at the end of a `docker run` command, use the ENTRY-POINT instruction.

Using the ENTRYPOINT Instruction

The ENTRYPOINT instruction lets you define the command executed when you run the container image. It does this in a way that is not overridden by arguments you put at the end of a `docker run` line. If your `Dockerfile` includes an ENTRY-POINT instruction and there is also a CMD instruction, any arguments on the CMD instruction line are passed to the command defined in the ENTRYPOINT line. Here is an example of a `Dockerfile` that uses an ENTRYPOINT instruction:

```
FROM fedora:latest
MAINTAINER John Jones
CMD ["/etc/hosts","/etc/os-release"]
ENTRYPOINT ["cat"]
```

Because the ENTRYPOINT used in this `Dockerfile` is set to run the `cat` command, that command is used by default with the container. However, if there is also a CMD line in the file, arguments on that line are passed to the ENTRYPOINT instruction. If you were to build that `Dockerfile` into an image named `myent`, here are a couple of examples of running the resulting image:

```
# docker build -t myent .
# docker run myent                 Runs cat on hosts, os-release files
# docker run -it myent /etc/issue  Runs cat on issue, ignore others
```

Notice that the command (`cat`) on the ENTRYPOINT line uses `/etc/hosts` and `/etc/os-release` files as arguments as long as no other argument is given on the `docker run` command line. However, if there is an argument when you run the image (`/etc/issue` here), anything on a CMD instruction is ignored.

An advantage of having the ENTRYPOINT only identify the command is that you might want to override the default way of running a command. Consider this example:

```
FROM fedora:latest
MAINTAINER John Jones
ENTRYPOINT ["cat","/etc/hosts","/etc/os-release"]
```

When you build and run the image you get these results:

```
# docker build -t myent1 .
# docker run myent1                 Runs cat on hosts, os-release
# docker run -it myent1 /issue      Runs cat all three files
```

Because the `hosts` and `os-release` files are on the ENTRYPOINT line, adding arguments to the end of the `docker run` line does not override them. Adding `/etc/issue` to the `docker run` line causes that file to be displayed to the shell after the other two files appear.

One last thing about ENTRYPOINT to keep in mind. Even though arguments at the end of the `docker run` command line don't override the command set by ENTRYPOINT, you can override the ENTRYPOINT command with the `--entrypoint=""` option. For example, this command line would run a `bash` shell instead of the default `cat` command set by the ENTRYPOINT inside the selected image:

```
# docker run -it --entrypoint="/bin/bash" myent1
```

Using the RUN Instruction

As noted earlier, the RUN instruction is only interpreted and used at the time you use the `docker build` command to create an image. The point of RUN instructions is usually to run commands that modify the image in some way. For example, you might install software packages or create a configuration file that becomes part of the image.

In this example, I create a file at build time and display it later with `docker run`:

```
FROM fedora:latest
MAINTAINER John Jones
RUN echo "This container was built on $(date)." > /tmp/built.txt
ENTRYPOINT ["cat","/tmp/built.txt"]
```

When I run `docker build`, that command reads in the current date and time and outputs it in a sentence to the `/tmp/build.txt` file. Because the `echo` command was run at build time, the exact same date is shown every time I do a `docker run` command:

```
# docker build -t myrun .
# docker run myrun              See the build time of the image
This container was built on Sun Jul  5 13:47:51 EDT 2015.
# docker run myrun              Notice the build time is the same
This container was built on Sun Jul  5 13:47:51 EDT 2015.
```

Adding Files to an Image from a Dockerfile

You can use the ADD instruction to add selected files into the container at build time. When you use ADD to add files and directories to your image, `docker build` uses the directory containing the `Dockerfile` on your host system as both the root directory (/) and the current directory. In this example, I make a file in the same directory as the `Dockerfile` and add it to the new image called `myadd` as follows:

```
# mkdir ~/Myadd
# cd ~/Myadd
# echo "This is the test.txt file." > test.txt
# vi Dockerfile
# cat Dockerfile
FROM fedora:latest
MAINTAINER John Jones
ADD /test.txt /tmp/test.txt
ENTRYPOINT ["cat","/tmp/test.txt"]
# docker build -t myadd .
# docker run myadd              See the contents of the test.txt file
This is the test.txt file.
```

On the ADD line, the `/test.txt` file identifies the file as being in the directory with the `Dockerfile` on the host system and `/tmp/test.txt` shows where it goes inside the container. Instead of `/test.txt`, I could have identified the host file as simply `text.txt`, since `docker build` sees the files in the directory where

`Dockerfile` is located as being the current directory. Again, remember to put all files and directories of content you want to build into the container in the same directory or a subdirectory in which the `Dockerfile` file is located.

> **NOTE**
>
> If you rerun a `docker build` often if an instruction is successful, the cached result of that instruction is reused by the new `docker build`. An exception to this is with an ADD or COPY instruction, which will do a fresh add or copy of the file if the underlying file has changed. See the "Manage How Caching is Done" section in this chapter for a more complete description of this issue.

EXPOSING PORTS FROM AN IMAGE WITHIN A DOCKERFILE

Adding an EXPOSE instruction within a `Dockerfile` lets you indicate that a particular port should be exposed from the image you build. When a port is exposed on a running container image, it allows two things to happen:

- **Linked containers**: Once you run the image, if you link the running container to another container, the exposed port will be available to the other container as though it were available on the same local system.

- **Run-time exposure**: Any port identified with an EXPOSE instruction when the image is built can be easily exposed from the same port number on the local host. By using the -p option to `docker run` on the image, you could assign any exposed port to the same or a specific different port on the local host. If you use the -P option of `docker run`, all exposed ports from within the container are assigned to random ports on the host system. You could then run the `docker port` command on the resulting container to see how the ports are mapped.

Here's an example of a web server `Dockerfile` for a container image with port 80 exposed from that image:

```
FROM fedora:latest
MAINTAINER John Jones
RUN yum install -y httpd
EXPOSE 80
```

```
# Start the service
CMD ["-D", "FOREGROUND"]
ENTRYPOINT ["/usr/sbin/httpd"]
```

When you go to run that image, here is how to expose port 80 from the container to port 8080 on the local system on the `docker run` command line.

```
# docker run -p 8000:80 -d myweb
# curl localhost:8000 | head
```

The `-p 8000:80` indicates that port 8000 on the host points to port `80` inside the container. The `curl` command line should show the first few lines of the Apache HTTP Server Test page.

If you don't designate the protocol with the port number, the TCP protocol is assumed by default. To identify a different protocol, such as the UDP protocol, you could follow the port number with a slash (/) and protocol name. For example, you could use 53/udp to expose UDP port 53.

Assigning Environment Variables in a Dockerfile

Using the ENV instruction, you can set an environment variable to any key that you choose. These variables are available to subsequent instructions as processing continues through a `Dockerfile`. You can assign multiple variables on a single line or have multiple ENV lines.

Environment variables in a `Dockerfile` can be useful for things like changing the location of data directories, adding passwords, or setting user names. The official WordPress image (`https://hub.docker.com/_/wordpress/`) sets multiple environment variables. You can change environment variables in a Dockerfile (`ENV variable key`) or change them at run time on the `docker run` command line (`-e variable=key`).

For example, the following environment variables could be built into a `Dockerfile` file to create a WordPress image:

```
ENV WORDPRESS_DB_HOST=host01.example.com
ENV WORDPRESS_DB_USER=root
ENV WORDPRESS_DB_PASSWORD=MYrut3pZwrd
```

When you go to run the WordPress image, you could change those variables on the `docker run` command line using the `-e` option. The WordPress repository on the Docker Hub Registry gives the following example of how to change these variables:

```
# docker run --name some-wordpress -e WORDPRESS_DB_HOST=10.1.2.3:3306 \
    -e WORDPRESS_DB_USER=... -e WORDPRESS_DB_PASSWORD=... -d wordpress
```

ASSIGNING LABELS IN A DOCKERFILE

Using the LABEL instruction in a `Dockerfile`, you can assign values to selected keys. You can use any key name that you want, as there are no restrictions on how you set these labels. That said, the Docker Project makes some recommendations for using LABEL instructions.

Here is a simple example of using a LABEL instruction:

```
LABEL description="Simple web server container"
```

If you were to build this LABEL to an image named `myweb`, you could see how that label is set using `docker inspect` as follows:

```
# docker inspect myweb | less
...
        "Hostname": "26bc48f09da7",
        "Image": "6396baf5ba25e16...",
        "Labels": {
            "description": "Simple web server container"
        },
...
```

Here are some tips for using LABEL instructions in a `Dockerfile`:

- **Many labels on one line**: If you need to set multiple labels for an image, setting them on one LABEL line prevents a separate container layer from being created for each label. Here are two different ways of setting multiple labels on a single LABEL line:

```
LABEL description="My game image" department="Sales" user="joe"
LABEL description="My game image" \
    department="Sales" \
    user="joe"
```

- **Use unique labels**: If you set a label more than once in a `Dockerfile`, the last value overwritten is the one used. When the Docker Project uses labels, it prepends each label with `com.docker.*`, `io.docker.*`, or `org.dockerproject.*`. It is good practice for you to also use reverse DNS notation for a domain you control when creating labels to make sure you avoid label conflicts—for example, `net.linuxtoys.mylabel`.

- **Characters in labels**: There are some restrictions on the characters you can use in a label. Although not enforced, you should use only letters (alpha), numbers (numeric), dots, and dashes in a key name. Make sure each key starts and ends with a letter or number. Don't use consecutive dots or dashes.

- **Filter by label**: After your image has been built, you can use the `--filter` option to list only those images or containers that include a label you set. For example:

```
# docker ps -a --filter "label=description=My game container"
CONTAINER ID IMAGE                   COMMAND       CREATED
   STATUS                  PORTS         NAMES
c35fe57d078c cricket/hangman:latest  "hangman"     4 minutes ago
   Exited (0) 4 minutes ago
# docker images --filter "label=description=My game container"
REPOSITORY        TAG       IMAGE ID       CREATED         VIRTUAL SIZE
cricket/hangman latest      1403322a81c5   10 minutes ago  427.3 MB
```

Now that you have seen many of the instructions you can use within a `Dockerfile`, the next section describes some of the additional options that you can use with the `docker build` command to build that `Dockerfile` into an image.

USING OTHER docker BUILD COMMAND OPTIONS

Although `docker build` is all you need to build a `Dockerfile` into a Docker image, you can add other options to `docker build` to modify the build process. Here are some `docker build` command lines that illustrate different options:

```
# docker build --force-rm=true .
# docker build --no-cache=true .
# docker build -f ~/Myweb/Dockerfile01 ~
# docker build --pull=true .
```

The `--force-rm=true` option tells Docker to force all intermediate images to be removed, even if the build failed at some point. However, removing intermediate containers doesn't remove the cached data. So to truly have the build start from scratch, use the `--no-cache=true` option. By setting the option `--no-cache=true`, the `docker build` does not use any cached data in the build. Each step is run from scratch.

By default, when you identify the build directory, which is often a dot (.) to indicate the current directory, the file named `Dockerfile` in that directory is used as the file to build from. By adding a `-f` option, you tell `docker build` to use a different file to build the image. Keep in mind that the build file you identify must be in the build directory or a subdirectory of that directory. In the example just shown, the build directory is the user's home directory (~), while the build file is named `Dockerfile01` and is located in a subdirectory of the build directory (`-f ~/Myweb/Dockerfile01`).

If the base image requested (on the FROM line) has previously been pulled by Docker to the local system, a `docker build` won't look for a newer version of that image by default. By adding `--pull=true` to `docker build`, Docker checks to see whether a later version of the image is available from any enabled repository.

TIPS FOR BUILDING CONTAINERS

If you are ready to start building containers, here are a few tips that can help make your build process better and more convenient.

Clean Up the Image

To keep the image as small as possible, clean out any software package or data you don't need from the image. If you use `yum` or `apt-get` to install packages, you should clean out any cached data that results (for example, `RUN yum clean -y all`). Likewise, you can remove packages in the image that you don't need (for example, `RUN yum remove -y vim-minimal`).

Keep Build Directory Small

As mentioned earlier, every file from the build directory is copied to the Docker daemon and stored (in `/var/lib/docker`, by default) before the build process begins. Before starting the build, removing files from that directory and any subdirectories speeds up the build and saves disk space.

In some cases, it might be inconvenient to remove files from the build directory structure so you can exclude them from a build. As an alternative, you can exclude files from the build directory structure by adding a `.dockerignore` file to the build directory and putting files in it that you want the build to ignore. Here are examples of the kinds of entries you could put in a `.dockerignore` file:

```
passwd
passwd*
*/passwd*
*/*passwd*
passw?
!passwd-local
mystuff/
```

Here is how each of those examples would cause files and directories to be prevented from being copied from the build directory to the Docker daemon during a build:

- **passwd**: Only the literal `passwd` file in the build directory is ignored.

- **passwd***: Any file in the build directory is skipped if it begins with `passwd`. For example, `passwd-stuff`, `passwd.5.gz`, and `passwd.html` would all be ignored. However, `passwd` in any subdirectory would not be ignored.

- ***/passwd***: Any file in an immediate subdirectory of the build directory that begins with `passwd` is ignored.

- **passw?**: Any file in the build directory that begins with `passw` and has one more letter in its name is ignored. For example, `passwd`, `passwa`, `passwb`, and so on.

- **!passwd-local**: If any rule causing a file named `passwd-local` to be ignored comes before this entry, the string shown here causes the file `passwd-local` to not be ignored. If a rule that causes `passwd-local` to be ignored comes after this rule, the file `passwd-local` is ignored.

- **mystuff/**: If there is a directory named `mystuff` in the build directory, ignore it and any files or subdirectories under that point in the build directory.

Keep Containers Simple

Creating containers that do only one thing (run a file server, start a web browser, or provide a simple database) makes it easier to manage and scale up your use of containers later. In general, each container should run only one process. If a container requires services from another container, you can link containers together or use an orchestration service (such as Kubernetes) to associate the services a container needs with the containers that provide those services.

Manage How Caching Is Done

Each time you rebuild an image from a `Dockerfile`, Docker checks to see whether the current instruction has been successfully run and therefore has the results of the instruction available in cache. If the results are successful and cached, Docker, by default, uses the cached data from the instruction and reuses it with the new build. This can be a huge time savings if, for example, the instruction does something such as download and install 100 packages.

There are times when using cache is the right thing to do. Other times however, you might want to use the `--no-cache=true` option. Take the case where you know that new versions of packages you installed during a `docker build` are available. If you build the image again, with the instruction exactly the same, Docker won't know to run the instruction again to pick up the new packages. An alternative to turning off the use of a previous cache is to change the instruction in some way. That also causes the instruction to run again without using cache.

If you use an ADD or COPY instruction to add files when you do a build, any changes to those files are noticed if you run a `docker build` again on the same `Dockerfile`. That is because Docker runs a checksum on each file pulled in with an ADD or COPY instruction, and if the contents of the file itself or metadata associated with the file (permissions, date/time stamps, and so on) have changed, the new file is copied to the image.

The tips just mentioned should give you a good start on building your first containers. For more advanced suggestions on building containers, see Chapter 17, "Developing Docker Containers."

SUMMARY

The `docker build` command is the preferred way to create a Docker container image. There are many advantages to using `docker build` for building an image, as opposed to modifying a running container and committing it to a new image. By building a new image with `docker build`, you can more easily verify its contents, reproduce the image, and pull in the latest software and configuration information.

The file used to build Docker container images is referred to as a `Dockerfile`. You create a `Dockerfile` by identifying the base image to build from, running commands during the build process to modify the container, setting the command to execute when the container image is run, and saving it to a new image you name. You can also add other instructions to a `Dockerfile` file to do such things as set environment variables, pull in files from the build directory, and identify the user account that should run the commands you include in the `Dockerfile`.

This chapter brings Part II of this book to a close. To this point, I have shown you how to work with individual images and containers. You have seen how to run, inspect, list, start, stop, attach to, and otherwise work with individual containers and images. The next part of the book helps you move your containers into cloud environments by running them in special container-oriented operating systems such as Project Atomic.

Part III

Running Containers in Cloud Environments

## CHAPTER 13

Using Super Privileged Containers

IN THIS CHAPTER:

- Understand super privileged containers
- Manage containers with the `atomic` command
- Use super privileged containers

Operating systems built to run containers are meant to be lean. By offering only a minimal feature set, container-oriented operating systems such as Atomic Host and CoreOS offer faster boot-up times, as well as smaller storage requirements and less CPU consumption than traditional operating systems. This makes them excellent operating systems to deploy to cloud environments.

The potential downside to these small, efficient systems is that they don't have all the tools built in that you expect in a full-featured operating system. So, you need to learn new ways to manage these systems.

This chapter focuses on how to add software tools to work on Atomic Host systems, using what are referred to as *super privileged containers (SPCs)*. With SPCs, you can not only get the tools you need to manage Atomic Host systems, you can also run them in such a way that those tools can break out of their containers to act on the host itself.

Although the SPCs described in this chapter can be used on regular Fedora, CentOS, Red Hat Enterprise Linux (RHEL), or Atomic Host systems, SPCs are most useful on Atomic Hosts. The reason is because it's easier to add software to regular RHEL or Fedora systems by simply using the `yum` (or `dnf`) and `rpm` commands. Because of the nature of RHEL Atomic Host (it uses Atomic upgrades to add software), it doesn't allow `yum` or `rpm` to add packages to the system. So all the special tools you might need to act on an Atomic Host system must be added by adding containers that include those tools. The SPCs described in this chapter were created specifically to make tools available on Atomic Host systems that would not be there otherwise.

> **NOTE**
>
> Although SPCs can be launched by adding special options to `docker run` commands, this chapter focuses on how containers can include preset `docker run` options that you can take advantage of on Atomic Host systems using the `atomic` command.

USING SUPER PRIVILEGED CONTAINERS IN ATOMIC HOST

Software is added to Project Atomic systems using atomic-style upgrades, and not by installing packages with traditional tools such as the `rpm` and `yum` commands. Although Atomic Host systems are built from RPM packages, you cannot add or remove RPM packages from an Atomic Host after an Atomic Host has been built.

So when you need more software on an Atomic Host system, the best way to add it is to put the software in a container and run that container on the host. Because, by default, containers are not given permission to act on the host itself, these types of containers need to be given extra privileges.

On Atomic systems, SPCs are granted special permission to see into the host system and change that system as needed. Whereas a regular container can only see processes running inside the container, an SPC can see and potentially act on all processes running on the host. Likewise, commands run from an SPC have direct access to devices on the host system and can see the host's network interfaces.

UNDERSTANDING SUPER PRIVILEGED CONTAINERS

Running an application from within a container typically lets you keep the processing of that application separate from other containers on the host system and from the host system itself. This is done by maintaining restricted privileges and separate namespaces for the container. SPCs are designed to break through those restrictions.

You can use command line options with the `docker run` command to tell the selected container image to use the host's namespaces instead of the container's namespaces. The `atomic` command is designed to read these options that you include within the container's metadata and pass them to a `docker run` command. So a prerequisite to understanding how SPCs work is seeing the options to `docker run` that provide those features.

The next sections describe the privileges and namespaces on the host that can be opened for an SPC with options on the `docker run` command line.

Opening Privileges to the Host

A running container typically has no direct access to devices on the host. Likewise, containers (by default) are run in systems that provide SELinux (Security Enhanced Linux) security (such as Fedora and RHEL) are constrained in their ability to access other files and processes on the host by the fact that they run in restricted SELinux security contexts.

With the `--privileged` option used with `docker run`, a container has almost all the same access to the host system as a process run from outside the container. To be able to use those privileges, however, you have to open different namespaces on the host so they can actually be seen inside the container.

Accessing the Host Process Table

By default, a running container sees only its own process table. So, process ID 1 for a container represents the process launched by the container and not the `systemd` or `init` process that you see on a normal, running Linux system. The only other processes on the containers process table are those started within the container.

Running a container without telling `docker run` to use the host process table limits that container's view of what is running on the host. For example, if you use `docker run` to start a bash shell and then run a `ps` command inside that container to see what processes are running, you might see something like the following:

```
# ps -ef
UID         PID    PPID  C STIME TTY          TIME CMD
root          1       0  2 16:06 ?        00:00:00 /bin/bash
root          7       1  0 16:06 ?        00:00:00 ps -ef
```

Notice that process ID 1 is the bash shell and the `ps` command is PID 7. If I had provided the `--pid=host` option when I ran this container, to set the container to use the host's process table instead of the container's process table, a `ps` from inside the container would look more like the following:

```
# ps -ef
UID      PID     PPID  C STIME TTY      TIME CMD
root       1        0  0 Apr24 ?    00:00:09 /usr/lib/systemd/systemd...
root       2        0  0 Apr24 ?    00:00:00 [kthreadd]
root       3        2  0 Apr24 ?    00:00:14 [ksoftirqd/0]
root       5        2  0 Apr24 ?    00:00:00 [kworker/0:0H]
...
root   18941    18864  0 17:02 ?    00:00:00 ps -ef
```

The list output from the ps command shows every process running on the host.

Accessing Host Network Interfaces

By default, the Docker daemon automatically provides an IP address to each container on the host's docker0 network via DHCP. Inside the container, that address is assigned to the eth0 interface. On Fedora and RHEL systems, the address range used by default for the docker0 interface is 172.17.0.0/16.

By running a container with the --net=host option, the container does not use a separate network interface within the container. Instead, processes run inside the container can interact directly with the network interfaces on the host system.

For example, with a container named myrhel-tools running the rhel-tools SPC image, I run the docker exec command to look inside the container. From there, I can use the ip command to see the physical network interface card on the host (ens3) and the docker0 network interface from within that container:

```
# docker exec -it myrhel-tools /bin/bash
# ip addr show
...
2: ens3: <BROADCAST,MULTICAST,UP,LOWER_UP> mtu 1500 qdisc...
    link/ether 52:54:00:22:e7:55 brd ff:ff:ff:ff:ff:ff
    inet 192.168.122.224/24 brd 192.168.122.255 scope global...
       valid_lft 2658sec preferred_lft 2658sec
    inet6 fe80::5054:ff:fe22:e755/64 scope link
       valid_lft forever preferred_lft forever
3: docker0: <BROADCAST,MULTICAST,UP,LOWER_UP> mtu 1500... state UP
    link/ether 56:84:7a:fe:97:99 brd ff:ff:ff:ff:ff:ff
    inet 172.17.42.1/16 scope global docker0
       valid_lft forever preferred_lft forever
    inet6 fe80::5484:7aff:fefe:9799/64 scope link
       valid_lft forever preferred_lft forever
```

Still inside the myrhel-tools container, I start the tcpdump -i command to listen on the docker0 interface. Then, from another container on the host (not necessarily an SPC), I try to install an RPM package. Because the SPC has access to the host's docker0 interface in this example, it can see packets from the other container being sent to request software from the `fedoraproject.org` site:

```
# tcpdump -i docker0
Utcpdump: verbose output suppressed, use -v or -vv for full...
listening on docker0, link-type EN10MB (Ethernet),...
17:59:30.332411 ARP, Request who-has atomic711.example.com
  tell 172.17.0.10, length 28
17:59:30.332455 ARP, Reply atomic711.example.com is-at 56:84:7a:fe:97:99
(oui Unknown), length 28
17:59:30.332465 IP 172.17.0.10.52036 > 192.168.122.1.domain:
  17163+ A? mirrors.fedoraproject.org. (43)
17:59:30.332747 IP 172.17.0.10.52036 > 192.168.122.1.domain:
  12722+ AAAA? mirrors.fedoraproject.org. (43)
17:59:30.472971 IP 192.168.122.1.domain > 172.17.0.10.52036:
  17163 9/0/0 CNAME wildcard.fedoraproject.org., A 152.19.134.142,
  A 66.135.62.187, A 67.219.144.68, A 209.132.181.15,...
```

Accessing Host Inter-Process Communications

A private inter-process communication (IPC) namespace is created for a container when it starts up, by default. By setting the `--ipc=host` option to `docker run`, the container uses the host's IPC environment (semaphores, message queues, and shared memory). If instead of `host` you set `--ipc=` to the name of another container, you can access the IPC environment of that container.

To work with the IPC environment on the host from within an SPC (with `--ipc=host` enabled), you can use the `ipcs` (to get IPC information), `ipcmk` (to create IPC resources), or `ipcrm` commands (to remove a shared memory ID, message queue, or semaphore set).

Accessing Host File Systems

Opening mount table access to the host is a bit different from opening other privileges from a container. One of the primary features of a container is that it maintains its own file system so the commands you run within that container have everything they need to start the containerized applications.

In the case of an SPC, however, you often want commands to run that are inside the container (and not available on the host). You then want those commands to act on files within the host's file system. For example, you might want commands run from the container to check the host's configuration files, log files, or devices.

To deal with the issue of an SPC wanting to look at both the file system within the container and the one on the host system at the same time, SPCs can mount the host file system on the /host directory inside the container. This is done using the -e HOST=/host option.

In anticipation of containers becoming more popular, some basic Linux administrative commands have been modified to be container aware. So, for example, if you run an sosreport command inside an SPC, that command uses /host as the root of the file system it queries (to gather configuration data only from the host's file system) and not the root file system (/) within the container itself.

Again, keep in mind that the -e HOST=/host option and other privileged options just described break down boundaries between containers and the host. You should not use these options carelessly in a production environment, since it gives a container the capability to gain access to other containers running on the host, as well as to the host itself.

As I mentioned, you can use these options directly with the docker run command. To use privileged features more effectively, however, consider installing an Atomic Host system and using the atomic command to install and run SPCs, as described in the upcoming sections.

Preparing to Use Super Privileged Containers

To try the SPCs in this chapter, I use a RHEL Atomic system. You can follow the instructions in Chapter 2, "Setting Up a Container Run-Time Environment," for getting and running a RHEL Atomic Host system. If you don't have a RHEL subscription, you can get an evaluation copy of RHEL Atomic Host or run the procedures on a Fedora Atomic Host.

The SPCs described in this chapter are made particularly to run on Atomic Host systems. Although you can start and use SPCs by adding options to docker run commands, an easier way to run SPCs is with the atomic command.

Using the atomic Command

The docker command is an excellent tool for manually working with an individual container. To automate how a container runs and connects into a host system, other tools are being developed to work with Docker-formatted containers. One such tool is the atomic command, which comes with Atomic Hosts for Fedora, RHEL, and CentOS.

The `atomic` command was created to install and run containerized applications on Atomic Host systems. To use `atomic`, you run that command with one of the following arguments:

- **`install`**: Pulls the selected container image to the local system. When you run this command, you can also specify a different image and container name to be assigned to the saved image. This option essentially does the same thing as a `docker pull` command.

- **`info`**: Gets information about a selected container image to help identify what it contains, where it is from, and how it is run. If the container is not on the local system, `atomic` tries to pull the image from any enabled repository.

- **`run`**: Runs the selected container using the command line identified on the LABEL RUN line inside the container image. If you add your own command to the `atomic run` command line, settings on the LABEL RUN line are ignored.

- **`uninstall`**: Uninstalls the container image from the local system. It does the uninstall based on the contents of the LABEL UNINSTALL line within the container.

- **`update`**: Pulls the latest version of the selected image from a repository to replace the current version.

The `atomic` command is especially useful for running SPCs. That's because `atomic` can read Docker metadata identified inside the container itself to open up the namespaces needed to run a container with privileges to act on the host system.

After starting up a RHEL Atomic Host system and logging in, here are some examples of `atomic` commands you can run to work with SPCs in particular. For these examples, I use the `rhel-tools` container, which I describe in detail later in this chapter.

NOTE

The `rhel-tools` container image is about 1G in size, so make sure you have enough space available on your Atomic Host to store that container image, plus any other container software you have on your system.

Installing an SPC Image with `atomic`

To pull the `rhel-tools` SPC to your RHEL Atomic system, you can use the `atomic install` command as follows (from a RHEL or Fedora system):

```
# atomic install rhel7/rhel-tools
Trying to pull repository registry.access.redhat.com/rhel7/rhel-tools
9a8ad4567c27: Pulling image (latest) from registry.access.redhat.com/
rhel7/rhel-9a8ad4567c27: Pulling image (latest) from registry.access.
redhat.com/rhel7/rhel-9a8ad4567c27: Download complete
Status: Downloaded newer image for registry.access.redhat.com/rhel7/
rhel-tools:latest
```

To check that the image is now available to your local system, type the following:

```
# docker images | grep rhel-tools
REPOSITORY                                       TAG       IMAGE ID
    CREATED              VIRTUAL SIZE
registry.access.redhat.com/rhel7/rhel-tools 7.1-9   9a8ad4567c27
    9 weeks ago       994.8 MB
registry.access.redhat.com/rhel7/rhel-tools latest  9a8ad4567c27
    9 weeks ago       994.8 MB
```

The image (9a8ad4567c27) is tagged with both the "latest" tag and a tag indicating the RHEL release in which the container image was built.

Getting Information about an SPC Image with `atomic`

To see information about this or any container built to use with the `atomic` command, run the `atomic info` command. This information is displayed only for SPCs and other images that have been prepared for use with the `atomic` command. This example shows information for the `rhel-tools` container:

```
# atomic info rhel7/rhel-tools
RUN          : docker run -it --name NAME --privileged --ipc=host
               --net=host --pid=host -e HOST=/host -e NAME=NAME
                 -e IMAGE=IMAGE -v /run:/run -v /var/log:/var/log
                 -v /etc/localtime:/etc/localtime -v /:/host IMAGE
Name         : rhel7/rhel-tools
Build_Host   : rcm-img01.build.eng.bos.redhat.com
Version      : 7.1
Architecture : x86_64
Release      : 15
Vendor       : Red Hat, Inc.
BZComponent  : rhel-tools-docker
Authoritative_Registry: registry.access.redhat.com
```

You can see from the output from `atomic info` that you can treat container images in ways that are similar to how you treat RPM or Deb software packages. This information lets you see who produced the image, the build host, version information, and architecture and release information. The RUN line shows the actual `docker` command that runs if you launch the container image without adding any other options to `atomic run`. I describe those options later.

Running an SPC Image with `atomic`

The `atomic run` command starts up the selected container and lets it continue running in the background. It does that by reading the LABEL RUN value inside the container and executing the complete `docker` command line included in that value. If the image includes no LABEL RUN value, `atomic run` falls back to a default behavior I describe later.

Typically, you pass two arguments to the `atomic run` command: the name you choose for the running container (`--name=`) and the name of the image (in this case, `rhel7/rhel-tools`). Here's an example using `atomic run` to start the `rhel-tools` SPC:

```
# atomic run --name myrhel-tools rhel7/rhel-tools
docker run -it --name myrhel-tools --privileged --ipc=host --net=host
--pid=host -e HOST=/host -e NAME=myrhel-tools -e IMAGE=rhel7/rhel-tools
-v /run:/run -v /var/log:/var/log -v /etc/localtime:/etc/localtime -v
/:/host rhel7/rhel-tools

#
```

You can see the `docker` command line launched by `atomic`. Notice that the container name and image name you passed to `atomic` are included in the `docker` command. The default action is to open a bash shell inside the container.

With the bash shell open inside the container, any commands you type at this point are run from within the container. But because the container has many host features open at this time, it might be hard to tell that you are inside the container.

Try typing the following from inside the container:

```
# ls /
bin    dev   home   lib     media   opt    root   sbin   sys   usr
boot   etc   host   lib64   mnt     proc   run    srv    tmp   var
# ls /host
bin    dev   home   lib64   mnt   ostree   root   sbin   sys       tmp   var
boot   etc   lib    media   opt   proc     run    srv    sysroot   usr
# exit
```

The /host directory should have shown up inside the SPC. Listing the contents of the /host directory (ls /host) you should see the root of the host file system, which should include the /ostree directory (in the case of a RHEL Atomic Host system). You can continue running any commands you want within the container. When you are done, type exit to exit the container and return to a shell on the host system.

Instead of just opening a shell, you can run the SPC with any command you choose. For example, the man command is not included on a RHEL Atomic Host, so you cannot read man pages about the docker command from the host. However, both the man command and the docker man pages are in the rhel-tools container. So, to see the Docker man page, you could type the following:

```
# atomic run rhel7/rhel-tools man docker
DOCKER(1)              APRIL 2014                    DOCKER(1)
NAME
   docker - Docker image and container command line interface
SYNOPSIS
       docker [OPTIONS] COMMAND [arg...]
DESCRIPTION
   docker  has two distinct functions. It is used for starting the
Docker daemon and to...
```

Stopping and Restarting an SPC with `atomic`

When you are done using a container that has a shell open to it, you can simply type exit to leave. For a container running in the background that you started with the atomic run command, you can stop the container with the docker stop command. For example:

```
# docker stop myrhel-tools
```

The docker command just shown stops the running container but doesn't automatically remove it (unless the image's RUN LEVEL value includes the --rm options for docker). If you want to use that same container image, you can restart it using the docker start command:

```
# docker start -i myrhel-tools
```

The container (not the original image) is started again and ready to use.

Updating an SPC Image

After a while, new versions of an SPC image may become available. To update the rhel-tools image with the **atomic** command, type the following:

```
# atomic update rhel7/rhel-tools
Trying to pull repository registry.access.redhat.com/rhel7/rhel-tools ...
9a8ad4567c27: Download complete
Status: Image is up to date for registry.access.redhat.com/rhel7/
➥rhel-tools:latest
```

Uninstalling an SPC Image

If you are done using the SPC image, you can remove it using the `atomic uninstall` command. For example, to remove the `rhel-tools` image from your system, you type the following:

```
# atomic uninstall rhel7/rhel-tools
```

Running `atomic uninstall` can do more than just remove the image from the local system. In some cases, `atomic uninstall` runs a script to change or remove files on the host system, presumably to get things back the way they were before the SPC was installed. You can see if there is an uninstall action defined using `atomic info` on the SPC.

Now you have seen descriptions of privileged options you can run with the `docker` command, as well as how those options are used with the `atomic` command. Next, I describe several SPCs available for RHEL Atomic to use to administer and otherwise work with a RHEL Atomic or Fedora Atomic Host.

TRYING SOME SPCS

In the Red Hat container registry (`registry.access.redhat.com`), you can find several SPCs designed specifically to add functionality to RHEL Atomic Host systems. If you plan to deploy containers into large enterprise environments, these SPCs can help you drop a range of troubleshooting and monitoring tools into your deployed containers.

Expect more SPCs to be available in the near future to allow you to add functionality to host computers running Docker-formatted containers. For the moment, if you have a RHEL Atomic or RHEL 7 host (which are, by default, configured to pull from the Red Hat container registry), you can try out the SPCs described in this section. These containers are also available on Fedora Atomic Hosts, without needing to point to an additional registry.

The SPCs described here include

- **RHEL tools container** (`rhel-tools`): Includes many tools for troubleshooting and debugging issues on your host systems

- **System logging container (`rsyslog`)**: Includes the `rsyslogd` daemon and configuration files for gathering and redirecting log messages to selected files or log hosts
- **System monitor container (`sadc`)**: Includes the system activity data collector (`sadc`), which monitors and gathers system activity data. It also includes other software from the sysstat package, including commands for displaying the gathered data, such as the `sar` command

Running the RHEL Tools SPC

The `rhel-tools` container is the Swiss army knife of SPCs. It contains nearly 400 commands that are not on a RHEL Atomic Host system. The aim is to include as many useful tools as possible inside the container for troubleshooting and otherwise checking on the host system. If tools are missing, you can add more software packages to the container with the `yum` command.

To get the right options to run `rhel-tools` as an SPC with Docker, you should run it with the `atomic` command, as illustrated previously throughout the "Using the `atomic` Command" section. No particular configuration is needed to use the container.

Here are examples of commands and features that the `rhel-tools` container adds to your ability to work with a RHEL Atomic system:

- **Documentation**: To save on space, all documentation was removed from RHEL Atomic Host. The `rhel-tools` container makes documentation available to the host by including documentation stripped from the `/usr/share/doc` directory, man pages, and info text. In particular, you can find man pages related to containers for components such as `docker` and Kubernetes (`kubectl` command).
- **Networking diagnostic tools**: Common tools for diagnosing networking problems were added to the `rhel-tools` container, including `tcpdump`, `tcpslice`, `netsniff-ng`, and `nfsiostat`.
- **Application debugging tools**: The `rhel-tools` container adds commands for debugging applications, such as the `strace`, `stap` (Systemtap run-time tool), and `ltrace` commands.
- **Block device troubleshooting tools**: Tools in the `rhel-tools` container for examining, monitoring, and fixing problems with block devices include `blkiomon`, `blkparse`, `blktrace`, `blkrawverify`, and `verify_blkparse`.

Hundreds of other commands are in the `rhel-tools` container as well. Some of the commands in the `rhel-tools` container have been modified to know that they are being run within a container. For example, when the `sosreport` command is run from within a container, it knows to use `/host` as the root of the file system instead of `/`, so it gathers data from the host system and not the container's file system.

Running the Logging (`rsyslog`) SPC

By adding the `rsyslog` container to an Atomic Host system, you can provide a central location for gathering log messages from the host system or from the containers on that system. To install the `rsyslog` container, type the following:

```
# atomic install rhel7/rsyslog
Trying to pull repository registry.access.redhat.com/rhel7/rsyslog ...
b5168acccb4c: Download complete
Status: Downloaded newer image for registry.access.redhat.com/rhel7/
➥rsyslog:latest
docker run --rm --privileged -v /:/host -e HOST=/host -e IMAGE=rhel7/
➥rsyslog -e NAME=rsyslog rhel7/rsyslog /bin/install.sh
Creating directory at /host//etc/pki/rsyslog
Installing file at /host//etc/rsyslog.conf
Installing file at /host//etc/sysconfig/rsyslog
```

In the case of the `rsyslog` container image, the `atomic install` command does more than just download the image. It also runs a script (`/bin/install.sh`) that sets up files the container needs to run. In particular, it shares configuration files between the container and the host system (such as `/etc/rsyslog.conf` and `/etc/sysconfig/rsyslog`) so you can work with the files from the host, but run the `rsyslogd` daemon from within the container.

With the container downloaded and installed, you can run the container image as follows:

```
# atomic run rhel7/rsyslog
docker run -d --privileged --name rsyslog --net=host -v /etc/pki/
rsyslog:/etc/pki/rsyslog -v /etc/rsyslog.conf:/etc/rsyslog.conf -v
/etc/rsyslog.d:/etc/rsyslog.d -v /var/log:/var/log -v /var/lib/rsyslog:
/var/lib/rsyslog -v /run/log:/run/log -v /etc/machine-id:/etc/machine-id
-v /etc/localtime:/etc/localtime -e IMAGE=rhel7/rsyslog -e NAME=rsyslog
--restart=always rhel7/rsyslog /bin/rsyslog.sh
36739324e1e1dd918aa2c93765a9de9201c43d816d71e2e5c16c80c5e38ea9c5
```

If you look at the `docker` command line that runs for this container, you can see the last option run a `/bin/rsyslog.sh` script, which starts the `rsyslogd` daemon with the proper options. The `rsyslogd` service runs in the background as a daemon process (`-d`), and several files and directories from the host are bind mounted inside the container (`/etc/rsyslog.conf`, `/etc/rsyslog.d/`, `/var/log/`, `/var/lib/rsyslog/`, and others).

Privileges are opened to the container from the host with the `--privileged` option, and the container can see the host's network interfaces (`--net=host`). The `restart=always` option ensures that the container is restarted when the system reboots.

To review information about this SPC, you can use the `atomic info` command as follows:

```
# atomic info rhel7/rsyslog
RUN     : docker run -d --privileged --name NAME --net=host
          -v /etc/pki/rsyslog:/etc/pki/rsyslog
          -v /etc/rsyslog.conf:/etc/rsyslog.conf
          -v /etc/rsyslog.d:/etc/rsyslog.d -v /var/log:/var/log
          -v /var/lib/rsyslog:/var/lib/rsyslog
          -v /run/log:/run/log -v /etc/machine-id:/etc/machine-id
          -v /etc/localtime:/etc/localtime -e IMAGE=IMAGE
          -e NAME=NAME --restart=always IMAGE /bin/rsyslog.sh
Name         : rsyslog-docker
Build_Host   : rcm-img04.build.eng.bos.redhat.com
Version      : 7.1
Architecture : x86_64
INSTALL      : docker run --rm --privileged -v /:/host -e HOST=/host
               -e IMAGE=IMAGE -e NAME=NAME IMAGE /bin/install.sh
Release      : 3
Vendor       : Red Hat, Inc.
```

Notice that a different `docker` command line is used when you install the image and run the image (RUN line). Other information displayed by `atomic info` shows the RPM-like information about the container, such as the system where the container was built (Build_Host), the RHEL version (7.1), and the architecture it is built for (x86_64).

To check whether the `rsyslogd` service is working, run the `logger` command from the host system and send a message you can check for with the `journalctl` command:

```
# logger "Testing that rsyslog is boffo"
# journalctl | grep boffo
Apr 27 22:43:32 node1 root: Testing that rsyslog is boffo
```

To see and possibly change how log messages are directed, you can edit the `/etc/rsyslog.conf` file on the host system. Keep an eye on the disk space being consumed in the `/var/log` directory on the host.

Running the System Monitor (`sadc`) SPC

The sysstat software package, which includes the `sar` and `iostat` commands, along with the `sadc` tool for monitoring system performance, has been around since the old UNIX days. That package contains the standard set of tools for doing ongoing monitoring of system performance of various components (network interfaces, block devices, CPU usage, and so on). Adding the `sadc` container to your RHEL Atomic Host lets you gather and display performance data for your host system.

From a RHEL Atomic Host system, using the `atomic install` command you can pull the `sadc` container from the RHEL registry and install it on the local system as follows:

```
# atomic install rhel7/sadc
Trying to pull repository registry.access.redhat.com/rhel7/sadc ...
1a97a9cc4d1b: Download complete
Status: Downloaded newer image for registry.access.redhat.com/rhel7
➥/sadc:latest

docker run --rm --privileged --name sadc -v /:/host -e HOST=/host
➥-e IMAGE=rhel7/sadc -e NAME=name rhel7/sadc /usr/local/bin/
➥sysstat-install.sh
Installing file at /host//etc/cron.d/sysstat
Installing file at /host//etc/sysconfig/sysstat
Installing file at /host//etc/sysconfig/sysstat.ioconf
Installing file at /host//usr/local/bin/sysstat.sh
```

Besides pulling the `sadc` container, you can see that several configuration files and scripts are installed on the host system to support the container when it runs. With the `atomic info` command, you can see the full `docker run` command lines used when the container image is installed (INSTALL) and run (RUN):

```
# atomic info rhel7/sadc
RUN : docker run -d --privileged --name NAME
      -v /etc/sysconfig/sysstat:/etc/sysconfig/sysstat
      -v /etc/sysconfig/sysstat.ioconf:/etc/sysconfig/sysstat.ioconf
      -v /var/log/sa:/var/log/sa -v /:/host -e HOST=/host
      -e IMAGE=IMAGE -e NAME=NAME --net=host --restart=always
      IMAGE /usr/local/bin/sysstat.sh
Name         : sadc-docker
License      : GPLv3
Build_Host   : rcm-img05.build.eng.bos.redhat.com
Version      : 7.1
Architecture : x86_64
INSTALL      : docker run --rm --privileged --name NAME -v /:/host
               -e HOST=/host -e IMAGE=IMAGE -e NAME=name IMAGE
               /usr/local/bin/sysstat-install.sh
```

```
Release        : 3
Vendor         : Red Hat, Inc.
UNINSTALL      : docker run --rm --privileged -v /:/host -e HOST=/host
                 -v /var/log:/var/log -e IMAGE=IMAGE -e NAME=NAME
                 IMAGE /usr/local/bin/sysstat-uninstall.sh ;
                 docker rm -f sadc
```

If you are ready to use the `sadc` container, start it with the `atomic run` command as follows:

```
# atomic run rhel7/sadc
docker run -d --privileged --name sadc -v /etc/sysconfig/sysstat:/etc/
sysconfig/sysstat -v /etc/sysconfig/sysstat.ioconf:/etc/sysconfig/
sysstat.ioconf -v /var/log/sa:/var/log/sa -v /:/host -e HOST=/host
-e IMAGE=rhel7/sadc -e NAME=sadc --net=host --restart=always rhel7/
sadc /usr/local/bin/sysstat.sh
c02b44ce7e4494571a7da13113a47873fd80d8d38201cbdb1e6c898c7df5caca
```

Once the `sadc` container is running, it is ready to start collecting system data. Data collection is started from the crond service on the host, from the `/etc/cron.d/ sysstat` file. Take a look at the contents of that file:

```
# Run system activity accounting tool every 10 minutes
# Customized for sadc container
*/10 * * * * root docker exec -d sadc /usr/lib64/sa/sa1 1 1
# 0 * * * * root /usr/lib64/sa/sa1 600 6 &
# Generate a daily summary of process accounting at 23:53
# Customized for sadc container
53 23 * * * root docker exec -d sadc /usr/lib64/sa/sa2 -A
```

Based on the contents of this file, you see that system activity data are gathered every 10 minutes and a daily report is generated at 11:53PM every night. If you are familiar with the sysstat software package, you will notice that this file has been modified to run the `sadc` tool with a `docker exec` command.

To change how data are gathered, you can modify that `/etc/cron.d/sysstat` file. Refer to the `sadc` and `crontab` (section 5) man pages for information on the format of that file. Because you are on a RHEL Atomic system with no man pages, however, you can use the `rhel-tools` container to read the man page:

```
# docker run --rm rhel7/rhel-tools man 5 crontab
```

To view the system activity data, you can use the `sar` command from within the container. For example:

```
# docker exec -it sadc sar
Linux 3.10.0-229.1.2.el7.x86_64 (node1)   04/28/15  _x86_64_   (1 CPU)
08:57:15     LINUX RESTART
09:00:01   CPU   %user   %nice   %system   %iowait   %steal   %idle
09:10:02   all   1.53    0.00    1.07      0.62      0.01     96.78
09:20:02   all   0.78    0.00    0.87      0.67      0.01     97.68
09:30:01   all   0.81    0.00    0.93      0.72      0.01     97.53
09:40:01   all   1.29    0.00    1.43      1.34      0.01     95.93
Average:   all   1.10    0.00    1.08      0.84      0.01     96.98
```

As development of the Atomic project continues, expect to see more SPCs such as rhel-tools, rsyslog, and sadc become available to monitor, troubleshoot, and manage Atomic Host systems.

SUMMARY

Because of the way container run-time operating systems, such as RHEL Atomic, are designed, they don't contain every tool you might want for managing and repairing those systems. For the Atomic project, this issue is dealt with by using super privileged containers (SPCs).

SPCs let you easily add and remove software from a lean, container-oriented operating system. You can create SPCs by adding options to the docker run command. However, several SPCs have been created for RHEL Atomic Hosts that can be managed by a special atomic command.

The atomic command sets options to docker run that define exactly which privileges and namespaces open on the host. It also does such things as copy files to the host and mount directories from the host to the container when the container is installed.

Three examples of SPCs are illustrated in this chapter. The rhel-tools container lets you add many troubleshooting and maintenance commands to an Atomic Host. The rsyslog container adds a logging facility to a host. The sadc container adds the sysstat package to collect system activity data from the host system.

The tools you can run from SPCs in your cloud-deployed Atomic Host systems make it possible to fix and monitor the container-based operating systems you have running in the cloud. The next chapter helps you understand different tools you can use to build your own SPCs, as well use other tools for deploying containers in cloud environments.

## CHAPTER 14

Managing Containers in the Cloud with Cockpit

IN THIS CHAPTER:

- Understand how Cockpit manages container-oriented operating systems
- Install and start Cockpit
- Add servers for Cockpit to manage
- Work with containers in Cockpit
- Configure networking and storage in Cockpit
- Use Cockpit tools to add user privileges and open Terminal windows

Once you have become comfortable starting up an Atomic, Fedora, RHEL, or other operating system to run your containers on, you might find yourself with multiple systems running in a cloud environment or on a virtualization host. Managing those systems individually can become a burden. Instead of using tools such as `ssh` to do remote login to each system, you can use a tool such as Cockpit to manage multiple systems from one interface.

Cockpit provides a web-based user interface for managing Fedora, RHEL, Atomic, and similar Linux systems. Because it includes tools for monitoring individual containers, as well as groups of containers orchestrated with Kubernetes, Cockpit is particularly good at managing systems deployed specifically for containerized applications. However, Cockpit also includes some nice features for doing general system management.

If working directly from a Linux command line has been a challenge for you so far in this book, I have good news for you. Cockpit is designed to discover and work with complex technologies, such as Docker containers and Kubernetes clusters, with an easy-to-use, point-and-click interface.

In this chapter, I demonstrate how to run Cockpit from a Fedora system. Through a single Cockpit interface, you can then add as many of your container-oriented systems as you want (running Atomic, RHEL, or Fedora) to monitor, start, stop, and otherwise work with containers on those systems.

NOTE

Cockpit is still in its early stages of development. The fact that it is not yet at version 1.0 is an indication that there is still more work to be done to make it stable. I show it here so that you can get a sense of the type of simple front-ends being developed to manage your individual or clustered containers. As the underlying container features continue to solidify, you can expect Cockpit and similar tools to make it easier to use them.

UNDERSTANDING COCKPIT

Cockpit runs as a service that listens for requests on TCP port 9090. To use the service, you simply open a web browser to port 9090 on the system where Cockpit is running and log in as an administrative user (usually just the root user at first).

When you first log in as root, you can assign Server Administrator privileges to other users with accounts on the system running Cockpit. Or you can just start working with Cockpit as the root user.

Once you are logged in to Cockpit, you are ready to start monitoring the local system for a variety of features. You can also add other systems to monitor. To do that, you simply provide the hostname (or IP address), administrative user name (such as root), and the password for that user.

If you have pushed Atomic, Fedora, Red Hat Enterprise Linux, or similar systems out to a cloud or to a host running virtual machines (such as a Linux KVM environment), you can watch over all those systems and the containers running on them from a single Cockpit dashboard. From Cockpit, you can select the system you want to view and then see the following types of information from a column on the left:

- **System**: Monitor the resource consumption on the selected system from this tab. General information identifies the type of hardware, BIOS, hostname, and other basic information. You can watch progressive use of CPU, memory, network traffic, and disk I/O resources. Figure 14.1 shows an example of the System tab for a Red Hat Enterprise Linux system installed directly on Dell hardware; Figure 14.2 is an example of Fedora installed in a KVM virtual machine.

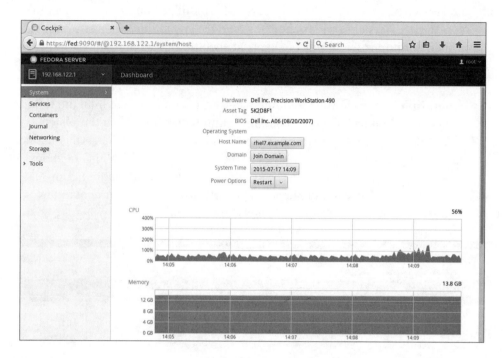

FIGURE 14.1 Cockpit displaying information on a RHEL 7 host on Dell hardware.

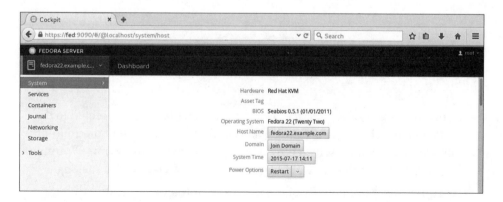

FIGURE 14.2 Cockpit displaying a Fedora virtual machine on a KVM host.

- **Services**: From the Services tab, you can see all the systemd assets on the selected host. For the selected system, you can see which of the enabled and disabled system services are currently running. You can also select to see Targets (sets of services), Sockets (service communications end points), Timers (unit files for setting of events at specific times), and Paths (unit files associated with actions to take when files/directories are accessed) configured on the system.

- **Containers**: Manage your containers for the selected system from the Containers tab. You can see each container running or stopped on the system. Consumed and available storage space is shown on a slider bar. All container images on the system are displayed in the Images box, which also includes a button to pull new images to the system (Get New Image button). This tab also provides a live view of memory and CPU usage from your containers. Figure 14.3 shows an example of the Containers tab.

FIGURE 14.3   View and manage containers from Cockpit's Containers tab.

- **Journal**: As a systemd service, Docker error messages are directed to the systemd journal. You can view Docker journal messages from the Journal tab. Messages can be selected by date or level of severity (Errors, Warnings, Notices, or All). Select any message for a detailed view of that message.

- **Networking**: View activity of the network interfaces associated with the selected host. Figure 14.4 shows the network interfaces for a physical computer that has multiple network interfaces. The docker0 interface provides network access to the containers on the system. There are two physical network cards (enp11s0 and enp12s2), one of which is active and providing access to external networks. Because the system is running virtual machines, the virbr0 network interface is defined as the virtual machine network by default. Network send and receive traffic is displayed at the top of the tab, while networking journal entries are at the bottom.

FIGURE 14.4   View and change network interfaces on the Cockpit Networking tab.

- **Storage**: Monitor the available disk space and disk usage on the selected host from the Cockpit Storage tab. If you need more storage, you can create RAID devices or volume groups from this tab as well. Each available disk is displayed, allowing you to mount, unmount, format, delete, or change file system options for each disk partition. Journal messages from storage-related services (such as udiskd and smartd) are displayed at the bottom of the tab.

- **Tools**: Tools for managing the system are listed under the Tools tab. For RHEL systems, the Subscriptions tab lets you see how the system is subscribed to Red Hat. Select Administrator Accounts to choose an existing user account on the system and optionally add Server Administrator or Container Administrator roles to that user account. Select Terminal to open a shell on the selected system as the user with which you are logged in to Cockpit.

As you can see, Cockpit provides a good set of features for managing operating systems being used to run containers. Cockpit is under active development at the moment. The current set of features, described in this chapter, help you track and work with individual containers on Atomic, RHEL, Fedora, and CentOS systems. I describe some of the new Cockpit features just being developed for managing sets of containers orchestrated with Kubernetes in Chapter 16, "Creating a Kubernetes Cluster."

STARTING WITH COCKPIT

The cockpit package is currently available on Fedora and Red Hat Enterprise Linux systems. This section describes how to install and run Cockpit on Fedora, but the same procedure works on Red Hat Enterprise Linux (provided that you have a RHEL system that has a proper subscription).

1. **Install Fedora**: Install the latest version of Fedora available (for this example, I use Fedora 22).

2. **Install cockpit package**: As root user (or using `sudo`), install the cockpit package (along with some dependent packages) as follows:

   ```
   # yum install cockpit -y
   ```

3. **Start the cockpit socket**: Type the following commands to enable and start Cockpit:

   ```
   # systemctl start cockpit.socket
   # systemctl enable cockpit.socket
   ```

4. **Open Cockpit in a browser**: Open a browser window from any system that has access to the system running Cockpit and go to port 9090 on that system. For example, if Cockpit were running on the local host, you could type the following into your location box:

   ```
   https://localhost:9090
   ```

   For this example, I use a host that is accessible via the hostname fedora22 (`fedora22.example.com:9090`). Figure 14.5 shows an example of the Cockpit login screen from that host.

NOTE

If the system on which you are running Cockpit has an active firewall that is blocking access to ports on the system, you need to open TCP port 9090. To do this temporarily on a host whose firewall is based on iptables, you could run the following command to open TCP port 9090. If the port is accessible after running this command, check your system's documentation on how to open that port on the firewall permanently:

```
# iptables -A INPUT -p tcp -m tcp --dport 9090 -j ACCEPT
```

FIGURE 14.5 Access the login screen from port 9090 on the Cockpit system.

5. **Log in to Cockpit**: Log in to Cockpit using the root login on the Cockpit system or another user with Server Administrator privilege to Cockpit. If the system running Cockpit is also running Docker, you can immediately begin working with containers on that system. If not, the next thing you want to do is select the button to start Docker and add one or more Docker systems that you want to work with into Cockpit.

ADDING SERVERS INTO COCKPIT

With the Cockpit web UI displayed from your browser, you can begin adding Docker containers to Cockpit. Follow these steps to add container server systems to Cockpit:

1. **Open the Dashboard**: Select the Dashboard tab at the top. You should see scrolling information on system resource usage and a list of servers at the bottom of the screen (there may just be the local system at the moment).

2. **Add the server**: Select the Add Server button (+) on the Servers tab and fill in the hostname or IP address of the server. If the new server uses the same

credentials (username and password), leave the Log in with My Current Credentials box checked. Otherwise, uncheck it. Then click Next.

3. **Add credentials**: From the Add Host pop-up (if it appears), enter the user name and password needed to access the new server. This should be a privileged user (such as root). Then click Next.

4. **Add host**: If the server can be found and accessed with the credentials, the host's address and fingerprint are displayed. If that looks correct, select the Add Host button. Figure 14.6 shows an example of the Cockpit Dashboard after two additional servers have been added to the fedora22 host, one by IP address (192.168.122.1) and one by hostname (rhel7.example.com).

FIGURE 14.6 Add servers you want to monitor on the Cockpit Dashboard.

By selecting any of the servers listed on the Dashboard, you can begin managing those servers through Cockpit, along with managing any containers running on those systems.

WORKING WITH CONTAINERS FROM COCKPIT

From the Containers tab in Cockpit, you can begin working with containers on the selected system. Any images or running containers already on the system appear on the Containers area. If you want to start adding your own images and running containers, you can do those tasks directly from Cockpit.

Adding Container Images to Cockpit

From the Containers tab, select the Get New Image button. Type in a search term to search any registries enabled from that system (at least the Docker Hub Registry and possibly others). Figure 14.7 shows an example of a search for an image named cricket/hangman.

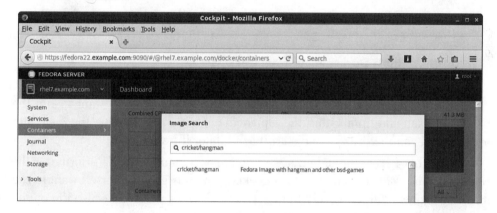

FIGURE 14.7 Search for images to download from the Cockpit Containers tab.

Select the image you want from the search results and click Download to begin downloading the image to the selected server. The image you download appears in the list of Images on the Containers tab.

Running Images from Cockpit

Once you have downloaded an image to a server being managed by Cockpit, you can run that image from Cockpit as well. Find the image you want under the Images heading on the Containers tab and select the play button associated with that image. A Run Image pop-up appears, ready to run that image, as shown in Figure 14.8.

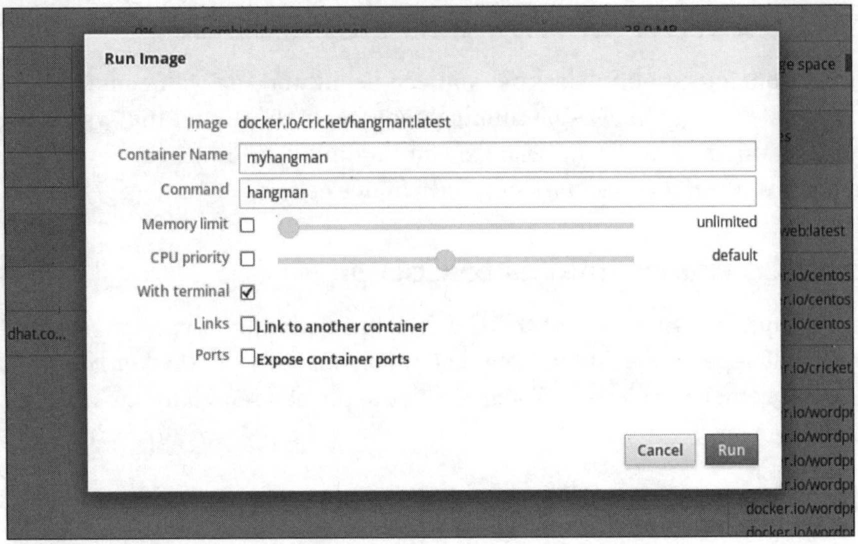

FIGURE 14.8 Run a Docker image from Cockpit.

The example in Figure 14.8 is a simple one. In this case, I want to run the hangman command from within the hangman container. By naming the container myhangman, I can recognize it and start it again later if I want to.

Notice that I have the option of setting memory limits or CPU priority for the container. The With Terminal box is checked, which is good because I want to run the hangman game interactively from a Terminal window. There is also the option to link the container to another container or expose ports from the container to the host.

If running the image is successful (essentially doing a docker run), the new, running container should appear on the Containers tab under the Containers heading. By selecting that container's name, you can see information about the container, manage the container, and work with the container from a Terminal window (assuming you ran the container that way). Figure 14.9 shows an example of the myhangman container I created, running hangman in a Terminal window within Cockpit.

Besides, in this case, being able to play a game of hangman from the displayed Terminal window, you can also work with the container in the following ways:

- **Stop, Start, and Restart**: Buttons on the page for the container let you stop the container (docker stop), start it (docker start), and restart it (docker restart).

- **Commit**: To save the container in its current state back as an image, you can select to stop it (Stop button) and then select the Commit button. You are prompted to provide a Repository name, Tag, Author, and Command to run from the image. The saved container image then appears in your Images list.

- **Delete**: Once a container is stopped, you can select the Delete button to delete it completely from the system. You can select Delete while the container is still running, but you are prompted to force a delete of the container.

- **Change Resource Limits**: As the container is running, you can change memory limits and CPU priority. Select the Change Resource Limits button and move the sliders representing Memory and CPU accordingly.

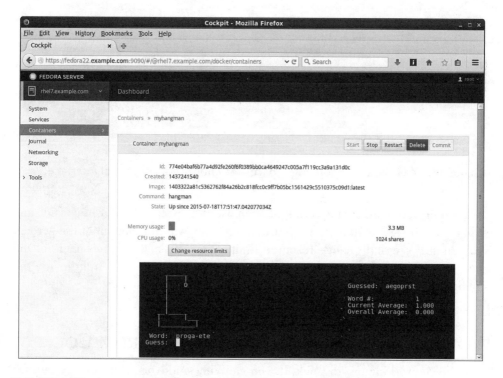

FIGURE 14.9 Interact with a running container from Cockpit.

If you are running a container image as a service, a Terminal interface is probably not required. By unchecking the With Terminal box, you can run a container image without opening a Terminal window to interact with the container. For example, Figure 14.10 shows a running web server container without a Terminal open to display standard output from the application.

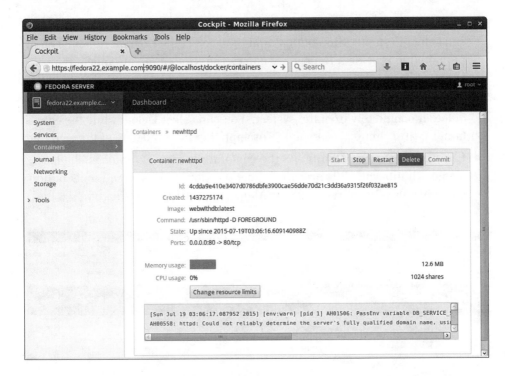

FIGURE 14.10 Containers running services may not need a Terminal interface.

Even though there isn't a Terminal open with this web service, you can see any output from the application displayed in a log window at the bottom of the screen. You can still see and change resource limits. You can also see the name of the image that generated the container and the fact that TCP port 80 from inside the container is mapped to port 80 on all network interfaces on the host.

WORKING WITH NETWORK INTERFACES FROM COCKPIT

From the Networking tab in Cockpit, you can view and work with all the network interfaces on the selected system. You can watch spikes in your network traffic as data packets are sent and received across those network interfaces. Figure 14.11 shows the network interfaces for a physical computer running a Red Hat Enterprise Linux system.

In Figure 14.11, the RHEL system is running the Docker service as well as running as a KVM host system (allowing the computer to run virtual machines). These facts are reflected in the docker0 and virbr0 network interfaces. The machine also has two physical network interface cards (NICs). The enp11s0 NIC is currently active and provides connectivity to the outside world. The enp12s2 NIC is inactive at the moment.

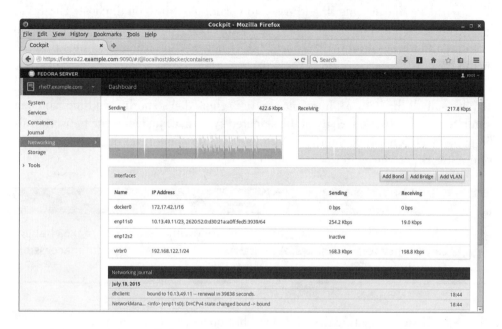

FIGURE 14.11 View and change network interfaces from Cockpit.

Select docker0 to see more details about that interface. From the Networking screen that appears for docker0, you can see that the IP address for the host system on the docker0 network is 172.17.42.1/16. As containers are started up, they are assigned addresses on the 172.17.0.0 network. From this screen, you can turn the docker0 bridge off or delete it (something you probably don't want to do).

One thing you might want to do to the docker0 interface is change the IP address on this interface if it conflicts with other IP addresses in use. You can make that change by selecting the Configure button for the IPv4 address associated with the docker0 interface on the host.

By selecting the active, physical NIC (enp11s0), I can see the type of NIC associated with the interface (Broadcom) and its MAC address. The Status shows the IP address associated with the interface and how it was set (in this case, via DHCP). The Carrier line shows that it is a 100Mbps NIC and that it connects to the network automatically upon boot. As with the docker0 interface, you can change the IP address for the enp11s0 interface if you want (although in this case, the NIC is receiving its IP address from a DHCP server).

The network interface on the virbr0 bridge is the last network interface to note in this example. By default, on RHEL systems configured to do KVM virtualization, the libvirtd service assigns IP addresses to virtual machines on the host. The KVM host itself is assigned the IP address of 192.168.122.1 and is able to give out up to 253 other addresses on the 192.168.122.0/24 network to virtual machines running on the host.

The Networking tab provides a way to get a detailed view of the setup and activities of all the network interfaces on the selected system. In real time, you can watch the total network activity of the selected system, or just view the network traffic of a selected network interface. You can also do some level of configuration of your network interfaces in Cockpit, such as

NOTE

Think carefully before using any of the following features to make changes to your network interfaces. A mistake could make your system inaccessible from the network.

- **Add Bond**: Selecting the Add Bond button allows you to bond together multiple network interfaces under the same IP address. You can choose the bonding mode, such as Round Robin (where network traffic to the address is divided across all the bonded NICs), Active Backup (where NICs are ready to take over if the primary NIC fails), and other bonding modes.
- **Add Bridge**: Choosing the Add Bridge button lets you add a bridge to an existing network interface so that the new bridge can use the existing network interface directly, without having to route to that interface.
- **Add VLAN**: Selecting the Add VLAN button lets you add a virtual LAN to your system.

Even though some of the networking features are not directly related to Docker containers, being able to watch over all the network interfaces on a system can offer a great way to see where potential bottlenecks are. At a glance, it can also show you the IP addresses assigned to the selected system's network interface, which can help you determine whether there will be conflicts with other IP addresses and ranges in use on your network.

CONFIGURING STORAGE FROM COCKPIT

Being able to see the storage configuration on the operating systems running your containers can help you to head off problems that can occur from running out of disk space. The Storage tab in Cockpit lets you not only see the file systems created on your selected server system, but also change those file systems or add new ones.

Figure 14.12 shows an example of the file systems and other storage information for a simple virtual machine server.

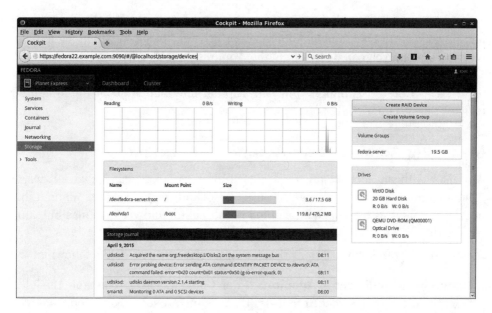

FIGURE 14.12 Display and change file systems on the selected server in Cockpit.

In Figure 14.12, under Drives you can see that there is a 20GB VirtIO Disk providing storage for the system. Most of that drive (19.5GB) is assigned to the fedora-server LVM volume group. Under the Filesystems heading, the root file system is configured to use 17.5GB of space from the logical volume /dev/fedora-server/root. The /boot file system is on a separate partition (/dev/vda1), consuming the remaining 500MB of disk space not in the fedora-server volume group.

If you attach an additional hard disk to the system you are viewing (either physically or by attaching network storage, such as iSCSI), that drive appears under the Drives heading. You can select that disk and then choose to format it, create file systems on it, and mount it.

Using buttons on the Storage tab, you can use existing disk space to create special types of storage. Select the Create RAID Device button to join together two or more disk partitions to form any of several different types of RAID device. Select the Create Volume Group button to create LVM physical volumes, volume groups, and logical volumes out of existing disk partitions.

Doing Other Administrative Tasks in Cockpit

Several other tasks can be done in Cockpit from selections under the Tools heading. If you want to grant Server Administrator privilege to a user with a login to the selected system, you can do that from the Administrator Accounts selection. Under Tools, you can also open a Terminal window to the selected system or (in the case of Red Hat Enterprise Linux) view subscription information about the system or register the system with Red Hat.

Managing Administrator Accounts in Cockpit

Any user with an account on the system running Cockpit can be given Server Administrator privilege to change settings on Cockpit server systems. Without that privilege, a user with an account can log in to Cockpit and view settings but can't change them.

To add Server Administrator privilege for a selected user, do the following:

1. **Select Administrator Accounts**: From Cockpit, select Tools from the left column and then select Administrator Accounts. A set of boxes representing users on the system appears, along with a Create New Account button.

2. **Select User**: Select the box identifying the user you want to give Server Administrator privilege to. If the user does not exist yet, you can select Create New Account to create a new user account for the system.

3. **Change Roles**: Select the Change Roles button. From the pop-up window that appears, select the Server Administrator box and click Change to assign the new privilege to that user.

Once the privilege has been assigned, the user can log in to Cockpit and begin working with available Server systems from the Cockpit interface. If the user does not have a password yet, you can set the password for any existing user from the Accounts screen for that user.

Open a Terminal in Cockpit

Not everything that you might want to do to manage containers and other system resources is available through Cockpit. You may find that you want to build a container from a Dockerfile or use options with the `docker` command that are not available through the Cockpit user interface. In those cases, Cockpit makes it easy for you to open a Terminal window to a selected server.

To open a Terminal window to any of the servers you have added to your Cockpit interface, start by selecting the server you want to access. To do that, select the Machines list from the upper-left corner of the Cockpit window and choose the system you want. Next select Tools and Terminal.

Using the credentials assigned to that server, Cockpit opens a Terminal window on the Cockpit screen and logs you in to that system. Figure 14.13 shows an example of a Terminal window open to a Fedora Atomic system after running a few commands:

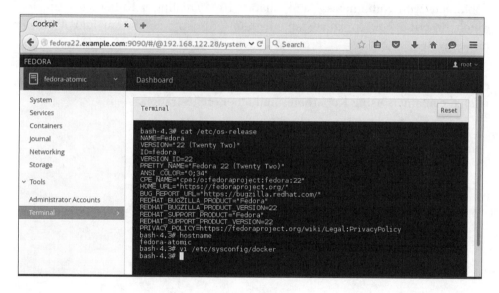

FIGURE 14.13 Run commands directly on a server from a Cockpit Terminal.

In the example shown in Figure 14.13, I displayed the `os-release` file to see what release the system is running. To check the name of the system, I ran the `hostname` command. After that, I wanted to change some settings for the Docker daemon, so I edited the `/etc/sysconfig/docker` file to modify how the Docker service on my system uses registries.

SUMMARY

As you create more and more systems for running containers, you might find those systems spanning multiple physical computers and cloud environments. Managing each of those systems can become tedious without a centralized way of managing them. Cockpit provides a new way of managing multiple container-oriented operating systems from a single web browser user interface.

Although still in early development phases, you can now use Cockpit to manage containers and images, as well as the underlying storage and networking interfaces associated with them. At the moment, Cockpit lets you manage systems based on Fedora, Red Hat Enterprise Linux, and Project Atomic Hosts.

This chapter stepped you through many of the uses of Cockpit for managing container-oriented operating systems and the containers that run on them. More advanced uses of Cockpit for orchestrating containers with Kubernetes are still in development. To learn more about those features, see Chapter 15, "Orchestrating Containers with Kubernetes," and Chaper 16, "Creating a Kubernetes Cluster," which describe how to create an all-in-one-Kubernetes system and a cluster, respectively.

So far, this book has focused on creating and using individual Docker containers. The next part of this book leads you into the practice of managing multiple related containers using Kubernetes and other orchestration.

Part IV

Managing Multiple Containers

## CHAPTER 15

Orchestrating Containers with Kubernetes

IN THIS CHAPTER:

- Understand Kubernetes
- Set up Kubernetes master and node on one system
- Start and manage pods in Kubernetes

Big Internet companies such as Google, Twitter, and eBay have been deploying applications in containers for years. While the Docker container format provides an elegant solution for building applications as microservices, it does not include everything required to deploy and manage many containers that need to work together and scale up as demand rises.

As each of these companies started creating its own tools for developing, deploying, managing, and scaling containerized applications, they realized that the job was too big for even the largest companies to take on alone. With some people building their own proprietary container management tools and different open source projects starting up to solve problems in different ways, the fledgling container movement was under a serious threat of becoming fragmented.

Enter Google and the Kubernetes project. Google released Kubernetes as an open source project with an aim at standardizing how containerized applications are managed. Kubernetes would act as an overlay on top of a company's data center, and open source projects could work on solving other aspects of container management (such as creating streamlined operating systems or graphical administration tools).

In July 2015, Kubernetes reached the 1.0 milestone, indicating that the project was ready to be used in production. With Kubernetes 1.0, Google also formed the Cloud Native Computing Foundation (CNCF). Created as a collaborative project in association with the Linux Foundation (http://collabprojects.linuxfoundation.org), CNCF has gotten off to a strong start. Companies joining the CNCF include Red Hat, eBay, AT&T, Cisco, IBM, Intel, Twitter, Mesosphere, VMware, and others.

The goal of this chapter is to take you through the features of Kubernetes and describe how it can enhance the entire experience of deploying Docker formatted containers in the data center. Becoming involved with the Kubernetes project gives you the opportunity to use the same tools that the largest, most successful companies deploying containers use today.

UNDERSTANDING KUBERNETES

Creating a single container to run for your own personal use doesn't require many resources or much planning. You can just start up the Docker service and run a few `docker` commands to get going. Creating containers that you need to rely on to provide your most critical applications in a secure, reliable, upgradable, and scalable way, brings a new set of challenges. For example, how do you do the following:

- Deploy an application that includes multiple services (such as a web server, database server, and authentication server) that you want to keep in separate containers but still interact with each other.

- Keep track of the services a container provides so another container knows where to find the services it needs (such as a web server that wants to know where the database is that provides the data it needs).

- Configure your system to bring up additional containers if a container crashes or if demand exceeds the capacity of existing containers.

- Centrally manage containers that run across a set of host systems.

- Move containers to other host systems so you can bring down a host for maintenance.

Kubernetes (https://github.com/GoogleCloudPlatform/kubernetes) in many ways presents a new way of thinking about creating and managing applications from development to production. Here are some ways in which Kubernetes could not only change the way in which you manage containers, but also change the whole way you look at data centers:

- **Operating in Devops model**: Kubernetes seeks to be part of a larger Devops movement, where closer communications between application developers and IT staff can make continuous deployment possible, without causing major disruptions in the data center. In the Devops model, software developers take greater responsibility for putting together all the software an application needs, rather than relying on system administrators to install compatible components on the host system.

- **Creating common sets of services**: Today, applications often ask for a service from another application by pointing to an IP address and port number. With Kubernetes, you can define containerized applications that provide services that are available for other containers to use. Kubernetes handles the details of making the connections between the container providing the service and the one asking for it. Groups of services can be defined by sets of labels.

- **Making host computers more generic**: Instead of configuring operating systems differently for the applications it runs, host computers would be more generic. So each organization within a company wouldn't have its own set of computers to deploy and maintain. Instead, an organization's services would run on the same pool of physical machines that everyone else in the company is using but be kept separate from the services of other organizations by using a different set of labels.

- **Stabilizing the data center**: Kubernetes aims to create consistent application programming interfaces (APIs) that result in stable environments for running containerized applications. Developers should be able to create applications that work on any cloud provider that supports those APIs. This reliable framework means that developers can identify the version of Kubernetes along with the services they need and not have to worry about the particular configuration of the data center.

Granted, much of the development that needs to be done to make these intentions real is still in its early stages. I want to lay out the goals here, however, so you can see the aims of Kubernetes and how those aims are intended to fit into the future of container-driven data centers. That said, I also want to show you what you can do with Kubernetes today.

The next sections describe features in Kubernetes that you can be using right now.

STARTING WITH KUBERNETES

While Docker manages entities referred to as *images* and *containers*, Kubernetes wraps those entities in what it refers to as *pods*. A pod can hold one or more containers and is the unit that Kubernetes manages. There are several advantages that Kubernetes brings to managing containers as pods over managing containers directly with Docker:

- **Multiple nodes**: Instead of just deploying a container on a single computer, Kubernetes can deploy a set of pods across multiple nodes. Essentially, a node (previously referred to as a minion) provides the environment where a container runs.

- **Replication**: Kubernetes can act as a replication controller for a pod. This means that you can set how many of a specific pod should be running at all times. Kubernetes starts more if more are needed to meet the replication number you defined.

- **Services**: The word "service" is used in many different computing contexts. In regards to Kubernetes, it means that you can assign a service name (ID) to a particular IP address and port, and then assign a pod to provide that service. Kubernetes keeps track of the location of that service internally, so Kubernetes knows how to direct any requests from another pod for that service to the correct address and port.

If you choose to set up Kubernetes yourself, as described in the next two chapters, you should understand the following concepts before you get started:

- **Kubernetes master**: A Kubernetes master acts as a controller from which you deploy and manage pods, replication controllers, services, nodes, and other components of a Kubernetes environment. To create a Kubernetes master, you need to set up and run systemd services that include etcd, kube-api-server, kube-controller-manager, and kube-scheduler. Commands for starting these services are described later in this chapter.

- **Kubernetes nodes**: A Kubernetes node (previously called a minion) provides the environment where containers actually run. To run as a Kubernetes node, a computer must be set up to run systemd services that include docker, kube-proxy, and kubelet services. These services, described later in this chapter, are required to run on each node in the Kubernetes cluster.

- `kubectl` **command**: Most Kubernetes administration is done on the master using the `kubectl` command. With `kubectl`, you can create, get, describe, or delete any of the resources that Kubernetes manages (pods, replication controllers, services, and so on).

- **Resource files (YAML or JSON)**: When you create a pod, replication controller, service, or other resource in Kubernetes, the `kubectl` command expects the information needed to create that resource to be in one of two types of structures: YAML or JSON formats. Examples of resource files in these formats are provided later in this chapter.

The best way to see how Kubernetes works is to configure one or more systems to run Kubernetes. For demonstration purposes, I create two different Kubernetes configurations (one in this chapter and one in the next):

- **Kubernetes all-in-one**: A simple all-in-one Kubernetes system has both master and node features running on the same host. This configuration lets you try out Kubernetes to see how it works but is not appropriate in production.

- **Kubernetes cluster**: A Kubernetes cluster has a master and should have at least two nodes, each running on separate systems. This is a configuration you could build on for production use by adding nodes as you need to increase capacity.

There are several different ways to get Kubernetes software to try out. Most importantly, you want to start with a Linux system that is following the ongoing development of Kubernetes. You can then deploy Kubernetes in any of these ways:

- Creating virtual machines on which to install Kubernetes
- Installing Kubernetes directly to hardware
- Using a virtual machine deployment tool, such as Vagrant (which could run a Linux virtual machine on Linux, MacOS, or Windows)
- Trying Kubernetes from a cloud provider

 NOTE

Refer to the "Creating a Kubernetes Cluster" page (https://github.com/GoogleCloudPlatform/kubernetes/blob/release-1.0/docs/getting-started-guides/README.md) for different ways of deploying and using a Kubernetes cluster.

For both examples of setting up Kubernetes in this book, I use Fedora 22 as the operating system. I installed Fedora 22 on virtual machines, but you can install it on bare metal if you prefer. In this chapter, I describe how to set up an all-in-one Kubernetes configuration, where all master and node features are on the same system.

Setting Up an All-in-One Kubernetes Configuration

To try out a Kubernetes configuration where Kubernetes master and node features are all available on a single system, I'm going to have you install Fedora 22. You can do this in a virtual machine or on bare metal. Here's what you do:

1. **Get Fedora**: Download and install a copy of the latest version of Fedora. The Fedora distribution is available from https://getfedora.org/. Media for either a workstation or server installation should work fine. I used a Fedora 22 workstation medium and installed from that medium.

2. **Install Fedora**: Install a single Fedora system. Kubernetes does not require that you have a desktop interface installed. It is fine to work from the command line. However, I did a basic server plus desktop install so I have the convenience of working from the desktop.

3. **Update Fedora**: To make sure you have the latest software, run the following command as root user:

   ```
   # yum update
   ```

4. **Reboot**: Once the updates are complete, reboot the Fedora system.

   ```
   # systemctl reboot
   ```

After the Fedora system comes back up, you are ready to start installing Kubernetes.

Installing and Starting Up Kubernetes

The kubernetes packages and related software are available from the basic Fedora repository without requiring any special configuration. However, to get the latest version of Kubernetes available, I recommend that you enable the update-testing repository. Here's how to enable that repository to install kubernetes and then begin configuring it.

WARNING

While using the update-testing repository gets the latest available Kubernetes software, this software may also be unstable. If you find that to be the case, uninstall kubernetes and reinstall without the `--enablerepo=updates-testing` option.

1. **Enable repo and install Kubernetes**: On the Fedora system, install Kubernetes from the update-testing repository:

   ```
   # yum install -y --enablerepo=updates-testing kubernetes etcd
   ```

   When I tested this, the resulting packages installed included kubernetes, kubernetes-master, kubernetes-node, kubernetes-client, etcd, and several other packages. The version of the kubernetes packages was 1.1.0.

2. **Turn off firewalld**: You need to have iptables installed for Kubernetes to work (`yum install iptables` if it is not there). However, since Kubernetes relies heavily on firewall rules for communicating between its components, I recommend that you turn off any competing firewall managers. Run these commands to make sure firewall features are inactive and disabled (if the iptables service is enabled on your system, disable that as well):

   ```
   # systemctl stop firewalld
   # systemctl disable firewalld
   ```

3. **Configuring master and node services**: Normally, you configure Kubernetes on the master and nodes in a way that tells them how to communicate together. Those configuration files are `/etc/etcd/etcd.conf` and files in the `/etc/kubernetes` directory. However, because most master and node services are set up by default to look for each other on the local host, that information doesn't need to be added to this all-in-one system.

   There is one change I suggest you make, however, to simplify launching a single pod. That is to edit the `/etc/kubernetes/apiserver` file and remove "ServiceAccount," from the KUBE_ADMISSION_CONTROL line. This allows you to bypass the ServiceAccount feature for a simple pod deployment. The next two lines show the original line (commented out) and the current line with ServiceAccount missing:

   ```
   #KUBE_ADMISSION_CONTROL="--admission-control=NamespaceLifecycle,
   NamespaceExists,LimitRanger,SecurityContextDeny,ServiceAccount,
   ResourceQuota"
   KUBE_ADMISSION_CONTROL="--admission-control=NamespaceLifecycle,
   NamespaceExists,LimitRanger,SecurityContextDeny,ResourceQuota"
   ```

4. **Starting master services**: To start up the services needed on a Kubernetes master and check that they are running, run the following commands:

```
# MSERVICES="etcd kube-apiserver kube-controller-manager
➥kube-scheduler"
# systemctl restart $MSERVICES
# systemctl enable $MSERVICES
# systemctl is-active $MSERVICES
active active active active
# systemctl is-enabled $MSERVICES
enabled enabled enabled enabled
```

5. **Starting node services**: To start up the services needed on a Kubernetes node and check that they are running, run the following commands:

```
# NSERVICES="kube-proxy kubelet docker"
# systemctl restart $NSERVICES
# systemctl enable $NSERVICES
# systemctl is-active $NSERVICES
active active active
# systemctl is-enabled $NSERVICES
enabled enabled enabled
```

6. **Check Kubernetes**: Run these commands to make sure your all-in-one Kubernetes system is ready to act as a node and begin running pods.

```
# kubectl describe node 127.0.0.1
Name:   127.0.0.1
Labels: kubernetes.io/hostname=127.0.0.1
CreationTimestamp:   Sun, 23 Aug 2015 12:05:23 -0400
...

# kubectl get node
NAME        LABELS                                STATUS    AGE
127.0.0.1   kubernetes.io/hostname=127.0.0.1      Ready     9m
```

With the master and node services running locally, you can now try out your Kubernetes configuration by starting up a pod.

Starting Up a Pod in Kubernetes

To illustrate how to make a pod in Kubernetes, I create a simple yaml file. The attributes of that file are as follows:

- The yaml file is a Pod type, as indicated by the kind label.
- When you create the pod (kubectl create command), it starts up one instance of a web server and one instance of a database server. Because I am only running one instance of the pod, a Kubernetes ReplicationController is not needed to start up multiple instances of the pod.

- Since only one node is defined (the local system), the containers start and run on the local system.

- There is no Kubernetes `Service` defined for either the web server or database server. So, to make the services running from the pod accessible, the web server exposes TCP port 80 on the local host, while the database server exposes port 3306 on the local host.

- If either container is killed, Kubernetes starts another instance of that container to take its place.

Follow these steps to define the pod and create it on your Kubernetes all-in-one system:

1. **Define pod yaml file**: The yaml file I create to define the pod is named `web-db.json`. If you copy this file to use this pod definition, be sure to maintain the indents. Also, as long as you have a connection to the Internet, you don't have to do anything special to get the containers it includes. The two container images are pulled from the Docker Hub when you create the pod. Here are the contents of the file:

```
apiVersion: v1
kind: Pod
metadata:
  name: web-db-pod
  labels:
    app: web-db-pod
spec:
  containers:
  - name: mywebdock
    image: "cricket/webdock"
    ports:
      - containerPort: 80
        hostPort: 80
  - name: mydbdock
    image: "cricket/dbdock"
    ports:
      - containerPort: 3306
        hostPort: 3306
```

The apiVersion must match the version of Kubernetes you are using (`v1` in this case). The "kind" of Kubernetes file is a Pod. The pod itself is named `web-db-pod`.

Two container images are used here: the `mywebdock` (from the image named `cricket/webdoc`) and another named `mydbdock` (from the image named `cricket/dbdock`). The `mywebdock` container exposes its service from TCP port 80 to the same port on the host system. The `mydbdock` container exposes TCP port 3306, also to the same port on the host system.

2. **Create pod**: With the content just described stored in a file named `web-db.json` in the current directory on your all-in-one Kubernetes system, start up the pod by typing the following:

```
# kubectl create -f web-db.json
pod "web-db-pod" created
```

3. **Check that the pod is running**: Using the `kubectl` command, you can check the status of the pod. In this case, there are two containers in the pod and both are running:

```
# kubectl get pod
NAME            READY       STATUS     RESTARTS    AGE
web-db-pod      2/2         Running    0           4m
```

4. **Check that the containers are running**: Use the `docker ps` command to verify that the containers are running:

```
# docker ps
CONTAINER ID  IMAGE           COMMAND            CREATED
  STATUS          PORTS     NAMES
eb79b0b640b8  cricket/dbdock  "/usr/bin/mysqld_saf  2 minutes ago
  Up 2 minutes              k8s_mydbdock.8c4ff0af_web-db-pod_default...
675532380c4d  cricket/webdock "/usr/sbin/httpd -D  2 minutes ago
  Up 2 minutes              k8s_mywebdock.65b9f0d7_web-db-pod_default...
b6fd829685d4  gcr.io/goog...  "/pause"            2 minutes ago
  Up 2 minutes 0.0.0.0:80->80/tcp, 0.0.0.0:3306->3306/tcp
                            k8s_POD.e80f0b79_web-db-pod_default...
```

From the `docker ps` output, you can see that the `dbdock` container image started up the `mysqld_saf` command and that it has been running for 2 minutes. Likewise, the `webdock` image is running the `httpd` command. Kubernetes started up its own container, which, as you can see, maps TPC ports 80 and 3306 to those same ports on the local system.

5. **Check that the application is working**: With the two ports exposed on the local system, you can use the `curl` command to query the web server container on port 80. The default web page for the web server (index.html) contains a "Web server check is successful" message. A script on the web server called action in the `cgi-bin` directory returns "Docker is cool" and "DB is working" messages if web server is able to communicate with the database. Here are examples of those commands:

```
# curl localhost:80
Web server check is successful
# curl http://localhost:80/cgi-bin/action

<html>
<head>
<title>My Application</title>
```

```
</head>
<body>
<h2>Docker is cool</h2>
<h2>DB is working</h2>
</body>
</html>
```

To make the output look nicer, you can type the URLs into the location box on your web browser.

Working with Kubernetes

With one pod (consisting of two containers) running on your all-in-one Kubernetes master and node, you can get a feel for how Kubernetes works and how you can expand beyond this simple example.

One thing to keep in mind is that creating a Kubernetes pod means that you want the containers in that pod to persist. So, if a container from the pod is killed, a new one starts up to replace it. Here is an example:

```
# docker ps | grep dbdock
CONTAINER ID   IMAGE           COMMAND              CREATED
  STATUS         PORTS   NAMES
eb79b0b640b8   cricket/dbdock  "/usr/bin/mysqld_saf  20 minutes ago
  Up 20 minutes          k8s_mydbdock.8c4ff0af_web-db-pod_default...
# docker kill eb79b0b640b8
34ea12d147de
# docker ps | grep dbdock
CONTAINER ID   IMAGE           COMMAND              CREATED
  STATUS         PORTS   NAMES
a1268d5d4603   cricket/dbdock  "/usr/bin/mysqld_saf  2 seconds ago
  Up Less than a second k8s_mydbdock.8c4ff0af_web-db-pod_default_...
```

Within a few seconds of killing the container, a new container is launched automatically by Kubernetes to replace the dbdock container that was killed. Notice that the container has a new container ID.

If something was wrong with the container and it did not come back up again, you could delete the pod and try to fix the container (or the image launching the container) before creating the pod again. For example:

```
# kubectl delete pod web-db-pod
pod "web-db-pod" deleted
# kubectl get pod
NAME        READY    STATUS    RESTARTS    AGE
# docker ps
```

```
CONTAINER ID   IMAGE   COMMAND   CREATED   STATUS   PORTS   NAMES
# kubectl create -f web-db.json        Fix pod and create again
pod "web-db-pod" created
```

Notice that after the pod is deleted, the pod no longer appears when you type `kubectl get pod`. Also, all containers associated with the pod are killed. After you make any corrections to the pod or its containers, run `kubectl create` again to recreate the pod.

Deleting the pod is a good idea if one of the containers in that pod refuses to start up. When I first created my web server container, there was a problem with it that allowed it to start originally when the pod was created but fail if Kubernetes tried to restart the container after it was killed. If that is the case, the container continues to try to restart every 10 seconds. The result is a massive amount of error message sent to your log facility and a list of many failed containers when you type `docker ps -a`.

Summary

This chapter illustrated a simple example of Kubernetes master and node features running on the same system. After starting up both Kubernetes master and node services locally, you deployed a pod on the local system that included two containers. With those two containers running, you could see how the two containers access each other through ports exposed on the host system.

The primary command for managing Kubernetes features is the `kubectl` command. In this chapter, you saw how to use `kubectl` to create pods, check that a pod is running, and delete pods when you are done. You also saw how when a container in a pod is killed, Kubernetes tries to restart the container to replace it while the pod is still active.

This chapter provided an introduction to a few basic features of Kubernetes. However, to realize the full potential of Kubernetes, you need to scale out beyond your local system and take advantage of other features I haven't touched on yet.

Kubernetes was meant to allow you to include hundreds of nodes in a Kubernetes cluster. The Kubernetes master was intended to be able to start and manage many pods of containers across those nodes and keep a defined number of replicas of those containers running at all times.

In the next chapter, I expand the coverage of Kubernetes in this book to describe features for deploying pods on multiple nodes, creating multiple replicas of containers across those nodes, and using Kubernetes services to simplify how containers find the connections they need to other containers.

## CHAPTER 16

Creating a Kubernetes Cluster

IN THIS CHAPTER:

- Understand how to use a Kubernetes cluster
- Build a Kubernetes cluster with a master and two nodes
- Deploy replication controllers, services, and pods on your cluster
- Delete replication controllers, services, and pods when you are done

To understand the scope of what Kubernetes can do to deploy, manage, and scale containers, you need to go beyond an all-in-one Kubernetes system (described in Chapter 15, "Orchestrating Containers with Kubernetes") and set up a Kubernetes cluster. A Kubernetes cluster that you can use as the foundation for a larger infrastructure to manage containers should consist of at least three systems to start with:

- **One master**: The Kubernetes master deploys and manages pods of containers, as well as the services, replication controllers, and other resources that need to be managed in Kubernetes.

- **Two or more nodes**: Nodes are where the pods are deployed. By setting up at least two Kubernetes nodes, the master system can load balance the workload across those nodes. If one node needs to go down, one of the other nodes can be assigned to run the pods.

This chapter is devoted to setting up a three-system Kubernetes cluster. Along the way, I describe in detail the services and features of each of those systems. Then I show you different ways of using this cluster.

Understanding Advanced Kubernetes Features

Now that you have deployed a pod on an all-in-one Kubernetes master and node system, it's time to start expanding into the more advanced features of Kubernetes. With a Kubernetes cluster with multiple nodes where containers can run, the features of Kubernetes become more useful.

With multiple nodes available for running containers, you can use features of Kubernetes that weren't really that useful when you had only one system for both the master and node. For example:

- **Scale up**: As demand rises, you can use replication controllers to add more replicas of each pod. As the nodes reach their capacity, you can add more nodes and continue to scale up.
- **Extend services across nodes**: Kubernetes can keep track of where services are being provided across all the nodes. When a container requests a service, Kubernetes can direct that request to the pod providing that service that is most available on any node.
- **Distribute storage**: Using distributed storage, containers can run on any node on which that distributed storage is available.

Because many of the methods of using distributed storage with Kubernetes are still in the works, this chapter focuses on features for scaling your use of containers and extending how containers are deployed across multiple nodes.

The next section helps you set up a Kubernetes cluster.

Setting Up a Kubernetes Cluster

To set up this Kubernetes three-system cluster, I use three virtual machines with Fedora 22 installed. Either a workstation or server installation works fine. Once Fedora is installed, you can install the packages and start up the services needed on each system as described in the following procedure. The following versions of Kubernetes, Docker, and etcd were used in this procedure:

- kubernetes-master-1.1.0
- kubernetes-node-1.1.0
- kubernetes-client-1.1.0
- etcd-2.0.13
- docker-1.7.1

Step 1: Install Linux

Follow these steps to install Linux:

1. **Install Linux**: On each of the three virtual machines (or you can use bare metal systems if you prefer), install Fedora 22. This procedure should generally work on other Linux distributions as well, but may need some modifications.

2. **Set up NTP**: It is important that time be in sync between the three systems. So, on all three systems, you can enable the network time protocol when you select the time zone during Fedora installation. That starts up the chronyd service and syncs with public time servers at pool.ntp.org. No further work is required unless you want to use your own time servers or use ntpd instead of chronyd for your time service.

3. **Set up DNS**: Make sure that all three systems can reach each other by name and IP address. You can either add each system to a DNS server (which is preferable) or just add the names and IP addresses of the systems to each system's /etc/hosts file. If you were to add each system to /etc/hosts, here is what the entries in that file might look like:

```
192.168.122.11        master
192.168.122.87        node1
192.168.122.170       node2
```

4. **Turn off firewall**: Because Kubernetes makes extensive use of iptables port forwarding rules to help pods communicate, you should turn off any competing firewall services that may be running on all three of your systems. In Fedora, the default firewall service is firewalld. Because that service is enabled by default, you need to disable it and stop the service by typing the following:

```
# systemctl stop firewalld
# sytemctl disable firewalld
```

Step 2: Set Up Kubernetes Master

Log in to the Kubernetes master system (root user or a user with sudo privileges) to install the packages and set up the systemd services needed by the Kubernetes master. In this process you enable and start the following services:

- **Kubernetes master data store (etcd) service**: The etcd systemd service stores the configuration data for your Kubernetes cluster. By default, etcd data are stored in the /var/lib/etcd directory. The etcd service includes watch support, which allows any changes in Kubernetes components to be noticed quickly and responded to.

- **Kubernetes scheduler (kube-scheduler) service**: When a pod has not yet been scheduled for deployment, the kube-scheduler service binds any unscheduled pods to available nodes.

- **Kubernetes API server (kube-apiserver) service**: Nodes don't communicate directly with the etcd database but instead make requests to the Kubernetes API server service. The kube-apiserver validates and processes REST operations before updating those objects in the etcd object store.

- **Kubernetes controller manager (kube-controller-manager) service**: Features not included in other services in the Kubernetes cluster are managed by the Kubernetes Controller Manager service. These features include managing node discovery and monitoring, as well as creating and updating endpoint controllers.

The following steps describe how to install the Fedora software packages needed on the Kubernetes master, configure the needed services, and then start up those services.

1. **Install Kubernetes master packages**: To install the kubernetes-master and etcd packages on the Kubernetes master, type the following:

   ```
   # yum install -y kubernetes-master etcd
   ```

2. **Configure the etcd service**: To configure the etcd service, edit the /etc/etcd/etcd.conf file so that it appears as follows (all other lines can be commented out):

   ```
   ETCD_NAME=default
   ETCD_DATA_DIR="/var/lib/etcd/default.etcd"
   ETCD_LISTEN_CLIENT_URLS="http://0.0.0.0:2379"
   ETCD_LISTEN_PEER_URLS="http://localhost:2380"
   ETCD_ADVERTISE_CLIENT_URLS="http://0.0.0.0:2379"
   ```

3. **Configure the kube-apiserver service**: To configure the kube-apiserver service, edit the /etc/kubernetes/apiserver file. Changes to this file include

   - **KUBE_API_ADDRESS**: Change this line to listen on all addresses (0.0.0.0) instead of just on localhost.
   - **KUBE_ETCD_SERVERS**: Set this value to the location of the master server (by name or IP address) followed by the port number 2379.

- **KUBE_SERVICE_ADDRESSES**: Set the range of addresses to be used internally by Kubernetes. In this case, I use 10.254.0.0/16 to allow Kubernetes to use addresses in the 10.254 network.

- **KUBE_ADMISSION_CONTROL**: Edit this line to remove the Service-Account value and the following comma. Removing this value makes it so you don't have to configure Kubernetes users before launching a pod.

Replace the IP address shown for KUBE_ETCD_SERVERS for the hostname or IP address for your Kubernetes master server. Otherwise, you can use the following lines in your /etc/kubernetes/apiserver file (notice that the last line wraps):

```
KUBE_API_ADDRESS="--address=0.0.0.0"
KUBE_ETCD_SERVERS="--etcd_servers=http://192.168.122.11:2379"
KUBE_SERVICE_ADDRESSES="--portal_net=10.254.0.0/16"
KUBE_ADMISSION_CONTROL="--admission-control=NamespaceLifecycle,Names
paceExists,LimitRanger,SecurityContextDeny,ResourceQuota"
```

4. **Configure other Kubernetes services**: Edit /etc/kubernetes/config to change settings that relate to different Kubernetes services. Only the KUBE_MASTER line needs to change to point to the hostname or IP address of the Kubernetes master (followed by port 8080). You can leave the other settings as they are. The resulting uncommented lines should appear as follows:

```
KUBE_LOGTOSTDERR="--logtostderr=true"
KUBE_LOG_LEVEL="--v=0"
KUBE_ALLOW_PRIV="--allow-privileged=false"
KUBE_MASTER="--master=http://master:8080"
```

5. **Start master services**: On the Kubernetes master, start and enable the etcd, kube-apiserver, kube-controller-manager, and kube-scheduler services. Here's one way to do that:

```
# MSERVICES="etcd kube-controller-manager kube-scheduler kube-
apiserver"
# systemctl restart $MSERVICES
# systemctl enable $MSERVICES
# systemctl is-enables $MSERVICES
enabled  enabled  enabled  enabled
# systemctl is-active $MSERVICES
active  active  active  active
```

The Kubernetes master is now ready. Next you want to configure your two (or more) nodes.

Step 3: Set Up Kubernetes Nodes

With the services configured and running on the Kubernetes master, you can now configure the Kubernetes nodes. Log in to each of the Kubernetes nodes (root user or one with sudo privileges) to install and configure the software needed to run each Kubernetes node. In this process you enable and start the following services:

- **Kubelet (kubelet) service**: The kubelet service manages different aspects of pods on each node and communicates with the API server on the master.
- **Kube Proxy (kube-proxy) service**: The kube-proxy service manages the load balancing and network proxy features needed by Kubernetes. It does this by controlling service endpoints. Environment variables stored inside the container are used to identify these endpoints. For example, *_SERVICE_HOST and *_SERVICE_PORT variables, with the asterisk replaced by some service name, can identify the IP address and port number that the container can use to find a service.
- **Docker (docker) service**: Although not part of Kubernetes itself, the docker service must be running on each of the nodes as well, so that it can ultimately manage the containers directed to each node.

On each node, follow these steps to add the software needed on the node, configure that software, and start up the required services:

1. **Install Kubernetes node packages**: To install the kubernetes-node and docker packages on the Kubernetes nodes, type the following on each node:

   ```
   # yum install -y kubernetes-node docker
   ```

2. **Configure the Kubernetes proxy service**: No configuration is required for the kube-proxy service. However, if you did want to configure that service, you could edit the /etc/kubernetes/proxy file.

3. **Configure the Kubelet service**: To configure the kubelet service, edit the /etc/kubernetes/kubelet file. Changes to this file include

   - **KUBELET_ADDRESS**: Change this line to listen on all addresses (0.0.0.0) instead of just on localhost.
   - **KUBELET_API_SERVER**: On this line, identify the location of the API server on the master.
   - **KUBELET_ARGS**: Edit this line to add the argument "--register-node=true" to cause the system to register itself as a node with the master.

   Replace the IP address shown for KUBE_API_SERVER for the hostname or IP address for your Kubernetes master server. Otherwise, you can use the following lines in your /etc/kubernetes/kubelet file:

```
KUBELET_ADDRESS="--address=0.0.0.0"
KUBELET_API_SERVER="--api-servers=http://192.168.122.11:8080"
KUBELET_ARGS="--register-node=true"
```

4. **Configure other Kubernetes services**: Edit /etc/kubernetes/config
   to change settings that relate to different Kubernetes services. Only the
   KUBE_MASTER line needs to change to point to the hostname or IP address
   of the Kubernetes master (followed by port 8080). You can leave the other
   settings as they are. The resulting uncommented lines should appear as
   follows:

```
KUBE_LOGTOSTDERR="--logtostderr=true"
KUBE_LOG_LEVEL="--v=0"
KUBE_ALLOW_PRIV="--allow-privileged=false"
KUBE_MASTER="--master=http://master:8080"
```

5. **Start node services**: On each Kubernetes node, start and enable the kube-
   proxy, kubelet, and docker services. Here's one way to do that:

```
# NSERVICES="kube-proxy kubelet docker"
# systemctl restart $NSERVICES
# systemctl enable $NSERVICES
# systemctl is-enables $NSERVICES
enabled  enabled  enabled  enabled
# systemctl is-active $NSERVICES
active   active   active   active
```

The Kubernetes cluster should now be operational. Next you can set up networking with Flannel.

Step 4: Set Up Networking with Flannel

Flannel is a feature you can add to your Kubernetes cluster to set the IP address
ranges used internally within Kubernetes. For this example, I set the address range
10.20.0.0/16. This range allows the Kubernetes cluster to have a few hundred nodes
each running a few hundred containers without running out of IP addresses.

The steps in this section install flannel package on the master and both nodes,
upload the Flannel network configuration to etcd, configure the flanneld service,
and then start and enable the flanneld service.

1. **Install the flannel package**: On the master and both nodes, install the
   flannel package as follows:

```
# yum install flannel
```

2. **Configure flannel**: On the master, open a file for editing and call it something like kube-flannel.config. To allow Flannel to use the 10.20.0.0/16
   address range, the contents of that file should be the following:

```
{
  "Network": "10.20.0.0/16",
  "SubnetLen": 24,
  "Backend": {
    "Type": "vxlan",
    "VNI": 1
  }
}
```

3. **Add Flannel configuration to etcd**: On the master, to load the `kube-flannel.config` file to the etcd service, type the following:

```
# etcdctl set coreos.com/network/config < kube-flannel.config
```

4. **Set options to the flanneld service**: On the master and both nodes, edit the `/etc/sysconfig/flanneld` file to identify the location of the etcd service, so the flanneld service can get its configuration information to start up. In that file, change the FLANNEL_ETCD line to identify the hostname or IP address of the etcd service and the port to connect to (2379). For example:

```
FLANNEL_ETCD="http://master:2379"
FLANNEL_ETCD_KEY="/coreos.com/network"
```

5. **Start and enable flanneld**: On the master and both nodes, start the flanneld service, enable it, and check that it is working as follows:

```
# systemctl restart flanneld
# systemctl enable flanneld
# systemctl is-active flanneld
# systemctl is-enabled flanneld
```

6. **Check flannel interfaces**: If everything works properly configuring flannel, you should be able to log in to the master and both nodes and see a flannel.1 interface. On the nodes, you should also see a docker0 interface in the same address range assigned earlier to flannel. Here's an example of what the new network interfaces look like on node2:

```
# ip a | less
3: flannel.1@NONE: <BROADCAST,MULTICAST,UP,LOWER_UP>
       mtu 1450 qdisc noqueue state UNKNOWN group default
     link/ether 02:78:75:5d:71:e3 brd ff:ff:ff:ff:ff:ff
     inet 10.20.8.0/16 scope global flannel.1
       valid_lft forever preferred_lft forever
     inet6 fe80::78:75ff:fe5d:71e3/64 scope link
       valid_lft forever preferred_lft forever
  4: docker0@NONE: <BROADCAST,MULTICAST,UP,LOWER_UP>
       mtu 1500 qdisc noqueue state UNKNOWN group default
     link/ether 9e:3a:23:25:68:47 brd ff:ff:ff:ff:ff:ff
     inet 10.20.8.1/24 scope global docker0
```

You can see that the address range assigned earlier is used for both the flannel.1 and docker0 interfaces. If you don't see the new address range being used by docker0, you may have to restart the docker service or reboot. With everything in place now, it is time to start using your Kubernetes cluster to manage containers.

STARTING UP PODS IN A KUBERNETES CLUSTER

In Chapter 15, I started up two containers in a single pod. While it's possible to do that, in an enterprise environment, where you expect demand for your applications to rise and fall, you want to have more flexibility in how you deploy your containers.

In this chapter, I deploy the same two containers. Instead of putting them in a single pod, however, I have them in separate pods, defined in what are referred to as *replication controllers*.

With replication controllers, I can not only define which pod I want to start up, but I can also say how many of those pods I want to stay up all the time. When I create the replication controller, Kubernetes tries to load balance those pods so they can be deployed across the available nodes. If a container dies or is killed, Kubernetes notices and starts another one to take its place.

The following procedure describes how to create one replication controller for a database service and one for a web service. Those replication controllers define that a set number of instances of each pod they contain be running at all times. For each of those pods, I also define a service that allows other pods to access that service based on a label. It is up to Kubernetes to keep track of the actual IP addresses and port numbers that fulfill each service.

1. **Create a database controller Kubernetes service**: On the master, to create a Kubernetes service representing a database container, I create a file called `database-service.yaml` with the following contents:

```
apiVersion: v1
kind: Service
metadata:
  name: database-service
spec:
  ports:
  - port: 3306
    targetPort: 3306
    protocol: TCP
  selector:
    app: db
```

2. **Create a web server Kubernetes service**: On the master, to identify the web server pod as a Kubernetes service, I create a `web-service.yaml` file, which includes the following content:

```
apiVersion: v1
kind: Service
metadata:
  labels:
    name: web
  name: webserver-service
  namespace: default
spec:
  ports:
  - port: 80
  publicIPs:
  - 192.168.122.170
  selector:
    name: web
```

3. **Create a database server replication controller**: On the master, to set the number of database server pods to launch, I create a `database-rc.yaml` file. This replication controller definition sets two replicas of the pod to be running at all times. The pod starts the container image `cricket/dbdock`, which it can pull from the Docker Hub, if it is not already available on the node when Kubernetes sets it to run. Here's what the file contains:

```
apiVersion: v1
kind: ReplicationController
metadata:
  labels:
    name: database-controller
  name: database-controller
  namespace: default
spec:
  replicas: 2
  selector:
    selectorname: db
  template:
    metadata:
      labels:
        name: db
        selectorname: db
    spec:
      containers:
      - image: cricket/dbdock
        name: db
        ports:
        - containerPort: 3306
```

4. **Create a web server replications controller**: On the master, to set the number of web server pods to run, I create the file named web-rc.yaml. This replication controller definition sets two replicas of a pod named web to be created. That pod launches container images named cricket/webdock, which can be pulled from the Docker Hub if it's not already available on the node. One thing to note here is that the web pod "uses" definition indicates that it needs to access the db service. Here's what the file contains:

```
apiVersion: v1
kind: ReplicationController
metadata:
  labels:
    name: web-controller
  name: web-controller
  namespace: default
spec:
  replicas: 2
  selector:
    selectorname: web
  template:
    metadata:
      labels:
        name: web
        selectorname: web
        uses: db
    spec:
      containers:
      - image: cricket/webdock
        name: mywebserver
        ports:
- containerPort: 80
```

5. **Check that the nodes are ready**: On the master, before creating the services and replication controllers, check that the nodes are available to start running the pods you define. To do that, run the following:

```
# kubectl get node
NAME      LABELS                            STATUS   AGE
node1     kubernetes.io/hostname=node1      Ready    1d
node2     kubernetes.io/hostname=node2      Ready    1d
```

6. **Create the service and replication controllers**: With the service and replication controller files you just created in the current directory, type the following commands to load those definitions into the Kubernetes database. Note that services should be loaded before replication controllers that need to use those services.

```
# kubectl create -f database-service.yaml
# kubectl create -f web-service.yaml
# kubectl create -f database-rc.yaml
# kubectl create -f web-rc.yaml
```

7. **Review the services, pods, and replication controllers**: If all goes well, on the master you should be able run some kubectl commands to see the results of the services and replication controllers you just created. After that, run the docker ps command on one or both nodes to see the actual running containers:

```
# kubectl get service
NAME                 CLUSTER_IP       EXTERNAL_IP   PORT(S)    SELECTOR      AGE
database-service     10.254.244.240   <none>        3306/TCP   app=db        1m
kubernetes           10.254.0.1       <none>        443/TCP    <none>        15d
webserver-service    10.254.153.159   <none>        80/TCP     name=web      1m
# kubectl get rc
CONTROLLER           CONTAINER(S)  IMAGE(S)        SELECTOR
     REPLICAS     AGE
database-controller  db            cricket/dbdock   selectorname=db
     2            53s
web-controller       mywebserver   cricket/webdock selectorname=web
     2            48s
# kubectl get endpoints
NAME                 ENDPOINTS                       AGE
database-service     <none>                          1m
kubernetes           192.168.122.11:6443             15d
webserver-service    10.20.40.3:80,10.20.8.3:80      1m
# kubectl get pod
NAME                         READY     STATUS     RESTARTS   AGE
database-controller-3nmmd    1/1       Running    0          1m
database-controller-8lcvy    1/1       Running    0          1m
web-controller-04fi2         1/1       Running    0          1m
web-controller-5dpjb         1/1       Running    0          1m
# kubectl get endpoints
NAME                 ENDPOINTS                       AGE
database-service     <none>                          2m
kubernetes           192.168.122.11:6443             15d
webserver-service    10.20.40.3:80,10.20.8.3:80      2m
# docker ps
CONTAINER ID    IMAGE             COMMAND               CREATED
   STATUS           PORTS      NAMES
e344dcee354a    cricket/webdock   "/usr/sbin/httpd -D   5 minutes ago
   Up 5 minutes                k8s_mywebserver.be5fd5c_web-controller...
cf23d47f75a8    cricket/dbdock    "/usr/bin/mysqld_saf  6 minutes ago
   Up 5 minutes                k8s_db.78b0f953_database-controller...
0515e52602f4    gcr.io/google_containers/pause:0.8.0
                                  "/pause"              6 minutes ago
```

```
      Up  5 minutes                 k8s_POD.3ef3f8d9_web-controller...
2740ef150c6a    gcr.io/google_containers/pause:0.8.0
                                     "/pause"              6 minutes ago
      Up  6 minutes                 k8s_POD.9665f93d_database-controller...
```

8. **Review containers**: Try to get some data from the containers to see that they are working. The first `curl` command displays the contents of the index. html file on the web server. The second `curl` command runs the action script on the web server, which, if successful, displays a "Docker is cool" message obtained from the database server. You can use the IP address from the Cluster IP field output from the `kubectl service` command for the service named webserver-service.

```
# curl -L 10.20.40.3:80
Web server check is successful
# curl http://localhost:80/cgi-bin/action
<html>
<head>
<title>My Application</title>
</head>
<body>
<h2>Docker is cool</h2>
<h2>DB is working</h2>
</body>
</html>
```

If any of the containers stop working, Kubernetes tries to launch new container pods to take their places.

DELETING REPLICATION CONTROLLERS, SERVICES, AND PODS

When you are done running the replication controllers, services, and pods you set up in the previous section, you can remove them using the `kubectl` command. The order in which you use the `kubectl` command to delete your configuration matters to some extent. In general you want to run `kubectl delete` commands in this order:

- Delete replication controllers
- Delete services

You don't need to stop the containers (`docker stop`) or delete the pods (`kubectl delete pod` *podname*). In fact, if you did, the replication controller would just start them back up again. Once you delete the replication controllers, however, the pods and containers automatically are stopped and the pods deleted. Another reason for deleting replication controllers first is that if you delete the services first, if the pods rely on being able to use those services, they will stop working anyway.

Here are the commands for deleting the replication controllers and services created in the previous examples:

```
# kubectl delete rc database-controller
# kubectl delete rc web-controller
# kubectl delete service database-service
# kubectl delete service web-service
```

To check that everything is deleted, you can run `kubectl get` commands. These commands should show no pods, replication controllers, or services defined for the Kubernetes cluster:

```
# kubectl get pod
# kubectl get rc
# kubectl get service
```

Your Kubernetes cluster should be back to where it was, ready to deploy more pods.

SUMMARY

A Kubernetes cluster provides the means of deploying containers in what are referred to as pods across a set of nodes. By configuring a Kubernetes cluster (in this chapter, with one master and at least two nodes), you can see that how you use your containers can easily extend into enterprise-level computing.

Descriptions in this chapter showed you how to install software on Kubernetes master and node systems, configure systemd services that implement Kubernetes, and run pods on the nodes, using definitions of replication controllers and services. From the examples, you can see how containers are distributed across the available nodes.

Once you are done running your Kubernetes pods, the chapter showed you how to use `kubectl delete` commands to delete the replication controllers and services you added. By deleting those items, the pods and containers they started are automatically stopped.

Part V

Developing Containers

Developing Contents

## CHAPTER 17

Developing Docker Containers

IN THIS CHAPTER:

- Create container development environments
- Set up OpenShift Origin to develop containers
- Use good container development practices

Application development in containers can be looked at as part of a larger transition to a Devops software development model. Containers give developers a greater level of control of the elements an application needs to run without having to think as much about the underlying data center infrastructure. Likewise, developers can be more assured that their applications will run as they pass from development to testing and finally into production.

This chapter describes things you need to know as someone who wants to develop containerized applications. First, it lays out some development tools available for you to put in place before starting to develop applications for containers. This includes the OpenShift Origin project, which offers a web-based user interface for container development. Next, the chapter goes through recommendations for efficient container development as well as techniques for making the resulting containers easier to manage and maintain.

SETTING UP FOR CONTAINER DEVELOPMENT

Before you begin developing your own Docker containers, you should consider the tools and work environment you want to get in place. You can use prebuilt environments to begin developing your Docker containers. You also should think about how your development is set up. Some of these issues are covered in the following sections.

Choosing a Container Development Environment for Red Hat Systems

To get started developing Docker containers, you don't have to do more than make a directory on the system you have running Docker and create a Dockerfile in it. However, there are ways you can set up your development environment so that a full set of development tools is at your fingertips.

Several different Docker development environments are available to help jumpstart your experience developing Docker containers. In some cases, you can get a full, bootable virtual machine to create your Docker environment. In others, you can simply download a container that you can run to provide the set of tools you need.

Running the Red Hat Container Development Kit

To encourage developers to build and certify their applications to run on Red Hat Enterprise Linux platforms, Red Hat Inc. offers the Container Development Kit (CDK). The CDK is available in different forms to Red Hat customers, partners, and those with a Red Hat Network account. You can apply to become part of the Red Hat Developers program (which gives you access to the CDK as well as other tools) here:

```
http://developers.redhat.com
```

After you log in using the Red Hat Developer program login (or any valid Red Hat account), visit the following download page to choose to install a Vagrant box in one of several different formats:

```
https://access.redhat.com/downloads/content/293/ver=1/rhel---7/1.0.0/
x86_64/product-downloads
```

The Vagrant box you download can be used to install RHEL Server or RHEL Atomic virtual machines preconfigured to run Docker, Kubernetes, and other software useful for developing containers. A big advantage to using Vagrant in this way is that you can install those virtual machines on your personal Mac or Windows system and still have full access to the RHEL container development environment.

Here is a list of those environments, along with links to articles that describe how to use Vagrant to install the CDK virtual machines on your laptop or desktop system:

- CDK on Mac OSX (https://access.redhat.com/articles/1487693)
- CDK on Windows (https://access.redhat.com/articles/1487723)
- CDK on Fedora (https://access.redhat.com/articles/1487733)

Once you have set up the virtual machines to run the Red Hat CDK, you can log in to those virtual machines and start using them to develop and test containers. Most of the container development and deployment tools in the CDK are text-based utilities.

Running OpenShift

OpenShift provides a platform for developing open source applications using a set of graphical tools to shepherd applications through development, testing, and production. Red Hat OpenShift version 3 incorporates tools specifically geared toward providing simplified methods for creating and managing Linux containers in Docker format.

For easy ways to try out OpenShift, you can refer to the upstream project named OpenShift Origin (http://www.openshift.org/). The OpenShift Origin site offers several different ways to get the OpenShift 3 Platform to begin trying it out:

- **OpenShift in a Container (https://github.com/openshift/ origin#getting-started)**: You can begin using OpenShift as quickly as you can pull and run the OpenShift container. This container can run as a privileged container on your system, which allows you to employ that container to run OpenShift from the command line or from your browser. With either interface, you can build containers, pull in existing containers, and deploy and manage containers in pods using Kubernetes.

  By visiting the OpenShift Origin Getting Started page, you can also find links to resources that help you create containers using Source-to-Image (STI) images for specific languages. There are STI images for Ruby, Python, NodeJS, PHP, and Perl that you can use.

  The procedure for trying out OpenShift in a container from OpenShift Origin is described later.

- **OpenShift from Ansible (https://github.com/openshift/openshift-ansible)**: Using an Ansible installer, you can set up a Kubernetes cluster of containers on a local virtual machine, Fedora, or Mac OSX.

- **OpenShift from Cloud Providers**: Setup instructions are available for running OpenShift in Amazon Web Services (https://github.com/openshift/ openshift-ansible/blob/master/README_AWS.md) or Google Cloud Engine (https://github.com/openshift/openshift-ansible/blob/master/README_ GCE.md).

OpenShift is available to run natively on Red Hat Enterprise Linux (RHEL), RHEL Atomic Enterprise, and RHEL Atomic host systems. So after you have tried OpenShift Origin, you can configure an enterprise-ready version of OpenShift on one of those Red Hat products.

The following procedure helps you get OpenShift Origin running on a system in a container. For details on installing and running OpenShift Origin, see the OpenShift Application Platform Getting Started guide on the project's website (https://github.com/openshift/origin#getting-started).

1. **Install Linux**: Start with a fresh Linux installation. I installed a Fedora 22 Workstation on bare metal (although a virtual machine would be fine). No special repo setup is needed for Fedora. However, if you were to run this procedure on RHEL, you would need to also subscribe the system and enable extras and optional repositories as follows:

   ```
   # subscription-manager register --auto
   # subscription-manager repos --disable=""
   # subscription-manager repos \
     --enable="rhel-7-server-rpms" \
     --enable="rhel-7-server-extras-rpms" \
     --enable="rhel-7-server-optional-rpms" \
     --enable="rhel-server-7-ose-beta-rpms"
   ```

2. **Install container software**: Install the software needed to run the system as a Kubernetes master and node as follows:

   ```
   # yum install docker kubernetes etcd
   ```

3. **Configure Kubernetes:** Configure a Kubernetes cluster as described in Chapter 16.

4. **Disable SELinux**: If you are getting AVC denial messages, you need to either correct the issue or disable SELinux. To put SELinux in permissive mode, open the /etc/sysconfig/selinux file and change the SELINUX= line as follows:

   ```
   SELINUX=permissive
   ```

5. **Trust Docker Registry service**: Edit the /etc/sysconfig/docker file to allow the Docker service to trust the docker registry service that will be started later. To do that, uncomment and modify the INSECURE_REGISTRY line so it appears as follows:

   ```
   INSECURE_REGISTRY='--insecure-registry 172.30.0.0/16'
   ```

6. **Start the Docker service**: Make sure that the docker service is enabled and started:

   ```
   # systemctl enable docker
   # systemctl restart docker
   ```

7. **Start OpenShift origin**: With Docker running, you can pull and run the openshift/origin container by typing the following. This causes the container to run in the background as a daemon:

```
# docker run -d --name "origin" \
  --privileged --net=host \
  -v /:/rootfs:ro -v /var/run:/var/run:rw \
  -v /sys:/sys:ro -v /var/lib/docker:/var/lib/docker:rw \
  -v \
  /var/lib/openshift/openshift.local.volumes:/var/lib/openshift/
openshift.local.volumes \
  openshift/origin start
```

8. **Use the OpenShift Origin container**: With the origin container running in the background, you can run `docker exec` to open a bash shell inside the running container and begin using OpenShift Origin. To do that, type the following:

```
# docker exec -it origin bash
[openshift]#
```

9. **Run some OpenShift commands**: From within the origin container, you can run some commands to start a registry, log in (no credential system is enabled, so type any username and password to create an account), and start a new project:

```
# oadm registry \
  --credentials=./openshift.local.config/master/openshift-registry.
kubeconfig
# oc login
Username: joe
Password: joe
# oc new-project joeproject
Now using project "joeproject" on server "https://10.13.49.45:8443".
# oc new-app -f \
https://raw.githubusercontent.com/openshift/origin/master/examples/
sample-app/application-template-stibuild.json
...
Service "frontend" created at
    172.30.8.90 with port mappings 5432->8080.
Build "ruby-sample-build" created and started -
    you can run 'oc status' to check the progress.
Service "database" created at
    172.30.40.239 with port mappings 5434->3306.
Run 'oc status' to view your app.
```

Once the container images are done building, they are deployed and you can test them to make sure they are working.

10. **Check the OpenShift web UI**: To check status and watch the progress of the docker images being built, you can use the web interface to OpenShift. Open a web browser on your local system to the following URL, log in (use the username and password just created), accept the insecure connection (self-signed certificate), and begin working with OpenShift:

```
https://localhost:8443
```

11. **Check out the project**: The project you added from the command line (in this case, joeproject) should appear when you log in to the OpenShift Origin web UI, as shown in Figure 17.1. From the Overview tab for this project, you see the service frontend for the Apache web server and the database service being created. Select the Browse tab and choose Pods to see the progress of the pods being built.

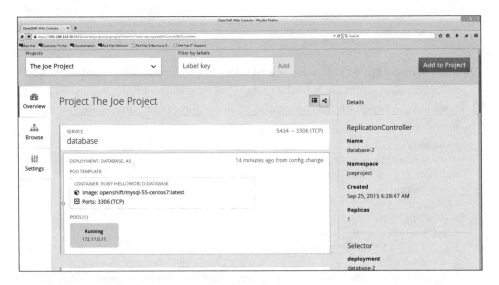

FIGURE 17.1 Manage container projects through the OpenShift web UI.

Once the pods are built and the containers are deployed, you can try to access the web server to make sure it is working. If you have any problems building your project, refer to the OpenShift Origin Troubleshooting guide (https://github.com/openshift/origin/blob/master/docs/debugging-openshift.md).

Container Development Environments from Docker

The Docker Project itself is offering container development tools that may interest you. Some of these tools give you the option of building and managing Docker containers using a graphical frontend instead of using command-line tools. These tools include the following:

- **Docker Kitematic (www.docker.com/docker-kitematic)**: Kitematic provides a graphical frontend to docker. Using Kitematic, you can build and run containers without having to rely on the Linux command line.

- **Docker Toolbox (www.docker.com/toolbox)**: Docker Toolbox provides an installer that lets you set up Docker on desktop or laptop systems. The Docker toolbox is available for Mac or Windows. Using VirtualBox to create the Linux environment on your personal computer, the Docker toolbox pulls in other docker tools (such as Docker Client, Docker Machine, and Docker Compose) to help you begin using Docker on your own system.

- **Docker Machine (www.docker.com/docker-machine)**: Docker Machine provides a way to provision Docker on to your own computer, a cloud provider, or to your data center. Using Docker machine, you can provision host systems and deploy Docker Engines on those systems. At the end, Docker clients are configured to use the Docker Engines.

For building larger container development environments, you can consider some of these tools from Docker:

- **Docker Compose (www.docker.com/docker-compose)**: Docker Compose is provided by the Docker Project to help developers form containers together into larger applications.

- **Docker Swarm (https://docs.docker.com/swarm)**: Docker Swam provides tools for scaling Docker to run multiple containers and multiple hosts.

These tools from the Docker Project can help you get an environment set up to work with Docker, but also extend your use of Docker beyond single-container applications. Many of the Docker tools just described also make it easier for you if you are more used to working with web-based interfaces than you are with command line interfaces.

USING GOOD DEVELOPMENT PRACTICES

Although building a Docker image is straightforward, there are techniques you can use to make your container development more efficient. Some of those techniques are described here.

Gathering or Excluding Files for a Build

I already talked about how it's usually best to create a new directory to contain your Dockerfile file, along with other files you need for the build. Because all files from that point down in the directory structure are directed to the Docker daemon during the build process and copied to the file system maintained by Docker, it's best to keep the number of files below that point in the file system to a minimum.

There are times when you might want to keep additional files in the directory structure where you keep your Dockerfile that you don't want included when you build containers with that file—or at least, files you don't want to include in every build. For example, you might want to use the same Dockerfile file to build container images that include different sets of configuration files. Or you might want to create a more streamlined version of an image that doesn't include documentation.

Using a .dockerignore file in the Dockerfile directory, you can exclude files you don't want to include in a build. In that file, you use text and special characters to tell what to exclude. The Dockerfile Reference page describes this file (https://docs.docker.com/reference/builder/#dockerignore-file). Here is an example of the contents of a build directory where you might want to exclude files from a docker build:

```
# ls ~/mybuild
. .. Dockerfile .dockerignore testbuild1/ testbuild2/ README
```

Each time you do a docker build, you can change the .dockerignore file to ignore different files or directories. Here are examples of entries you could include in that file to exclude different files and directories:

```
testbuild1
testbuild?
testbuild[12]

*

!README
```

You wouldn't want to use all those lines in the same .dockerignore file, but you might want to use them individually. The line testbuild1 would cause the README file and all files under the testbuild2 directory to be included in the build. The line testbuild? would cause both testbuild1 and testbuild2 directories to be excluded, leaving only the README file to be included in the build. If there were many testbuild? directories, testbuild[12] would specifically only exclude testbuild1 and testbuild2 directories, but it wouldn't exclude testbuild3, testbuild4, and so on.

If you were to simply put an asterisk (*) in the file, no files from your build directory would be included in the build. If, however, you wanted to include some files back in after excluding them with an asterisk, the exclamation point (!) is a way to do that. In this example, !README causes the README file to be included.

Keep in mind that including or excluding files in the build does not cause them to be included in the image you are building. You do that with ADD and COPY instructions in the Dockerfile. Excluding files simply keeps you from wasting time waiting for unneeded files to be copied to the Docker daemon and unnecessarily consuming storage space in the Docker directory structure.

Taking Advantage of Layers

Docker images are created from base images with additional file systems overlaid on to them in layers. The type of file systems used to do this are called *union file systems*. Understanding how these layers work helps you manage the way in which you use these layers when you run docker build.

Using layers efficiently can help you at every level of your interactions with Docker. If every container image in your data center uses the same base image, you need only one copy of that base image on each node where the container will run. Only additional layers need to be downloaded when you pull an image that does a specific job.

By making layers build on each other logically, you can further add efficiency. For example, you might add layers that include the libraries and other components needed for your run-time environment (such as JBoss or Ruby). Then that resulting container could be used by many applications that need that same environment. So, for example, each service you added on top of the run-time environment would result in a new container that could be pulled efficiently, since it needs to add only the application layer to the run-time environment.

When it comes to actually building the containers, keep in mind that each time an instruction is run during the build process, it creates a new layer. There are ways in which you can use instructions in a Dockerfile that result in more or fewer layers being created.

Putting multiple commands on the same line in a RUN instruction results in only one layer being created from the multiple commands in that RUN instruction. Here are some of the implications of doing that:

- Including a RUN instruction that has several commands can help set a good boundary between the intermediate layers in an image. For example, a RUN line that included yum -y update && yum clean all would update all packages in the container and then clean out cached data left behind by yum. If the next instruction were to fail in the build, after you correct the problem, the next `docker build` could start up with an updated, cleaned up container from the RUN instruction I just described.

- On the down side, a RUN instruction that includes too many commands can be inefficient in some cases as well. If one of several commands fails from a RUN instruction, you have to go back and re-run the entire instruction. If they had been on separate RUN lines, you could just start from the one that failed.

Once a container image is created, you can consider trying to squash layers together. Tools are being developed to help you do that. This can result in fewer layers to manage but can itself result in some inefficiencies. For example, if multiple layers are in a container, they can potentially be pulled to your system more efficiently since they can all be downloaded simultaneously. Also, as mentioned earlier, if some of the layers are already on your system when you do the pull, they don't have to be pulled again. But if the layers are not separate, any change requires the entire image to be pulled again.

Managing Software Packages in a Build

Grabbing software to put in a container image from any old place is not a good idea. Software that you just take from random sites on the Internet may include, at worst, malicious software and, at least, few guarantees that it will work well with other software in your container.

Here are a few things to think about when you are choosing the software packages to put inside your containers:

- **Choose a trusted Linux**: Many well-established Linux distributions offer a base image that includes the minimal components you need to create a container based on their distribution. Often, those base images are also configured to let you immediately install more software within that container. If you are used to using Fedora, Ubuntu, CentOS, Red Hat Enterprise Linux, or other popular Linux distributions, starting with that distribution's official base image gives you a trustworthy place to start.

- **Remove unnecessary packages**: If you don't need a certain text editor, troubleshooting tools, or other software that is in a base image, you can simply remove the package it contains from the base image and save the new image. Every package you remove saves you time in upgrading and managing the image. It also makes the image smaller, and therefore more efficient to store and move around.

- **Don't install packages not needed at run time**: Avoid including packages with software used to investigate or troubleshoot the container, as that software can be added in other ways as needed (for example, by adding a tools container to the system or installing a package temporarily to a running container and then removing it). In general, you don't want impermanent components to be in the containers you build.

- **Exclude parts of packages**: Some package management systems offer you a way to prevent certain software in a package, that you might want otherwise, from being installed. The `yum filter` command lets you filter out particular types of software when you install software packages in Fedora, Red Hat Enterprise Linux, or CentOS. For example, if you were to run the following `yum fs` command, any `yum install` commands run during the `docker build` will have documentation files excluded from any packages being installed:

```
RUN yum fs filter documentation
```

Learning More about Building Containers

As people learn more about the best ways to develop and work with containers, more information will become available. I suggest keeping an eye on some of the following locations for information to help you develop containers:

- **Review best practices for writing Dockerfiles (https://docs.docker. com/articles/dockerfile_best-practices)**: The Docker Project has come up with a list of what it calls best practices. Included in these best practices are specific suggestions related to how to best use each instruction available in Dockerfiles.

- **Refer to Dockerfile Reference (https://docs.docker.com/reference/ builder)**: The Dockerfile Reference provides an extensive reference to the instructions and ways of using those instructions inside Dockerfiles. This is the place to go if you are not sure exactly how to use a particular instruction.

- **Docker Official Images Project (https://github.com/docker-library/ official-images)**: Find guidelines for creating and maintaining official Docker images from this Docker Official Images page. It talks about not only how to make efficient and reusable images but also how to create secure images.

Summary

As someone who wants to develop containerized applications in Docker format, you want to get a good set of development tools in place that will scale up with you from creating small, individual containers to large enterprise-scale applications. Open source projects such as OpenShift provide the means for creating and managing scalable containers in pods, using Kubernetes on the backend.

Once you are comfortable with the set of development tools you have, the second part of this chapter takes you through recommendations for making the most of your container development. This includes best practice recommendations from the Docker Project and other ideas for making your Docker container development efficient and secure.

## CHAPTER 18

Exploring Sample Dockerfile Files

- View Dockerfiles for Linux distributions
- Look at Dockerfiles from open source projects
- Examine Dockerfiles for personal applications

The fact that many people publish their Dockerfile files (on GitHub and other locations) offers you the opportunity to see how people create the Docker images they use for work or play. To illustrate different types of Dockerfiles, I chose some Dockerfiles to feature here and divided them up into different categories:

- **Linux distributions**: Many Linux distributions publish the Dockerfile they use to produce the official Docker images of their distributions. Viewing those Dockerfiles, and sometimes the tarballs they include, lets you see how those images were created.

- **Open source projects**: Some open source application projects create container images that provide an easy way to launch their applications. The Dockerfiles that create those images often include things such as environment variables and recommend run commands to help you configure those applications at the time you run them.

- **Personal applications**: Many people just create containers to provide convenient ways to run the applications they want on their desktops or personal servers. Sometimes these containers are specific to a particular Linux distribution since they need to tap into particular sound, video, or other desktop features to work efficiently on the local system.

In this chapter, I show you some of the Dockerfiles that organizations and individuals have published so you can see the techniques they used to build Docker images. Although these techniques are not necessarily best practices for creating Dockerfiles (check out best practice guides at Docker.com for that), they can offer some insights into how others work through issues that you may encounter as you create your own containerized applications.

 WARNING

The sample Dockerfiles described in this chapter are here to demonstrate the techniques people are using to containerize their Linux distributions or applications. As you should with any software you run, I recommend that you investigate the security of the components that go into these Dockerfiles before using them to build and run your own container images.

EXAMINING DOCKERFILES FOR OFFICIAL DOCKER IMAGES

Before containers, to run a Linux application you would typically set up a Linux system and then install and configure the application to run on that system. With containers, the same concept usually holds true. To run an application in a container, you typically choose a container based on a particular Linux distribution and then add software from that distribution (and possibly your own software) to prepare a new container image to run that software.

The Dockerfiles described in this section show you how Linux distributions such as CentOS and Busybox create their own base containers. Many of these containers begin with the `scratch` container (available from the Docker Hub) and then add what the distribution considers to be the basic software that most applications need to run from within the container.

Viewing a CentOS Dockerfile

CentOS is a popular Linux distribution for people who want to run a Linux system tailored for enterprise use but don't need support or update guarantees. CentOS is built from Red Hat Enterprise Linux source code and provides a way to test the same software available through subscriptions to Red Hat Enterprise Linux.

Originally, the official CentOS container image didn't include the init system that comes with the CentOS distribution (which is systemd by default) to start and manage applications within the container. Recently, they added a special version of systemd software to the CentOS base image (via the systemd-container and systemd-container-libs packages). Now you can install services inside a CentOS container that are configured to be used with systemd (such as the httpd web service), and then start and otherwise manage them with `systemctl` commands.

The next section describes the Dockerfile used to build the CentOS base image. After that, I describe how you can use that base image to install and start the httpd web server as a systemd service using the CentOS base image.

Using the CentOS Base Image Dockerfile

An official CentOS project Docker image is available from the Docker Hub (`https://hub.docker.com/_/centos/`). From that page, select the Dockerfile for the version that interests you (for example, centos7) to see the contents of that Dockerfile. Next, go to the directory containing that Dockerfile (select the `docker` directory) to find the tarball that the Dockerfile includes.

The following is a recent Dockerfile used to build the official CentOS image for CentOS 7:

```
FROM scratch
MAINTAINER The CentOS Project <cloud-ops@centos.org> - ami_creator
ADD centos-7-20150616_1752-docker.tar.xz /
# Volumes for systemd
# VOLUME ["/run", "/tmp"]
# Environment for systemd
# ENV container=docker
# For systemd usage this changes to /usr/sbin/init
# Keeping it as /bin/bash for compatibility with previous
CMD ["/bin/bash"]
```

Here are a few things to note about the contents of this Dockerfile:

- The `scratch` image (`https://hub.docker.com/_/scratch/`) is pulled from the Docker Hub (on the FROM line) to provide the underlying image on which the CentOS base image is built. On the Docker Hub, the `scratch` image is described as being useful for building base images for Linux distributions or creating "super minimal images." Other major Linux distributions start with the `scratch` image as well.

- The MAINTAINER line lists the CentOS project as the maintainer of this image. If you have questions about the image, an email address is provided for you to contact the maintainers of this Dockerfile and the images it creates.

- The ADD line causes a tarball, consisting of the entire contents of the CentOS container, to be expanded and placed into the root (/) of the container's file system. As mentioned earlier, that tarball is in the same directory at GitHub as the Dockerfile.

- The CMD line at the end of the Dockerfile causes the running container to simply open a bash shell, by default.

To see how the tar file is built, from the sig-cloud-instance-build GitHub page (`https://github.com/CentOS/sig-cloud-instance-build/tree/master/docker`), select one of the Kickstart files. These Kickstart files can be used with the standard CentOS installer to install minimal CentOS systems. Each installed system can then be copied into a tarball used to build the container for the associated CentOS version.

If you were to examine those Kickstart files, you would see that only a minimal set of packages is installed. One package added that is not part of the standard CentOS distribution is the systemd-container package. That package contains the components needed to start and stop systemd services without including those components that are only appropriate on the host system (such as targets that change the states of the host system as a whole).

Some packages that would be installed automatically are removed or excluded, such as firmware packages, the GRUB2 bootloader, CentOS logos, and firewall software (firewalld package). To keep the base image small, the Kickstart files also block documentation within any packages from being installed and remove large files that are known to not be needed. The resulting tarball files from each Kickstart (there are different Kickstart files for different releases of CentOS) provide a lean foundation for you to use to run applications in a CentOS container.

As someone using the CentOS base container, you would create your own Dockerfile and add the CentOS base container to your FROM line. The rest of your Dockerfile could add packages (`yum install whatever`) and your own software and configuration files. The next section describes how to add the httpd package to the CentOS base system container and then start that web server as a systemd service.

Adding a systemd Service to a CentOS Dockerfile

To run a systemd-enabled application to a Dockerfile built on a CentOS image, you simply install the package containing the service and use the `systemctl` command within the new Dockerfile to launch that service when the container is run. Here's an example of a Dockerfile to do that:

```
FROM centos:7
RUN yum -y install httpd; yum clean all; \
systemctl enable httpd.service
EXPOSE 80
RUN echo "Web Server Works!" > /var/www/html/index.html
CMD ["/usr/sbin/init"]
```

To build that Dockerfile into an image for running the httpd server, you could type the following:

```
# docker build -t systemd-httpd .
```

With the systemd-httpd image created, you can run that image with the following command:

```
# docker run --privileged -d -v /sys/fs/cgroup:/sys/fs/cgroup:ro \
    -p 80:80 systemd-httpd
```

The command just shown runs the httpd systemd service. Since the Dockerfile was set up to enable the httpd systemd service, the `/sys/fs/cgroup` directory needed to be mounted in the container from the host system. The `-p 80:80` option exposes TCP port 80 from the container to the same port on the host, and the `-d` option leaves the container running in the background. To check that the service is working, type the following:

```
# curl http://localhost
Web Server Works!
```

You could use the same Dockerfile as a model for starting any service that has a systemd unit file included in its package.

Viewing a Busybox Dockerfile

Busybox is a tiny operating system often used to run simple executables in embedded systems. You can find the busybox image at the Docker Hub (`https://hub.docker.com/_busybox/`). The busybox Dockerfile pulls in a tiny tarball (only about 2.7M) that includes just enough utilities to run a statically compiled binary.

Like the CentOS base image Dockerfile, the Dockerfile used to build busybox itself starts with the scratch image and adds a tarball. Here is an example of a busybox Dockerfile available from the Docker Hub:

```
FROM scratch
MAINTAINER Jerome Petazzoni <jerome@docker.com>
ADD rootfs.tar /
CMD ["/bin/sh"]
```

To create a Docker image to run your own statically compiled binary, you can create your own Dockerfile that includes the busybox base image and add your binary. Here is an example from the busybox Docker Hub page:

```
FROM busybox
COPY ./my-static-binary /my-static-binary
CMD ["/my-static-binary"]
```

You would have to compile your own binary, since the busybox image doesn't contain the tools needed to do that. Once you have compiled the binary, you could place the binary in the same directory with the Dockerfile (replacing `my-static-binary` with the name of your binary). When you run `docker build`, the new image includes the binary and sets it up to run by default when the container is run.

EXAMINING DOCKERFILES FROM OPEN SOURCE PROJECTS

A growing number of open source projects have created container images to run their software and made those images available from the Docker Hub. The Dockerfiles for those projects that I illustrate here are different from base operating system container images. These Dockerfiles are meant to create images that you run directly, instead of using them to build other images.

Seeing how Dockerfiles are created for WordPress and MySQL can give you ideas about how to create images that run your own applications. These two cases represent daemons that run in the background, providing services where they are run. When using these images, you are offered ways of changing environment variables to direct how these images behave when they are run.

Viewing a WordPress Dockerfile

WordPress is a popular content management system and blogging tool available as an open source project. An official WordPress image is available on the Docker Hub (`https://hub.docker.com/_/wordpress/`). A Dockerfile and related software are also available for you to view or use to build your own WordPress container image.

Select one of the Dockerfile links from the WordPress Docker Hub page. The following is an example of one of those Dockerfiles:

```
FROM php:5.6-apache
RUN a2enmod rewrite
# install the PHP extensions we need
```

```
RUN apt-get update && apt-get install -y \
  libpng12-dev libjpeg-dev && rm -rf /var/lib/apt/lists/* \
  && docker-php-ext-configure gd --with-png-dir=/usr \
  --with-jpeg-dir=/usr && docker-php-ext-install gd
RUN docker-php-ext-install mysqli
VOLUME /var/www/html
ENV WORDPRESS_VERSION 4.3
ENV WORDPRESS_SHA1 1e9046b584d4eaebac9e1f7292ca7003bfc8ffd7
# upstream tarballs include ./wordpress/
# so this gives us /usr/src/wordpress
RUN curl -o wordpress.tar.gz -SL \
  https://wordpress.org/wordpress-${WORDPRESS_VERSION}.tar.gz \
  && echo "$WORDPRESS_SHA1 *wordpress.tar.gz" | sha1sum -c - \
  && tar -xzf wordpress.tar.gz -C /usr/src/ \
  && rm wordpress.tar.gz \
  && chown -R www-data:www-data /usr/src/wordpress
COPY docker-entrypoint.sh /entrypoint.sh
# grr, ENTRYPOINT resets CMD now
ENTRYPOINT ["/entrypoint.sh"]
CMD ["apache2-foreground"]
```

Here is some information about this Dockerfile that you might find interesting:

- Because WordPress software is based on PHP, the base image identified on the FROM line is the php image (5.6-apache version) based on Ubuntu.

- The first RUN instruction loads the Apache rewrite module.

- The next RUN instruction runs several commands. First it updates all the Ubuntu packages inside the container and installs a few more packages. After that, it adds the gd PHP extension and sets the location of a couple of directories used by PHP.

- The `docker-php-ext-install` command on the next RUN instruction installs the mysqli extension of PHP.

- The `/var/www/html` directory is mounted from the host, using the VOLUME instruction, to store the data used by WordPress.

- Two ENV instructions set the version number of the WordPress release and the SHA1SUM used later to check that the WordPress tarball is valid when it is downloaded in the next step.

- Several things happen on the next RUN line to get and prepare WordPress software. The `curl` command gets the wordpress-4.3.tar.gz tarball (using the version number set earlier), checks it using the SHA1SUM (also set earlier), and untars it to the `/usr/src` directory. It then removes the tarball and changes the ownership of the `/usr/src` directory to the `www-data` user and group.

- The COPY line copies the `docker-entrypoint.sh` script from the build directory to the `/entrypoint.sh` file in the container.
- Finally the ENTRYPOINT instruction sets `/entrypoint.sh` as the command to start when the container is run later, and CMD sets `apache2-foreground` as the option passed to the `entrypoint.sh` script.

To use the resulting image, you could link the wordpress container you start up with an existing mysql container you already have running on the system. You could do that as follows:

```
# docker run --name new-wordpress --link new-mysql:mysql -d wordpress
```

Inside the wordpress container itself, there is a set of environment variables that you can change to modify the behavior of the wordpress container. Using the -e option you can set those options on the `docker run` command line. Here are a few examples:

- **-e WORDPRESS_DB_HOST=**: Sets the IP address and port of the MySQL server. By default, wordpress finds the MySQL service from a linked container.
- **-e WORDPRESS_DB_USER=**: Changes the user name used to access the MySQL database. By default, the user is root.
- **-e WORDPRESS_DB_PASSWORD=**: Changes the password set for the root user of the MySQL database. By default, the MYSQL_ROOT_PASSWORD environment variable is used from the linked MySQL container.
- **-e WORDPRESS_DB_NAME=**: Changes the name of the MySQL database used from the default name `wordpress`.

Setting environment variables is a technique used by many container images so that you can modify the location of components, change user names and passwords, and generally adapt the container to work in your environment.

Viewing the MySQL Dockerfile

MySQL is the most popular open source database for web applications. You can get the Dockerfile used to build the official MySQL image (`mysql`) from the Docker Hub (`https://hub.docker.com/_/mysql/`). Here is an example of the Dockerfile of the latest version of the mysql image:

```
FROM debian:wheezy

RUN groupadd -r mysql && useradd -r -g mysql mysql
RUN mkdir /docker-entrypoint-initdb.d
```

```
RUN apt-get update && apt-get install -y perl --no-install-recommends && rm
➥-rf /var/lib/apt/lists/*
RUN apt-key adv --keyserver ha.pool.sks-keyservers.net --recv-keys
A4A9406876FCBD3C456770C88C718D3B5072E1F5

ENV MYSQL_MAJOR 5.6
ENV MYSQL_VERSION 5.6.26

RUN echo "deb http://repo.mysql.com/apt/debian/ wheezy mysql-${MYSQL_MAJOR}"
➥ > /etc/apt/sources.list.d/mysql.list
RUN { \
echo mysql-community-server mysql-community-server/data-dir select ''; \
echo mysql-community-server mysql-community-server/root-pass password ''; \
echo mysql-community-server mysql-community-server/re-root-pass password ''; \
echo mysql-community-server mysql-community-server/remove-test-db select
false; \
} | debconf-set-selections \
&& apt-get update && apt-get install -y mysql-server="${MYSQL_VERSION}"* &&
➥ rm -rf /var/lib/apt/lists/* \
&& rm -rf /var/lib/mysql && mkdir -p /var/lib/mysql

RUN sed -Ei 's/^(bind-address|log)/#&/' /etc/mysql/my.cnf \
&& echo 'skip-host-cache\nskip-name-resolve' | awk '{ print } $1 ==
➥"[mysqld]" && c == 0 { c = 1; system("cat") }' /etc/mysql/my.cnf > /tmp/
➥my.cnf \
&& mv /tmp/my.cnf /etc/mysql/my.cnf

VOLUME /var/lib/mysql
COPY docker-entrypoint.sh /entrypoint.sh
ENTRYPOINT ["/entrypoint.sh"]
EXPOSE 3306
CMD ["mysqld"]
```

The Dockerfile for the mysql container images follows many of the same techniques used in the Dockerfile for the wordpress image. Here is a description of some of the highlights of this file:

- The FROM line sets the debian image (wheezy version) as the base image.
- The first RUN instruction creates the mysql user and group inside the container, while the next RUN instruction creates the directory `/docker-entrypoint-initdb.d`.
- After updating the software in the container (`apt-get update`), the next RUN line installs the perl package and cleans out the `/var/lib/apt/lists/*` directories.

- The `apt-key` command on the next RUN line sets the keys used to check the validity of the MySQL software.
- Environment variables are set (ENV instruction) to identify the MySQL major release (MYSQL_MAJOR 5.6) and version (MYSQL_VERSION 5.6.26).
- The location of the mysql software is set on the next line (incorporating the MySQL major release number set earlier in the name of the software).
- The next RUN command does some MySQL database cleanup.
- More cleanup is done on the next RUN line to change a few configuration values and to tell MySQL to not do reverse hostname lookup.
- The VOLUME instruction sets the location of the mysql database to the `/var/lib/mysql` directory on the host (which this instruction mounts inside the container at the same location).
- The COPY instruction copies the `docker-entrypoint.sh` script from the build directory to `/entrypoint.sh` in the root of the container.
- The MySQL service listens on port 3306 by default, which is exposed outside the container from the EXPOSE line.
- Finally, the CMD instruction sets the command to run by default as the `mysqld` command (which is the MySQL daemon).

As with the wordpress image, when you run the `mysql` image you can change the value of various environment variables to adapt how MySQL is used in your own setup. For example, you can set some of the following:

- **-e MYSQL_ROOT_PASSWORD=**: Sets the root password used to access the MySQL database.
- **-e MYSQL_DATABASE=**: Sets the name of a MySQL database to be created when the image first starts.
- **-e MYSQL_USER=**: Sets the name of a user granted super-user privilege to the database you create with the MYSQL_DATABASE variable.
- **-e MYSQL_PASSWORD=**: Identifies the password to use with the user account identified with MYSQL_USER.
- **MYSQL_ALLOW_EMPTY_PASSWORD**: This optional variable if used (MYSQL_ALLOW_EMPTY_PASSWORD=yes) causes the container to be started with a blank MySQL password.

When you go to run a container image built from the MySQL Dockerfile described here, you can add options to the `docker run` command line to modify the container's behavior. Besides setting environment variables just described, you can also identify a different host directory to use to provide the MySQL database. For example:

```
# docker run --name new-mysql              \
    -v /my/custom:/etc/mysql/conf.d        \
    -v /my/own/datadir:/var/lib/mysql      \
    -e MYSQL_ROOT_PASSWORD=my-secret-pw    \
    -d mysql:latest
```

The `docker run` command line just shown runs the `mysql` image as the container name `new-mysql`. The first volume mount option (`-v`) illustrates how you could use your own MySQL configuration files from the host (`/my/custom` directory) and mount them over the configuration files in the container (`/etc/mysql/conf.d` directory).

Likewise, you can have data files from your host (`/my/own/datadir` directory) mounted over the MySQL data directory (`/var/lib/mysql`) inside the container. The `-e` option here sets the MySQL root password to `my-secret-pw`. The last options on the command line run the `mysql:latest` image and run that image in the background as a daemon process (`-d`).

Examining Dockerfiles for Desktop and Personal Use

Many people begin learning how to use Docker by containerizing desktop applications. There are many advantages to making desktop applications into containers.

If you want to use different versions of an application on the same computer, putting them in containers lets you avoid potential library conflicts on the host system. Likewise, if you decide later that you don't want that application on your system, you can easily just stop the container and remove the image without otherwise disrupting your system.

In this section, I show two different ways that people have created images for adding a containerized web browser to their system. The first example shows a Chromium browser image that integrates directly with the host system's X Window System display. In the second example, the image illustrates how `vnc` can be used to open a virtual desktop to hold Firefox or any other X Window System application you want to use.

Viewing a Chrome Dockerfile

The Google Chrome web browser is a popular addition to a Linux desktop, especially those offering only Firefox. Jessie Frazelle (`https://blog.jessfraz.com`), an employee at Docker, created a Chrome container image that you can pull from the Docker Hub or build yourself using the Dockerfile displayed here.

This Chrome image works by mounting the X11 socket from your desktop system directly into the container. By doing this, it avoids the overhead (both in size and performance) you get using X11 forwarding over ssh. You can also mount the audio device (/dev/snd in Debian and Ubuntu) so you can play audio directly through the browser as well.

Here's the Dockerfile used to create the container (check here for updates: https://github.com/jfrazelle/dockerfiles/blob/master/chrome/stable/ Dockerfile):

```
FROM debian:sid
MAINTAINER Jessica Frazelle <jess@docker.com>

ADD https://dl.google.com/linux/direct/google-talkplugin_current_amd64.
➥ deb /src/google-talkplugin_current_amd64.deb

ADD  https://dl.google.com/linux/direct/google-chrome-stable_current_
➥ amd64.deb /src/google-chrome-stable_current_amd64.deb

# Install Chromium
RUN mkdir -p /usr/share/icons/hicolor && \
        apt-get update && apt-get install -y \
        ca-certificates \
        gconf-service \
        hicolor-icon-theme \
        libappindicator1 \
        libasound2 \
        libcanberra-gtk-module \
        libcurl3 \
        libexif-dev \
        libgconf-2-4 \
        libgl1-mesa-dri \
        libgl1-mesa-glx \
        libnspr4 \
        libnss3 \
        libpango1.0-0 \
        libv4l-0 \
        libxss1 \
        libxtst6 \
        wget \
        xdg-utils \
        --no-install-recommends && \
        dpkg -i '/src/google-chrome-stable_current_amd64.deb' && \
        dpkg -i '/src/google-talkplugin_current_amd64.deb' \
        && rm -rf /var/lib/apt/lists/*
```

```
COPY local.conf /etc/fonts/local.conf

# Autorun chrome
ENTRYPOINT [ "/usr/bin/google-chrome" ]
CMD [ "--user-data-dir=/data" ]
```

Here are some things you can take away from the chrome Dockerfile:

- The base image identified on the FROM line is the debian image (sid version).
- Two ADD instructions copy Debian packages from the Google download websites. The google-talkplugin_current_amd64.deb and google-chrome-stable_current_amd64.deb packages are added by copying them to the /src directory inside the container. These two packages get you the Google Talk plugin and the latest stable Chrome browser.
- After making a directory for icons and updating all the software in the container, the next RUN instruction installs a bunch of packages needed to provide such things as sound and video drivers inside the container. It also installs the two packages just downloaded from Google.
- The COPY instruction copies the local.conf file from the build directory to the /etc/fonts/local.conf file inside the container.
- The last two instructions set the command to run. The ENTRYPOINT instruction runs the google-chrome command to start the browser and the CMD instruction identifies the /data directory as the location for the browser to get user data.

If you want to build this image, you can get the local.conf file defined in the Dockerfile from the same place the Dockerfile itself is available on GitHub (https://github.com/jfrazelle/dockerfiles/tree/master/chrome/stable).

Keep in mind that this Dockerfile is tailored to run on a Debian-style system. You may need to modify the locations of devices on the host and deal with some permissions issues to get it to work on a different Linux system. (Adding –privileged overcomes permission issues in Fedora). To avoid this issue altogether, you could use VNC or X11 forwarding (as shown in the coming example of a Firefox container), but that approach has much more overhead.

Here is the docker run command that Jess Frazelle suggests for running the Chrome container image:

```
# docker run -it    \
   --net host        \
   --cpuset-cpus 0 \
   --memory 512mb   \
```

```
-v /tmp/.X11-unix:/tmp/.X11-unix        \
-e DISPLAY=unix$DISPLAY                  \
-v $HOME/Downloads:/root/Downloads      \
-v $HOME/.config/google-chrome/:/data   \
--device /dev/snd  \
--name chrome         \
jess/chrome
```

In this example, there are a few interesting ideas related to running the Chrome browser in a container. The `--cpuset-cpus` and `--memory` options provide an easy way to limit CPU usage and memory usage, so you can limit the harm that Chrome can do to your desktop performance.

The directory containing the X sockets (`/tmp/.X11-unix`) is mounted inside the container to provide access to the display. Your local display is identified to the DISPLAY environment variable. For convenience, the `/root/Downloads` directory is mounted in the container so anything you download is stored on the host by default.

Your Chrome settings and data are stored in the `.config/google-chrome` directory in your home directory, so that information persists. To be able to play audio from Chrome, the `/dev/snd` device is mounted inside the container. Figure 18.1 shows an example of the Chrome browser running from a container on the local desktop.

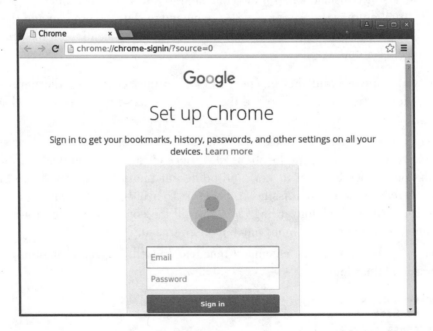

FIGURE 18.1   Run Chrome from a container by mounting host resources inside the container.

Viewing a Firefox Dockerfile

Firefox is the other popular web browser on Linux systems. Firefox is maintained by the Mozilla project and has roots that go back to the first web browsers in existence. The Firefox Dockerfile I describe is part of the fedora-cloud initiative (`https://github.com/fedora-cloud/Fedora-Dockerfiles`), which has created a bunch of Fedora-based container images to provide individual applications or technology other containers can build on (such as Java or python).

What is interesting about the Firefox Dockerfile described here is that it installs remote desktop software (vnc) along with Firefox into a container image. As noted earlier, there is more overhead than you get by just mounting desktop sockets and devices inside your container. But this approach provides a more generic solution that can work for many different desktop applications.

The Firefox Dockerfile (`https://github.com/fedora-cloud/Fedora-Docker-files/tree/master/firefox`) requires an `xstartup` script be added to the build directory if you want to build the image yourself. That script is in the same directory as the Dockerfile on GitHub. Here's an example of what the Firefox Dockerfile looks like:

```
FROM fedora
MAINTAINER http://fedoraproject.org/wiki/Cloud

# Install the appropriate software
RUN yum -y update && yum clean all
RUN yum -y install firefox \
xorg-x11-twm tigervnc-server \
xterm xorg-x11-font \
xulrunner-26.0-2.fc20.x86_64 \
dejavu-sans-fonts \
dejavu-serif-fonts \
xdotool && yum clean all

# Add the xstartup file into the image and set the default password.
RUN mkdir /root/.vnc
ADD ./xstartup /root/.vnc/
RUN chmod -v +x /root/.vnc/xstartup
RUN echo 123456 | vncpasswd -f > /root/.vnc/passwd
RUN chmod -v 600 /root/.vnc/passwd

RUN sed -i '/\/etc\/X11\/xinit\/xinitrc-common/a [ -x /usr/bin/firefox ]
&& /usr/bin/firefox &' /etc/X11/xinit/xinitrc

EXPOSE 5901

CMD     ["vncserver", "-fg" ]
# ENTRYPOINT ["vncserver", "-fg" ]
```

Here is what this Firefox Dockerfile does:

- The FROM indicates that the container starts with the `fedora` base image.
- The first RUN instruction updates all the Fedora software in the container (`yum -y update`) and cleans out any cached files left behind. The next RUN instruction installs the packages needed in the container, including the browser itself (`firefox`), a tiny window manager (`xorg-x11-twm`), the remote desktop VNC server (`tigervnc-server`), software to boot up Firefox (`xulrunner`), and some font packages.
- To hold the xstartup script, the next RUN instruction creates the `/root/.vnc` directory. After that the `xstartup` script is copied from the build directory to that `/root/.vnc` directory in the container with an ADD instruction. To make the script executable, the RUN command that follows runs the `chmod` command on that script.
- The password for VNC is set with the next RUN instruction. Later, when you try to connect to the container using a VNC client, you need to provide the password 123456. The password file (`/root/.vnc/passwd`) is assigned read/write permission by the root user, with no permission assigned to anyone else (`chmod -v 600`).
- The `sed` command on the following RUN line adds the `/usr/bin/firefox` command to the `/etc/X11/xinit/xinitrc` file.
- TCP port 5901 is exposed from the container with the EXPOSE 5901 instruction, which provides access to the VNC service inside the container to the outside world.
- The last instruction (CMD) is used to start the vncserver process.

Before moving on, it's useful to take a look at the `xstartup` script, which is run when the VNC server starts up from the container. Here are the last few lines of that file:

```
if [ -f /etc/X11/xinit/xinitrc ]; then
   exec sh /etc/X11/xinit/xinitrc
fi
[ -r $HOME/.Xresources ] && xrdb $HOME/.Xresources
xsetroot -solid grey
xterm -geometry 80x24+10+10 -ls -title "$VNCDESKTOP Desktop" &
twm &
```

If the `xinitrc` file exists (which it does), that file is executed. That's where Docker added the `firefox` command earlier so it runs from there. If there are X settings in the `$HOME/.Xresources` file, those are included when the X resource database utility (xrdb) is run. After that, the xsetroot command sets the VNC background color to grey, and an xterm (Terminal window) is opened with a certain size and title with a twm window manager running inside it. If you wanted to change the look or behavior of your VNC session, you could add commands here or provide your own .Xresources file.

If you are ready to try out your Firefox web browser in a VNC container, get the Dockerfile and the xstartup script from GitHub and, with those two files in the current directory, run the following docker build command:

```
# docker build -rm -t myfirefox .
. . .
Successfully built c5c9e7e770db
```

Then to run the VNC server and Firefox from the container, type the following:

```
# docker run -d -p 5901:5901 myfirefox
```

The vncserver daemon should now be running in the background.

To try it out run a VNC client from your local system. For example, you can select Remote Desktop Viewer from your desktop, choose Connect, choose VNC, type localhost:1 into the Host box, and click Connect. When prompted for the password, type 123456. The simple VNC desktop and twm window manager should appear with Firefox running.

To start a VNC client from the command line instead, you could type the following from the local system:

```
# yum install tigervnc -y
# vncviewer localhost:1
```

Again, type the password 123456 when prompted and the VNC desktop, with Firefox running it in, should appear on your local desktop. Figure 18.2 shows an example of the VNC/Firefox container running on a Fedora system.

Because you are running Firefox in a VNC window and not as a containerized application, all your settings and any files you save are inside the container. If you want to use settings from your desktop, save files there, or connect to the sound system, you can mount volumes, sockets, or devices as needed, as was done in the Chrome example.

Using the Dockerfile described here, you could modify it to launch any desktop application available with your distribution.

FIGURE 18.2   Launch a desktop application, like Firefox, in a VNC container.

SUMMARY

Seeing how others create images from Dockerfiles can help you figure out how you want to create your own Docker images. In this chapter, I showcased several different Dockerfiles being used today to create base images as well as images for running particular applications.

For base images, I showed a simple Dockerfile for creating a CentOS base image. Most of the work for creating that base image is done from a Kickstart file (to initially install the packages needed) and the `tar` command (for gathering up the files to be included in the container). A much smaller example of a Docker base image is the busybox image. As with the CentOS image, the busybox Dockerfile mostly just pulls in a tarball (although just a tiny one of about 2.4MB).

Open source application projects such as WordPress and MySQL offer their own official Docker images on the Docker Hub. From the Dockerfile and other files they use to create their images, you can see interesting uses of environment variables to be able to modify how the containers are used at run time.

The last couple of Dockerfiles described in this chapter show different ways of launching a web browser on your local desktop from a container. The example of using a Chrome browser from a container connects directly to desktop features by mounting sockets, directories, and sound devices. The example of a Firefox browser in a container relies on a VNC server to launch a slimmed-down remote desktop in which to manage Firefox.

Index

I

J-K

Q-R